From Wooden Ploughs to Welfare

MCGILL-QUEEN'S NATIVE AND NORTHERN SERIES
Bruce G. Trigger, Editor

1 When the Whalers Were Up North
Inuit Memories from the Eastern Arctic
Dorothy Harley Eber

2 The Challenge of Arctic Shipping
Science, Environmental Assessment, and Human Values
David L. VanderZwaag and Cynthia Lamson, Editors

3 Lost Harvests
Prairie Indian Reserve Farmers and Government Policy
Sarah Carter

4 Native Liberty, Crown Sovereignty
The Existing Aboriginal Right of Self-Government in Canada
Bruce Clark

5 Unravelling the Franklin Mystery
Inuit Testimony
David C. Woodman

6 Otter Skins, Boston Ships, and China Goods
The Maritime Fur Trade of the Northwest Coast, 1785–1841
James R. Gibson

7 From Wooden Ploughs to Welfare
Why Indian Policy Failed in the Prairie Provinces
Helen Buckley

From Wooden Ploughs to Welfare

Why Indian Policy Failed in the Prairie Provinces

HELEN BUCKLEY

McGill-Queen's University Press
Montreal & Kingston • London • Buffalo

© McGill-Queen's University Press 1992
ISBN 0-7735-0893-7

Legal deposit second quarter 1992
Bibliothèque nationale du Québec

Printed in Canada on acid-free paper

This book has been published with the help of a
grant from the Social Science Federation of Canada,
using funds provided by the Social Science and Hu-
manities Research Council of Canada. Funding has
also been received from Multiculturalism Canada.

Canadian Cataloguing in Publication Data

Buckley, Helen, 1923–
    From wooden ploughs to welfare
    (McGill-Queen's native and northern series; 7)
    Includes bibliographical references and index.
    ISBN 0-7735-0893-7
    1. Indians of North America – Prairie Provinces –
    History. 2. Indians of North America – Canada –
    Government relations. I. Title. II. Series.
    E92.B83 1992   323.1'1970712'09   C91-090619-X

This book was typeset by Typo Litho composition inc.
in 10/12 Palatino.

For Marg, Ruth, and Carol

Contents

Acknowledgments   ix

1 Behind the Headlines   3

2 The Reserve System: Early Days
(1870s–1945)   28

3 New Adjustments (1945–1975)   67

4 The Government's Role:
Some Perspectives   97

5 The Road Ahead   126

6 Changing Course   162

Notes   177

Bibliography   191

Index   203

Acknowledgments

The author wishes to recognize the assistance provided by many individuals and organizations both in Ottawa and the West. Particular importance attaches to conversations with officers in several tribal councils in Manitoba and Saskatchewan and in the Assembly of First Nations. These officers were kind enough to give me their time. Stan Fulham of Kinew Housing in Winnipeg, Principal Jerry Arshinoff of Plains Indian Survival School in Calgary, and consultant Bill Hanson in Saskatoon deserve a special word of thanks. Acknowledgment is also owing for conversations with officers of Indian and Northern Affairs Canada (INAC), both at national headquarters and in the West, and with J. S. Frideres, University of Calgary; Robert Bone, Jack Stabler, and Frank Tough at the University of Saskatchewan; Tom Carter, director of the Urban Institute at the University of Winnipeg; and officers of Nova Corporation in Calgary. I am in debt to a long list of librarians at INAC, Carleton University, and the Public Library in Ottawa; Winnipeg's Centennial Library; the Saskatchewan Indian Cultural College and the Saskatoon Public Library; and the library of the Glenbow Museum in Calgary (thanks to Mrs Lindsay Muir). Finally, a special thanks to my good friend and word processor, Deirdre Nishimura-Jones, who produced successive versions of the manuscript and maintained my spirits throughout; to Claire Gigantes, editor; and to the editorial staff at McGill-Queen's University Press.

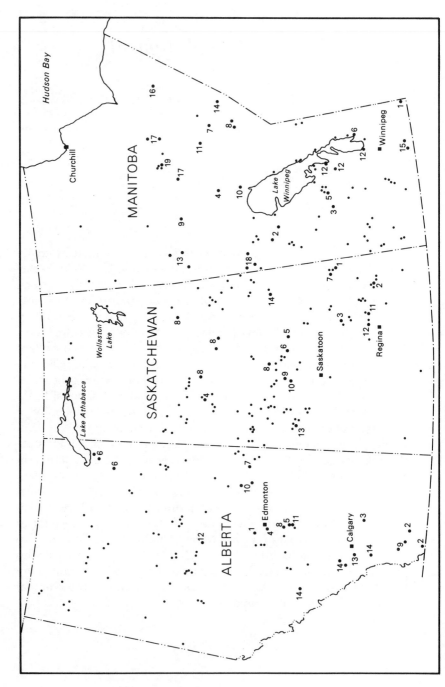

Indian Bands, Reserves, and Settlements in Manitoba, Saskatchewan, and Alberta

ALBERTA

1 Alexander
2 Blackfoot
3 Blood
4 Enoch
5 Ermineskin
6 Fort Chipewyan
7 Kehewin
8 Louis Bull
9 Piegan
10 Saddle Lake
11 Sampson
12 Sawridge
13 Sarcee
14 Stoney

SASKATCHEWAN

1 Coté
2 Cowessess
3 Day Star
4 Ile à la Crosse
5 James Smith
6 John Smith
7 Key
8 Lac La Ronge
9 Mistawasis
10 Muskeg Lake
11 Pasqua
12 Piapot
13 Poundmaker
14 Red Earth

MANITOBA

1 Buffalo Point
2 Chemawawin
3 Crane River
4 Cross Lake
5 Fairford
6 Fort Alexander
7 God's Lake
8 Island Lake
9 Nelson House
10 Norway House
11 Oxford House
12 Pequis
13 Pukatawagen
14 Red Sucker Lake
15 Roseau River
16 Shamattawa
17 Split Lake
18 The Pas
19 York Landing

From Wooden Ploughs to Welfare

Behind the Headlines

This is the story of the people of the western plains and forests who lost their lands to the settlers in the 1870s. They have lived since, in the provinces of Manitoba, Saskatchewan, and Alberta, on parcels of land that were reserved for them, of necessity taking up a new life, but never becoming part of the larger society or regaining their independence. Some Canadians wonder why it all turned out so badly, while many have simple explanations which ignore or distort the facts. This account has been written to make the history more accessible, in the hope that with greater understanding on the part of Canadians generally the need for a new relationship will at last be perceived and supported.

To see it from a larger perspective, consider the immigrant experience. In the first one hundred years after Confederation, an estimated nine million immigrants entered Canada. Many of them subsequently left Canada (the numbers are unknown), but even allowing for a considerable outflow, the ones who stayed on and were absorbed into the main fabric of Canadian life could probably be reckoned in millions. Yet a tiny population of native people whose ancestors signed the western treaties with the Crown still live separately from Canadian society, many of them in conditions that resemble those of the Third World. Numbering only 150,000-odd at the present time – and fewer in the 1870s – the people are spread across three provinces, further fragmented by the numerous reserves and the growing beach-heads in all the major cities. They make up roughly five percent of the population in Manitoba and Saskatchewan, three percent in Alberta.[1]

On the face of it, it makes no sense. Granted that absorption hinged on overcoming differences in culture and experience, these were obvious enough at the time of the treaties and we have had more than a hundred years to find ways of bringing them in. The most curious part is how easily we other Canadians accept the situation. We don't see it as strange, much less embarrassing, that these particular Canadians live as they do, for we have managed to see it as their preference to live separately and their fault for clinging to old ways.

We do not all see it this way, of course, but enough of us do that the government feels no pressure to heed the bands' requests for better programs, more money, real power. Critics are ignored. One such, Stephen Lewis, former Canadian ambassador to the United Nations, has said that the moments when he was most embarrassed at the UN were when incidents of Canada's treatment of her native peoples were thrown at him.[2] He might have had in mind such a place as Pukatawagen, a tiny dot on the map of northern Manitoba; a recent feature story in the *Winnipeg Free Press* begins as follows: "Poverty beyond imagination – like a shanty-town in Mexico or São Paulo, with sometimes 10 to 15 people in one shack. The people are conditioned to live on welfare; more than 70 percent don't work. There is no work, apart from a little trapping and fishing along the Churchill. Life has improved in recent years thanks to band initiatives and good leadership, but there is still no work ... People have nothing to do here. Especially the young people. Children start drinking as early as six. Smoke marijuana, sniff glue, contact cement, gasoline etc."[3]

Pukatawagen is an extreme case, but poverty is near universal, as are welfare and people who have been dependent on a government department for several generations. Pukatawagen is cited at the outset in an attempt to nudge complacency by showing the true dimensions of the problem today; but this account will be a balanced one, giving due attention to reserve communities that work well, progress that is being made, and problems for which solutions are being found.

THE PEOPLE, THE PROMISES, THE PRESENT SITUATION

Certain aboriginal nations in the West have been there for thousands of years, others are relative newcomers, pushed out of their ancestral homelands in the East by spreading settlement in the eighteenth and early nineteenth centuries. These are the nations of this story: the Crees, Chipewyan, Saulteaux (known as the Ojibwa in Ontario), Nakota (also called the Assiniboine), Dakota (Sioux), Siksika (Blackfoot), Kainai (Blood), Piegan, and Sarcee; it is as members of these ancient nations that the people see themselves today. The name "Indian" originated with Columbus's mistake in identifying his land-fall, and its continued use is evidence of the relationship which has prevailed between conquering Europeans and indigenous people, not only in western Canada but across two continents. The present account centres on the Canadian West, and its primary purpose is to explain the course of events after the treaties, in particular the discrepancy between the aboriginal and immigrant experiences.

The western treaties marked the end of independence and an ancient way of life, and were supposed to open doors that would enable a nomadic people to take up the new. They were signed by chiefs representing virtually all the bands in what are now the Prairie provinces and the odd one missed, whether by oversight, design, or the band's own preference, may be seen in Alberta's Lubicon, now negotiating terms. These treaties record specific commitments on the part of the Canadian government: tracts of land to be set aside; a small annuity; a school on each reserve; seed, implements, and livestock in all areas where farming could provide the economic base. And there were other entitlements as well, for the western bands were brought under the Indian Act and, as "registered" (or "status") Indians[4] would have a special agency to safeguard their lands, provide certain services, and be responsible for their welfare. This was the Department of Indian Affairs, already operating in eastern Canada. It has had exclusive responsibility for the people to this day, although some of the services in recent times have been supplied by other federal departments.

The commitments and entitlements are the things that stick in the minds of Canadians. Given the land, instructors, and equipment to get them farming, housing, and schools, it might seem that the western bands had only to pitch in and adopt the new life. Many Canadians do see it this way, but it was not that simple, and the difficulties encountered by the bands at the outset are by no means absent from the scene today.

My account is limited to the bands that signed the treaties because these are the people to whom the promises were made and on whose behalf the government has laboured ever since, attempting to fulfil its promises. In pursuing this single theme, the Métis are necessarily left out, along with other aboriginal people who never had "status" or who lost it, usually through marriage. Theirs is another story, marked chiefly by neglect, but the treaty nations and their member bands share a particular history in association with the Canadian government, including a degree of control that was not imposed in the eastern provinces or in British Columbia. By most indices, they are worse off today than registered Indians in other parts of Canada, and this is at least partly a result of their history.

It is a history laced with misunderstanding and shaped by bureaucrats. Government, in the early days, saw the problems in simple terms, with a keen eye for cost and low expectations. Many Canadians at that time believed that the former hunters would be unable to adapt, perhaps would not survive, for they had been much reduced by epidemics and starvation. The official plan, on the other hand, called for assimilation into Canadian society. The results, as they may be seen today, confound both extremes. The people did not disappear; although decreasing for a time, their numbers rose rapidly after World War II, when modern health services reached the reserves. Nor did they assimilate as a group, and only rarely as individuals. Although a process which allows the individual to relinquish status dates back to the early nineteenth century, statistics for the whole of Canada for 1876–1948 show that only 4,100 persons did so. Later figures for 1955–75 rise to 13,000, but more than eighty percent of these were Indian women who married a non-Indian man.[5] In a word, it has been a society with a strong sense of identity, in the West as elsewhere, despite poverty and other ills.

The Prairie provinces today account for forty percent of all registered Indians in Canada. This does not make them a large minority, because the provincial population is relatively small (only sixteen percent of Canada as a whole), but the ratios do run higher here than elsewhere. In some local areas, notably in the North, Indian people take a majority position (over fifty percent in northern Manitoba) and they are a growing presence in all the major cities.

For more than eighty years after the treaties were signed, life was lived on the reserves and sometimes, in the North, in little settlements on provincial Crown land, often shared with the Métis. And when, in the 1960s, a movement to the cities began, it was not a sign of growing readiness to join the majority society, but rather a desperate response, on the part of a people most unready to leave the security of the reserve, to the shrinking demand in rural job markets. This much had been accomplished in nearly a hundred years, that the alien cities could draw people who had neither the education needed for most jobs nor the likelihood of acceptance by employers, fellow workers, neighbours, or society in general. It is a measure of how poorly they were living on the reserves.

Eventually, the exodus slowed and reserve population stabilized, although the people today are still moving – to the city on the one hand, and back to the reserve on the other. Overall figures show a quarter to a third of band population living "off-reserve," and they may be understated.[6] The percentages vary greatly among reserves and commuters raise the numbers in the cities. But the reserves remain very much the centre of Indian life, even for many city dwellers, and are, together with the bands and nations, the primary source of identity.

Not many reserves enjoy a situation where regular employment is available in sufficient quantity, or where there is a combination of employment and traditional pursuits that permits the people, by and large, to be self-supporting. They are basically small communities, most with fewer than a thousand people and many numbering in the low hundreds or even less, yet the resource base is usually smaller still. The larger reserves – two to five thousand people perched on the shore of a northern lake or on farmland that could perhaps support thirty families – tend to be seriously overpopulated. Some locations are remote from jobs of any kind; some are close enough to town or industry for people to get work, provided town employers will hire them.

There is no one pattern that can describe the typical reserve, but it is safe to say that unemployment is endemic on most. In some communities, the unemployment rate soars to eighty or even ninety percent, especially in winter, and thirty to forty percent is common. Statistics for social assistance confirm the melancholy reality: sixty percent of the population in Alberta, seventy-nine percent in Saskatchewan, and eighty-five percent in Manitoba (these figures are for 1980–81, the latest currently available). The corresponding percentages in Ontario and Quebec were thirty and forty-two percent, respectively.[7]

This said, statistics will be used sparingly because they mainly prove what is already known: that there isn't much employment on or near the reserves and, as a direct result, a great many people have to be supported by the government. As a further result, stemming from both unemployment and dependency, the reserves contend with social problems that would tax the resources of much more prosperous communities.

A chief from northern Manitoba, citing a long list of criminal offences in his community, added: "Even these staggering figures fail to reflect the scale of crime, alcohol, drugs, vandalism, and the mindless violence which we suffer."[8] The year is 1989, the setting Manitoba's Aboriginal Justice Inquiry. All of it is plainly related to the underlying conditions – not only the absence of jobs but also the lack of purpose in people's lives, the hopelessness of the outlook. Perhaps most important is a deep-seated resentment. Their present plight is plainly a measure of their worth to Canadian society and to the government which has insisted on running their lives for more than a hundred years.

Alcohol and the frustrations of reserve life form a common thread which runs through several measures of a society at odds with its situation. The consequences, which have a long history, are duly reflected in the figures. For example, in Manitoba, the suicide rate for status Indians under thirty is four times the rate for the province; in Saskatchewan, it is four times the provincial rate for ages twenty to twenty-nine and six times for teenagers. Twenty-two percent of the inmates of federal prisons in Manitoba and thirty-six percent in Saskatchewan are aboriginal people (registered or not). In 1986, the Indian Association of Alberta declared war on alcohol and drug abuse, calling it the number one problem among the province's forty-five thousand status Indians. On some reserves, over eighty percent of deaths were alcohol-related.[9]

The statistics for incarcerations are to some extent misleading because Indian offenders are usually in for relatively minor offences and serve time where the white offender might pay a fine. It should also be said that only a small minority of Indian people get into trouble with the law; of these, many are repeat offenders. However, the essential point is that far too many are in jails and prisons because society refuses to deal with the problems that put them there.

Violence, suicide, and trouble with the law are primarily associated with young males, but women and children are not unaffected. Family life has been strained by poverty and by a system which has failed to get men into jobs, while making welfare easily available to families which lack an earner. In Regina and Winnipeg, women in the younger adult years outnumber the men two to one, and although many are working, too many have been living on social assistance in bad housing and poor neighbourhoods, worrying about the children who are doing poorly in city schools.

Attention turns, eventually, to the system which takes care of Indian people, the main thrust of which has always been provision of services. This is one reason for poor results, for the obligation to provide services became a preoccupation in itself, obscuring the more sensible course of helping people to become self-supporting and able to pay for services in the ordinary way. Over the last thirty years, as people grew less able to support themselves in a world of advancing technology, their dependence on the Department of Indian Affairs increased, when it should have been declining. Social assistance (welfare) is entirely a modern phenomenon, begun in the 1960s.

Health, education, and housing have been the main services provided by the government. None of them could be claimed to be of reasonable quality, although health services have much improved in modern times, so much so that life-expectancy rates on the western reserves are now only nine or ten years below the provincial averages. That being said, reserve residents still suffer disproportionately from tuberculosis (long a scourge and still five times the provincial rate in Manitoba), illness associated with contaminated water and poor sanitary systems, and higher mortality rates among young men, mainly due to accidents and violence.

Low performance levels in the schools have been tolerated by the authorities throughout the history. Lacking education, the people were limited to the lowest-paying jobs – the ones that would eventually disappear – which reinforced the view in white society that they were different, less competent than other people. In the last decade or so, education has been taking hold on the western reserves, with high-school and post-secondary completions rising, but it has been late in coming and still leaves too many out.

Of housing on the reserves, a recent report states that seventy-five percent fails to meet basic standards of safety and decency; forty-seven percent falls below minimum standards, thirty-six percent is seriously overcrowded, and thirty-eight percent lacks water and fixtures.[10] These are national figures (all many times higher than for the general population) and conditions are termed "worse" in rural areas (where most western reserves are located) and "worst" in Manitoba. The life expectancy of reserve housing declined in the 1980s, a result of efforts to improve energy efficiency, and now stands at only five to fifteen years. New design features, combined with poor construction, overcrowding, and much cooking, have produced high moisture build-up, so that houses become uninhabitable within a matter of a few years.

On the Piapot Reserve in southern Saskatchewan, a contractor comes in each year and builds about twelve houses – all Department of Indian Affairs subsidy units, the cheapest option, since most of the population is on welfare. In 1987, the maximum construction cost was $28,000. Higher-quality housing is available to bands which choose the models funded by the Central Mortgage and Housing Corporation (CMHC), but they cost more. All the housing built at Piapot since 1982 is suffering from condensation problems. The use of woodstoves has been found to help and, although wood costs fifty dollars a cord, some people have replaced their electric heaters and furnaces with stoves.

The housing problems reveal in miniature something which ails the system as a whole. Housing is a government obligation, and the houses have always been shoddy, a clear sign of the value society assigns to Indian people, who feel cheated rather than grateful and unable to experience pride in ownership. Yet positive attitudes to housing are found in places "where band members were properly trained to build and operate high performance housing." Involvement of people has always been the missing factor in the Department's long reign. Reserve residents have been recipients: education, health services, and housing, all provided as a matter of entitlement, but in a way that reflected the primacy of cost considerations and the unimportance of the people themselves.

Living separately and as government wards has been another dimension in the history. Shopping in the same stores, working whenever possible for white employers, the people have always known the low opinion their neighbours had of them, and their attachment to the reserve could not but increase. On the other hand, the system set in place to settle the nomadic people was rooted in a nineteenth-century mindset, harsh and paternalistic, which could not but fail. Thus the course was set.

The department responsible for the people's welfare did not see to it that education took hold, that farming was developed or employer resistance combatted; the people on the reserves had no power to do these things on their own. The result is "dependency" – a continuing need for government assistance because the reserve communities never got the help they needed to build their own economy or get jobs in the mainstream. Dependency is a term now used to describe the state of mind engendered in the course of a hundred-odd years of having their lives run for them. Today's Indian leaders see it as one of the most serious problems they face.

The 1980s brought new hope, including the first concerted attempt to inject life into the reserve economy since the farm instructors were hired a century before. Today's people are freer from petty regulations, they can vote both federally and provincially, and the bands have taken over delivery of the all-important services. On the other hand, unemployment levels are still very high, money paid out in social assistance far exceeds the money made available for economic development, social problems are still present, as are children dropping out of school and the hostility that people feel over broken promises and poor treatment. Most critically, the bands still have no power. Every important decision affecting their lives is still made by the federal government – a circumstance wholly at variance with that of all other Canadians.

Such a history raises many questions. These people have been living on the fringes of mainstream society since the 1870s – on the southern reserves, in tiny northern settlements and, increasingly in recent years, in the poorer parts of Prairie cities. Yet these long years of stewardship have not made them full citizens in the sense of having access to jobs or to Canadian standards of health and education. The whole situation – the poverty, the social problems, the basic isolation from the rest of society – is deeply disturbing, and in particular the continuing dependence on an agency whose mandate was to ready them for full participation in society.

The situation can be dismissed with a shrug, written off as hopeless, or we can go behind the headlines to see what keeps the people poor and separate. These two dimensions are obviously related, the awkward locations of the reserves and limited resources that are a prime reason for poverty, and the wish or need to stay there nonetheless. But the reserves must also be seen as communities where people do choose to live, the real home to countless city dwellers and the one place on earth that truly belongs to them, providing continuity with their history. The next section turns to the reserves themselves, which are virtually unknown to the dominant society, yet central to an understanding of the people who live there.

INDIAN HOMELANDS

The isolation of the reserve is the very essence of its being. In one sense, it can be measured in kilometres – the distances which separate so many in the North from anything approaching a city; the remoteness of so many southern reserves, located where the land is poor and the surrounding area largely undeveloped. In another sense, isolation can be seen in the special status as wards of the government, a category that applies to no other people in the Canadian mosaic.

Originally envisaged as a staging ground, the western reserves are still home to a majority of the people entitled to live there and those who have left are mainly in the cities. There have never been normal relations with neighbouring communities where people from the reserves go to shop; reserve and town are separate worlds, linked only by the money which one spends in the other. Lethbridge, a city of about sixty thousand in southern Alberta, has two large reserves close by, which spend an estimated $30 million a year in the city; yet a recent survey found that only six percent of Lethbridge businesses hired Indian people.[11]

Indian people have lived like this since the treaties were signed, and they resent the one-dimensional relationship and the disapproving looks that mark them as inferior. They see themselves as having tried hard to be self-supporting, but having been frustrated in their efforts by a white society that has seldom been willing to employ them. Free housing and other entitlements do not begin to make up for what they have lost or what they have endured through the years.

What they do have are these lands where they have lived for several generations, which provide a link to their past and a place where they can live as a people. Did they choose separateness, or was it thrust upon them? There are elements of both. In early days, the Indian people held on to their culture as best they could, as defeated peoples tend to do, and the more so as the Department tried hard to root it out, seeing it as a barrier to assimilation. In this sense, they "chose" separateness. But as white society gave no sign of accepting them, or any sign even that they could become acceptable in time, the Indian people were not so much making a choice as trying to salvage what they could from the débâcle. The reader can assess the degree of choice involved in the course of the next chapter.

The strength of their culture has enabled the western nations to survive as a people, and they are still living cultures, with meaning both for those who have adopted western ways and for those whose values and outlook are more traditional. Retaining their culture has made adjustment more difficult, but it has also served as armour against a hostile world, just as the reserves have served as a refuge. In view of the hostility they still encounter in white society, the system of separate living suits most Indian people. Everyone has been through it: the schoolrooms where Indian children feel the low opinion of their classmates, the snide comments of fellow workers on the job, the small-town stores where Indian people were likely to be last served.

So it is that the reserves remain as tiny islands in a sea of white culture, *terra incognita* to all but their own people. Approximately 170 reserves are scattered about the three provinces, their locations determined in a rough sort of way by where the bands happened to be in the 1870s, although none were living in one place at the time and some moved considerable distances to take up residence on their reserve. In terms of population, they range in size from the Blood Reserve with more than five thousand people, down to tiny Sawridge in northern Alberta and Buffalo Point in Manitoba, neither of which can claim forty residents. These two, incidentally, enjoy a prosperity that is far above average, their resources and population being better aligned than is usually the case.

In terms of land size, the Blood Reserve is the largest in Canada, but it takes very large acreage in the short-grass country to support an economic farm and the Blood haven't nearly enough. Some bands have never received the full allotment to which they were entitled by the treaties, and many have lost land they once had through sell-offs, notably in the years surrounding World War I.

At the national level, it has been estimated that Canadian Indians have one of the smallest land bases per capita in the world: "Indians represent 3 percent of the population of Canada, but retain less than 0.2 percent as reserves. Indians in the United States constitute just over 0.5 percent of the population, yet retain nearly 4 percent of the land." Moreover, according to the same source, the Department itself admits that," as an economic resource of potential benefit to Indians, their land base is now a fraction of the acreages originally provided by Treaties and other forms of entitlement during a period when the population was much smaller."[12]

Most reserves have a distinctly rural air, with houses built in a random pattern, linked by paths and usually well separated because the people like privacy. There is likely a central cluster of buildings – a band office, a school, a store, a community centre, a rink or other sports facility – and commercial malls, which offer a range of services, are found on many reserves. There is a certain sameness about the government-provided housing on the best-housed reserves, and more serious problems elsewhere. The settings vary. In the North, pine and spruce trees and crystal lakes make for sites of great beauty, something that seems to have a deeper meaning in Indian culture than in Euro-Canadian culture generally. The southern reserves have their own kind of beauty; a Saskatchewan writer who loved the Prairies put it this way: "things to be seen and felt that exalt or soothe the spirit: wheatfields merging into a green or golden ocean, unbounded save for a remote horizon rim at times indistinguishable from the sky itself ... and the occasional vista, when a man sees all the kingdoms of the earth stretched out at his feet and feels himself a creature of utter insignificance in the scheme of things or else the very centre of the universe."[13]

A few bands with outstanding good fortune managed to locate on oil- or gas-producing lands, which yielded riches beginning in the 1970s. Some reserves in the North work well enough, either through access to employment in the mines and forest industries, or with good fishing or trapping and not too many people. On most northern reserves, population outstripped the resources at hand long ago, so that living there involves heavy dependence on social assistance. The situation is particularly difficult in northern Manitoba where an overgenerous supply of Precambrian Shield wilderness has limited the extent of road building.

Roughly one-third of Manitoba's reserves are accessible only by small aircraft and the tractor-trains which haul in supplies over winter roads in a brief two-month season, so that the cost of everything is high. At Shamattawa, on God's River, one of the most isolated communities in the province, homes are limited to fifteen-amp power from a diesel generator, barely enough for a refrigerator and two light bulbs. At God's Lake Narrows, the Indian owner of a small grocery store has a monthly electricity bill of $300. His supplies are trucked from the airport to the lake, and he moves them across in his motor boat. Much of northern Manitoba is like this, small population clusters which are nevertheless too large for the people to live off the land as they used to do, and poorly situated from the standpoint of development.

Much the same could be said of the agricultural South, for the rural areas have been losing population for the better part of four decades, the small farmers being pushed out as efficient farm size increased and small-town businesses failing as their customers departed. The reserves, however, are still there, their populations much increased since the 1870s and now vastly exceeding what farming could support, supposing that it had been successfully established in the first place.

In a 1960s Canada-wide survey, the three lowest-income reserves included two from Saskatchewan.[14] And beginning in the sixties, the heaviest flow of people from the reserves to the cities has taken place in southern Saskatchewan. This exodus has slowed in recent years, thanks to some strengthening in the reserve economies, but the basic parameters are not greatly changed.

Unemployment and social assistance are not the whole story, however, for the reserve is not exclusively an economic entity, nor are they all the same. Some reserves work well, although they don't have much to work with, while others, seemingly better endowed, are overwhelmed by problems. Such differences can sometimes be traced to the quality of the leadership, to the strength or weakness of the attachment to the culture or the Church, or to any number of special factors in a band's particular history.

Island Lake, which I shall come to shortly, is one example of a special history. On the map just one of hundreds of lakes in northern Manitoba, this one happens to be on a boundary line – between the Cree nation to the north and the Ojibwa to the south. Over the centuries, the Island Lake people drew on the culture and traditions of both, producing a unique heritage, including a dialect which is a mixture of the two languages. This special history is thought to be one reason for the social cohesion which underlies much of the progress recorded in recent years. Neighbouring Red Sucker Lake, also on the Cree-Ojibwa line, has a similar history and a famous native son, Elijah Harper, who spoke for all native people when he opposed the Meech Lake accord in the summer of 1990.

The world of the reserves contains a wide range of experience: at one end, there are hard-working, go-ahead places that wrest all possible income from a scanty endowment; at the other, there are places where people are demoralized from years of welfare and failed efforts. Five thumbnail sketches are presented next in an attempt to convey something of this variety and, it is hoped, a little flavour of life on the reserve. They should not be taken as representative, for the choice was influenced in part by the availability of information, and also by a wish to document some positive situations to balance the opposite bias in the media. They should at least dispel certain stereotypes and demonstrate the real efforts being made to build a better life, as well as the heavy odds which the people and their leaders are battling.

Peguis (Population: 2,779)

This is Manitoba's largest reserve in terms of acreage, but its location deep in the Interlake Region, with its thin soils and long winters, is far from favourable for farming. Only a little over half the band lives on Peguis, but it is nevertheless a busy place. Many people farm, which cannot be said of most of the reserves which are blessed with good farmland. There is a business section, including a band office, an adult-education centre, a library, and a community hall where bingo is a frequent event and a good money raiser. Several band members run businesses: a service station, a bulk-fuel dealer, a laundromat, a grocery, etc.

By and large, the people are poor. Although better off than they were some twenty years ago, when the Hawthorne Report revealed that one hundred percent were on welfare, there is still much of the Third World look that applies to so many Prairie reserves. The present chief, Louis Stevenson, a man with a lively imagination, made headlines in 1987 by inviting the South African ambassador to visit his reserve. The ambassador did visit, briefly, accepting a request for $99 million in foreign aid, exchanging gifts, and going to see a family of seven living in a two-room shack. His appropriate dismay was well covered by the media, and Chief Stevenson had a good line for the press: "Canada is grandstanding and ego-tripping trying to solve the problems of 26 million blacks in South Africa and they can't even solve the small problem here with half-a-million Indians."[15]

Peguis is a place where many people try hard. They paint their houses and cut their grass; many of them go to church. The band-operated school system runs from kindergarten through grade twelve and has a good ratio of pupils continuing through high school, which is by no means a common achievement on the western reserves. It is said that Peguis has always had good leadership, and it is a matter of record that under the original Chief Peguis this band took up farming in the 1830s. It was a response to scarcity and though not a "first" (other examples of early farming can be found in chapter 2), it still speaks well for the leadership.

The Peguis band lived then at St Peter's (a later name), just north of what is now the city of Winnipeg. This raises the question of what the Peguis people might have accomplished had they been left on the rich black soil of the Red River Valley, instead of banished, early in the twentieth century, to the inferior soils and climate between the lakes. According to the story, there was a deal involving a faction in the band and some government officials: the band got a cash settlement and a poorly located reserve, while the consortium got land that could be sold at very high prices. [16]

Eighty years later (1989), Peguis fortunes took a sudden upturn as construction began on a $6-million shopping mall, financed mainly by the federal and provincial governments. Was it the ambassador's visit that unleashed this largess? It is impossible to say, but Chief Stevenson did comment on the absence of fanfare which usually accompanies such grants.

John Smith (Population: 671)

A short twenty-kilometre drive from Prince Albert, this reserve in central Saskatchewan was the first choice of the Department's officer when he was asked to name a band that was doing well. "Good farming," he said, "good leadership, church-going people." [17] And certainly, the band is blessed compared with poor Peguis, for it has good farmland, with more than twenty thousand acres under cultivation in 1989. The leadership is active: John Smith was the third band in Canada to enter into agreements with the Department to transfer responsibility for programs to the bands. Education has been seen as important, and the numbers in and completing high school have risen well in recent years.

But John Smith is not truly a success story and, in a dramatic way, can illustrate the historic failure to settle the bands and provide them with a future. The fact is that up to sixty percent of the cropland is farmed not by band members but by neighbouring whites, who lease the land. And since leasing returns very little, the income which could be had from farming has, in large measure, been lost. It is still further diminished by the weak development of reserve farming: only one band farmer operates on the scale that is average for the district, while another four or five farm in a smaller way. This is a common pattern in reserve agriculture, the result of a sad history which will be recounted in due course.

The original John Smith (a surname said to be translated from the Cree) came west from Red River, bringing with him the nucleus of the present band. A history of the band has been written by one of its members, Paulette Bear, who describes the Old Chief as a great friend of the white people,[18] and perhaps he was less attentive than some to the welfare of ordinary band members. In any event, the good relationship that the Old Chief established with government officials appears to have lasted through to modern times. Paulette Bear's account is entirely confined to ordinary people on the reserve, who are described as hard working, church going, and very poor, but also helpful to each other, full of enjoyment at social occasions, and proud of their accomplishments.

Saskatchewan south of the tree line offers few opportunities other than farming for people who make their home in rural areas, so this failure in farming explains the high rate of exodus from all the reserves in the South, Saskatchewan leading all other provinces in this regard. John Smith has been fortunate in its location, for Prince Albert is handy and offers educational opportunities as well as employment; many residents commute and some choose to live in the city. They also work in other cities and in northern industries, and have done so for many years.

Piegan (Population: 2,500)

One of three nations in the Blackfoot Confederacy in buffalo days, the Piegan have lived since on their reserve in southwestern Alberta, a short distance from Lethbridge. There is not much farming now, nor has there been for a long time, despite the fact that the Piegan took it up with much enthusiasm in the 1880s (see chapter 2). Now, there is only a thin sprinkling of farmers and a band-owned ranch which offers a little employment. Beyond that, the Piegan have a crafts-manufacturing enterprise, a construction company, and a few small businesses; it doesn't add up to nearly enough. A recent consultant's report put on-reserve population at ninety-seven percent, with an unemployment rate of "95 percent of more."[19] Social assistance remains a major source of income, much of it spent in Lethbridge.

Over the years, the Piegan have done many things; they have worked as ranch hands and in the construction and logging industries in both the US and Canada, raised race horses, and ridden broncos in rodeos. But the reserve at Brocket has always drawn them back. This tendency to stay or to come back is generally strong in Alberta, compared with neighbouring Saskatchewan. One reason, in the case of the Piegan and their confederates, might be that their reserves are part of their traditional homelands, with features and memories that go back for centuries, keeping their heritage in view. Much more commonly, in Manitoba and Saskatchewan, the bands were settled on lands with which they had no historic ties, and also in smaller groups, which made for small reserves with perhaps fewer landscape features that cement attachment or places where people could walk with the ancient spirits undisturbed. But regardless of the reason, there can be no question concerning the Piegan's attachment to their land.

A major concern at the present time is school drop-out. Only about seven percent of the children finish school, and the Piegan have been pressing for money for special programs to combat low ambition and feelings of hopelessness among the students.

What the Piegan do have is staying power. In the early 1980s, they got a cash settlement for a claim they had been pressing since 1922, involving water diverted from the Oldman River. A few years later, they got a second settlement for a claim dating from 1909 when substantial reserve acreage had been sold off with the Indian agent's connivance. These monies are helping to implement a development strategy drawn up by the band, beginning with an historical site, Head-Smashed-In Buffalo Jump and Interpretive Centre. Designated a world heritage site by UNESCO, the Centre is among the best preserved such jump sites where, in the millenia before they had the horse, the Plains people stampeded herds of buffalo to their deaths. A second project concerns the Oldman River which runs through the reserve. The plan is to build two low-head hydro units to supply the reserve and to sell irrigation services. In 1985, the date of the consultant's report just mentioned, the Piegan had been waiting five years for funding and they were still waiting at the end of the decade when the province began implementing its own plans for the Oldman.

As further evidence of staying power, the *Calgary Herald* reports that a group of Piegan film makers are engaged in a project to show six thousand years of Piegan life, only one hundred of which have been spent on the reserve.

Norway House (Population: 2,700)

This is a reserve with a beautiful natural setting, like so many in the North, on the rocky shoreline of the Nelson River a mile or two from the town of the same name which dates from the fur-trade era. Norway House was then a major post in the Hudson's Bay network; it is now an administrative centre for northern services, which extend to all the reserves that spread east, north, and west from Norway House.

The amount of government employment in the town has not done much for the Crees on the reserve. In the winter of 1987, sixty percent of the population was on welfare, which has been a way of life for two generations. A teacher interviewed by the *Winnipeg Free Press* expressed concern for children growing up without seeing their parents as people who go off to work every day.[20] He said they are bright kids, with as much potential as any, but they just don't have a sense of striving. He blamed the welfare system, which he saw as a strong disincentive to learning, as do most observers. There is a high school which has 250 students, but few are interested in completing their schooling.

Employment opportunities available to band members are limited. Some Crees are employed by the government agencies – mainly at the lowest levels – and the band employs many more, as bands do nowadays, administering many or most of the services that used to be run by the Department. There are a few small businesses, while seasonal work in logging, trapping, and fishing provides part-time employment for perhaps 150 individuals. The welfare figure suggests the size of the shortfall.

Heather Robertson, who wrote an exposé of conditions on the western reserves in the late 1960s, spent some time at Norway House. One thing that struck her was the amount of time spent on the activities of daily life, such as fetching water from a communal tap, chopping firewood, going to the Hudson's Bay store, and so on. She saw such activities as a substitute for the paid work which was not available in her time and is still in short supply today.[21]

The log shacks described by Robertson have been replaced to a considerable extent, but by small, cheaply constructed frame bungalows, heated with woodstoves and intolerably cold in winter temperatures of minus forty degrees. There is also a housing shortage; as many as fifteen people have been reported living in one three-bedroom house. There are still no sewers or running water. Twenty-odd years ago, Robertson reported pollution in the Nelson River, the result of untreated waste being dumped by the hospital. In the late 1980s, the water is again suspect, but this time mercury readings are high, the fish are gone, and, although the trouble seems to stem from hydro works completed more than a decade earlier, remedies have not yet been devised, nor compensation paid.

Island Lake (Population: 4,934)

Island Lake itself is a large lake, and the three bands located on it have formed a tribal council which goes by that name. Roughly 150 kilometres east of Norway House, they are infinitely more remote since access is limited to small aircraft and the winter road. The three reserves – Garden Hill, Wasagamack, and St Theresa Point – will have to be treated as a collective for the sake of brevity, but in reality they are far from losing their individual identities.

This is a much more independent situation than Norway House with its large community of white caregivers. The people of Island Lake have an airport, a small Bay store, and the occasional service worker coming in, but otherwise they are pretty much on their own. In the brochure produced by the tribal council, Island Lake is described as "a quiet, placid place to live." Shortly thereafter, however, come references to square dancing, picnics, banquets, celebrations, bingo, various sporting events, and a new arena under construction, which suggest that life might be considerably more eventful than the brochure implies.[22]

The people describe themselves as following a "partially traditional" way of life. There are some who live mainly by fishing, trapping, and hunting, while others move out into the bush a couple of times a year, partly to offset the high cost of living and partly because they enjoy the outdoors. There is also modern employment: band offices, the Child and Family Agency, the school, the Hudson's Bay store, the airport, and some dozen or more Indian-owned businesses. As elsewhere in the North, it does not add up to nearly enough and leaves considerable numbers on welfare for part of the year. But the other factors still stand out: the degree of autonomy, the level of resource utilization, the quality of life.

That the Island Lake people are poor is beyond doubt; nor are they without social problems, for the brochure lists alcohol- and drug-abuse programs and several kinds of family services established by the tribal council. But they are moving to deal with these problems and they have been education-oriented for a long time. Their schools go to grade ten and many students go out for higher education. University graduates from Island Lake have found employment with bands across the West.

The Island Lake Tribal Council has launched a new housing program based on R-2000 – the energy-efficient units that reduce heating costs and make homes more comfortable – as well as an economic-development program based on joint venturing. One such project, already underway, is a resort; another is an airline. In addition to passenger traffic, the airline is intended to fly fish directly to American markets, so that the fishermen can get a better price than the provincial marketing agency pays.

What seems to mark Island Lake is a high degree of social cohesion, although it is by no means a monolithic community. Traditional customs, morals, and values are still respected and followed, yet Christian churches, in several denominations, are also a living part of the communities. Somehow, the two are reconciled. Elders in the community play a large part in decision making and are sought out for their wisdom and advice. Traditional practices appear to fit with modern band councils and to give the people a good sense of themselves; the elders stress that "they must not forget who they are or where they came from or their grass roots.[23]

It is difficult to generalize. Their remote location has given these people more opportunity than most to manage for themselves, yet there are other reserves, equally remote, that do far less well. The singular history, mentioned earlier, of living with and merging two cultures, the Cree and Ojibwa, seems likely to be part of it, but any further insights would have to be sought from the Island Lake people themselves.

SOME COMMON THEMES

These five sketches should dispel the stereotype that all reserves are cut from the same cloth, by showing something of the variety that prevails in real life. The same sketches, however, may also be used to pick out the common elements which explain the poverty and related problems which apply more or less across the board. All of them relate to the system within which these people have lived for more than a hundred years.

Weakness of the Resource Base

Resources are always the starting point, and this weakness is well nigh universal – in many cases, it has been present since the communities were first settled. Jean Lagassé, heading a 1950s inquiry into the circumstances of the Métis in northern Manitoba, spoke bluntly about some of the communities he saw, most of which adjoined an equally impoverished reserve: "One can find no economic justification for continued existence of such Métis communities as Brochet, South Indian Lake, Norway House, Pelican Rapids, Anama Bay, Duck Bay and several others. The population increases each year while no new source of income is discovered. These people will have to lean more heavily on welfare assistance or face a decline in the standard of living."[24] In the more than thirty years since these lines were written, the prophesy has proved true: the population is larger, the economy is still stagnant, and welfare has become the primary source of income.

Lagassé's conclusion was echoed recently by the Department, whose view of a northern Manitoba reserve was thus conveyed to a consultant: "There is no economic activity in the area and no economic reason for the band being there. There is no potential for future development on the Reserve as there is nothing there to build on."[25] In fact, there was some potential, as the band knew well enough; confirmed by the consultant, it was subsequently taken up by the band. Yet the basic problem remains, for this, as for so many reserves where population has outstripped any reasonable prospect for development.

The Prairie reserves are in equally unnatural locations for sizeable communities. The allocations agreed to at Treaty Six were based on the amount of land deemed necessary for supporting a family of five, but they were made at a time when motive power was supplied by horses or even oxen, and grain was often harvested with hand tools. A viable farm today requires several times as much land, while reserve size, far from increasing, has been significantly reduced through sell-offs in all three provinces. Population, on the other hand, has substantially increased. The fact that the land is mainly leased, as seen at John Smith, hardly improves the picture, and what are people to do in farm country if they don't farm? In essence, the reserves, both north and south, need access to additional sources of income. This leads to the second common theme.

Separateness

Special status and the whole apparatus of living separately from the rest of society are obviously major reasons for poverty, since the people are tied to a particular piece of real estate, irrespective of its ability to generate jobs and income. Why, then, are they there?

The reserve as a concept seems reasonable enough, going back to the days when the West was being opened for settlement, for the nomadic hunters would need time to learn new ways and the reserve system seemed acceptable to the bands in eastern Canada. But the outcome is not at all reasonable. The people are not supporting themselves by farming, and although they managed with casual wage work for many decades, those jobs dried up in the 1950s and 1960s. Since then, the people have been stranded. So many of them lacked access to jobs in the mainstream economy that welfare became the mainstay. Education, confidence, and, most of all, acceptability have been the missing ingredients.

Throughout their long association with Canada, these people in the West have lived separately, actively excluded from white society in ways both large and small, by hostile teachers and co-workers, employers who won't hire them, and landlords who won't rent to them in the city. George Manuel tells of his boyhood experience in a small town in British Columbia, where Indians were seated separately in a small corner of the theatre. "For a long time this seemed to me just a part of the way things were, like the distance to town or the rain that soaked you on the way home. It was only as I grew older that I developed a resentment and realized that this movie house reservation was not as fixed and certain as the Creator's will."[26] It would be hard to explain why this separate world has been sustained over so many years, unless one assumes a collective wish in Canadian society that the Indian people should live separately, no matter how poorly.

Dependency

The five communities described above all depend in varying degrees on social assistance; it is needed both for non-earners and for workers who have long gaps in employment during the year. On many reserves, the unemployment rate runs right off the charts and however these rates are calculated, they reflect the reality that hardly anybody works year-round. That is why the government brought in social assistance nearly thirty years ago, and it is a sad comment on the way things are run that it is just as much needed today.

But dependency of this kind is only on the economic side. In its most basic sense, dependency goes back to the beginnings of reserve life when true independence ended. In the South, where the people had to be equipped for a completely new life, the Department took over the management of their lives, leaving them to follow orders while failing to provide the kind of assistance that could have established farming and encouraged the children to see schooling as worthwhile. Such a system would be unthinkable today, but the Department put men to work on small plots and preached the work ethic to farmers who earned next to nothing. Ancient beliefs and practices were seen as standing in the way, and the Department did its best to root them out.

Some Indian people became self-supporting, but many did not; nor did the communities in which they lived. The Department is still the sole source of power and the system, although partially dismantled, is still very much a presence, a key dimension in the lives of Indian people, marking them as different.

Failures in the system have held the people back in the crucial areas of schooling and job skills, and have induced feelings of inferiority and incompetence. Children in school, as well as adults, are affected by the sense that they are bound to fail. An officer in a tribal council whose job it is to promote economic development names as one of the main problems the fact that people on the reserve don't learn to achieve.[27]

David Courchene, when he was president of the Manitoba Indian Brotherhood, put the problem this way: "One hundred years of submission and servitude, of protectionism and paternalism have created psychological barriers for Indian people that are far more difficult to break down and conquer than the problems of economic and social poverty. Paternalistic policies of the past, based largely on the idea that we must shelter and protect the ignorant savage, have created complex problems for those who want to shelter and protect themselves."[28]

Rents in the Social Fabric

Despite a harsh system and the hostility in white society, the Indian people have found deep sources of strength in their culture and in their belief in themselves. They could not otherwise have survived as a people. But the difficulties have been enormous – the difficulties of living for several generations in circumstances that generate high levels of stress and in communities that offer little support.

Poverty is itself a source of stress. So is the inferior status assigned to Indian people, and the feelings of resentment, for shoddy housing, for example, or the sheer meanness of life on the reserve. The Indian family has been subjected to stress from several sources and conflict between the generations is a recurrent theme. Children are pulled two ways: to the white society that seems to offer riches, but equally to their own society because it is theirs and heals the wounds of unsuccessful encounters with the other. Discouragement has been another constant and it has reached beyond the reserve to those who hoped to find a better life in the city, only to find themselves defeated by the problems there. Above all are the feelings of helplessness on the part of people who could find no way to improve their lives.

Another side has been a weakness at the community level. The Department has been too commanding a presence for the powers that are needed to solve the problems do not lie with the bands. Some bands have managed better than others and, in many cases, have provided a strong sense of belonging to the group and a shared history. But some have gone through times when leaders were co-opted by the Department or the band split into factions, so that individual band members were left to deal with problems on their own and without a sense of identity. This is a main cause of the disaffection to be found in many communities and of the social problems which reach alarming proportions.

This kind of difficulty is another facet of dependency. A parliamentary committee reporting in the mid-1980s named dependency as the basic source of the problems today and a transfer of power as the essential starting point from which solutions can emerge.[29]

FUTURE AND PAST

This first chapter has not, thus far, allowed for changes in the last few years that make the future look better. In fact, the 1980s brought the first concerted attempts to inject life into the reserve economy since the farm instructors were hired in the 1880s. There are new federal efforts, new help from the provinces and the private sector, and band councils are delivering most services. Education levels are rising and university graduates are taking jobs in many fields, both on the reserve and off. All these are important changes when set against the years of stagnation, although their impact is as yet discouragingly small. Unemployment rates seem not much affected; a spokesman for an Indian-owned development corporation said recently, "The plight of the Indian economy is quite constant, despite the higher employment figures."[30]

More growth will come as new factors take hold, but a question remains as to how much. On this point, the unfavourable factors come crowding in: the awkward locations of the reserves, wardship, the whole legacy of problems accumulated over a hundred years. To make the future better, it will be necessary to take account of problems inherited from the past.

In the original plan, the hunters would learn farming and support themselves and their families thus. They would also be civilized. Indeed, "civilizing" would come first, for in the thinking of those far-off times, language, religion, and proper dress were the essential beginning, assuming far more importance than tools and instruction for farming. The newly established Canadian government also saw itself as part of a larger European mission to "backward" societies the world over and, faced with the daunting task of settling several thousand nomadic hunters, set up a system of tutelage that left no room for old beliefs, initiative, or advancement. This system, which failed to establish farming and had little success in the schools, occupies much of chapter 2.

Not for a long time would the failure in farming be recognized, much less admitted. Years without progress were explained away on the grounds that time is needed to make adjustments. But in fact, as settlers became prosperous farmers and towns became cities, the reserves fell ever further behind. This widening gap confirmed the general view, including the government's, that most Indian people would prove unable to adjust and that it was better, therefore, that the two societies should continue to live separately. This, of course, they have done, with one society growing in wealth and power, while the other remains poor, without power or resources to tackle its problems.

The separation of the races has long been taken for granted, and white society lives with a clear conscience because it never sees the fault as its own. In the prevailing view, Indian people were offered the gift of civilization but failed to take advantage of it. At a conference on reserve agriculture in the 1960s, I heard a high-ranking federal official declare that the government had been overly generous with its gifts of farm equipment, for the Indian people, given everything they needed, had still failed, whereas the immigrants, empty handed and given nothing, became prosperous. This is a widely accepted version of events in the West; but it ignores both the capital which immigrants brought with them in the form of farming knowledge, and the harsh and ill-conceived regime imposed on the aboriginal hunters, a regime which denied them knowledge, initiative, and capital.

The more recent history has also been seen in a one-sided way as the government providing programs while Indian people insist on failing. But the later government programs have also missed the mark. Meanwhile, the continuing role of government in managing their affairs has sapped the people's initiative and stifled growth. The people have survived, largely through their own strength and efforts, but they have also lived separately from their neighbours, and as people who are seen as different, inferior, and incapable. This is as much their heritage today as the thin soils of the Interlake Region, or the cost of freight and heating in remote northern settlements.

The past confronts Indian leaders who deal with apathy and hopelessness, and equally the communities where leadership fails to emerge. It clouds the outlook of young people who, unable to see themselves in a job, fail to get the education they need. A century of being managed by and excluded from a more powerful society has had many damaging effects, both for individuals and the society.

All this is known to Indian people, but Canadians generally accept the anomalous status, the apparatus of control, the absence of an economic base, the abysmal poverty, and the welfare expenditures that keep the whole thing afloat. Some don't see it as an issue, others have simple explanations: Indian people didn't try hard enough; government is doing the best it can. Such views hold back real change because white society controls the political decision that would be needed to change the policies.

To change the situation, simple explanations would have to give way to questions, most of them contained in one that could be put this way: What on earth has the government been doing all these years that people should be living in the circumstances that describe most western reserves?

The next three chapters describe the hundred-year history that begins with the treaties and the government's plan for a people which had lost both its land and its livelihood.

CHAPTER TWO

The Reserve System:
Early Days (1870s–1945)

The chiefs who signed the western treaties represented nations with very different histories. The Blackfoot and their confederates – the Blood and the Piegan – had roamed the western plains for thousands of years, and the Chipewyan in the northern forests were also long-term residents. But the others were newcomers, relatively speaking, pushed out of their historic homelands in the East by the press of white civilization, or moving West with the fur trade.

The Assiniboine count as early comers: in 1688, Henry Kelsey recorded in his journal that he met them in what is now western Manitoba.[1] They are a Siouan people who had broken away from the main Sioux (Dakota) nation, probably in Minnesota, and eventually made their way north to share the plains with the Blackfoot to the west.

The Crees cannot have been far behind. A meeting with them on the Winnipeg River is recorded in the early seventeenth century, but their main movement out of the James Bay region followed the arrival of the Hudson's Bay Company in 1670.[2] The Crees joined the fur trade. In their great canoes they took the waterways to the West, where they exchanged trade goods for furs with the western nations, sometimes doing a little trapping for themselves. But mainly they were traders, middlemen in the system, connecting the trappers in the West with European civilization on Hudson Bay. The Crees secured this position by making alliances, first with the Assiniboine, who became attached to the fur trade as suppliers of pemmican and buffalo robes, and later with the Blackfoot. They also controlled the inland river systems and, thus, access to the inland posts, once they were built.

Although first introduced to European goods and weapons through the Hudson's Bay Company, the western nations had long-established trading connections to the south. The Assiniboine went each year to the upper Missouri, where the agricultural Mandans supplied them with corn and tobacco; it was also through the Mandans that the Assiniboine had access to the horse markets, their only source of horses since the supply was strictly controlled by the American tribes. The Blackfoot had southern trading partners as well, and these took on new importance as the horse became a key piece in Plains society, both for hunting and for war. By the 1750s, both the Blackfoot and the Assiniboine were "well mounted," and shortly thereafter the Cree river traders had begun to acquire horses as well.

By this time, the Crees and the Blackfoot had cemented their mutual interests, economic and military, in a formal alliance, the Crees supplying weapons for the Blackfoot wars and the Blackfoot supplying horses. Some Crees had taken up buffalo hunting, while others still plied the rivers, but with the Hudson's Bay Company and the Northwest Company now building posts, there was a diminishing need to make the long trip to York Factory on Hudson Bay. These same posts offered the Plains people a new economic opportunity, that of killing buffalo to provision the posts, and it was taken up with a will. The Blackfoot were the first to give up fur trading; not long after, it could be said of the Crees that "all are tenting in the plains, killing buffalo for themselves to eat."[3] The speakers were Hudson's Bay men, who equated these pursuits with idleness and want of purpose.

It may also be seen as a choice the Crees made at a time when choice was possible, demonstrating both the attractions of the free life and the independent spirit of the people. By and large, they seem to have been good years, from the late eighteenth century to the middle of the nineteenth. Vast herds of buffalo ensured that there was plenty to eat; the country was beautiful and life changed with the seasons. In the spring, the people moved out onto the prairie, where they spent the summer killing buffalo; in the fall, they moved back to the shelter of the park belt. At all seasons, they lived in large groups, for sociability was one of life's great pleasures. The capabilities of their chiefs are amply attested to by historians, who also say that the Crees maintained a good view of themselves from their first contact with the whites. The Europeans' goods were not taken as evidence of a superior civilization, whatever the Bay men might say. Indeed, says historian James Milloy, "as a general rule, they saw themselves as the norm, and the more the European differed from an Indian ... the more ridiculous that European appeared."[4]

By the eighteenth century, the Ojibwa in Ontario were also moving westward, pushed by white settlement. The name "Saulteaux" was attached to them in the days when they traded at the Sault. There, the westbound groups diverged, some moving west and north through the forests, eventually bumping against the Crees, while a southern stream emerged on the Plains, not far from Red River. Here, they allied themselves with the Assiniboine, as the Crees had before them, but took up the buffalo hunt with the Métis. As the century drew to a close, there were still many years of the free life ahead, yet a dark shadow was cast by the first smallpox epidemic (1780–82) which took a terrible toll. David Thompson estimated that half the Indians of the prairies and woodlands died of this plague[5] and it must have planted a fear of uncontrollable forces that the people had not previously known.

In the nineteenth century, important trading relationships broke down. The essential connection through the Mandans for the supply of horses was the first to go, leaving both the Crees and the Assiniboine without an assured source. Then the Blackfoot experienced similar difficulties and the Blackfoot-Cree alliance split apart under the strain. Warfare became more frequent. But the heaviest toll in terms of lives came with the second smallpox epidemic in 1837. The Crees escaped the worst of it (many of them were vaccinated at the trading posts), but the Mandans in the United States disappeared altogether; in Canada, the Assiniboine lost whole bands and the Blackfoot two-thirds of their population. The former, thought to have numbered around 28,000 at the beginning of the nineteenth century (counting both Canada and the US), were down to 2,600 in a 1904 count, largely because of losses in the 1830s. One of the bands that came through the epidemic gathered as many orphaned survivors from other bands as it could find and fled, through Blackfoot territory, to the foothills of the Rockies. The descendants of this band, now known as the Stonies,[6] live there to this day.

The second outbreak of smallpox fell in the same decade as the US government's decision to relocate the eastern tribes to the lands west of the Mississipi. In a sense, this was the beginning of the end. Entailing great hardship, the relocation also increased the competition for hunting in the West and raised the level of warfare among the tribes. Soon, the landhungry settlers were pressing again, demanding access to the western plains. The tribes, still free, were assigned to reservations; some of them resisted, fighting pitched battles with the US army. They were also easy prey to the seductions of the whiskey traders, who offered a temporary respite from fear and harassment. In 1860, a new technology made it possible to use buffalo hides in the leather trade and, in short order, ten thousand white hunters descended on the Plains, raising the scale of the slaughter to unimagined proportions. But even earlier, on the eastern side of the Canadian range, the herds had begun to disappear. Captain John Palliser, who was to give his name to a vast triangle of land deemed unsuitable for agriculture, went through in 1857 and was told that the Crees were beginning to know scarcity. He also reported that many were anxious to try farming[7] – indeed, a start had been made, by Indian as well as Métis, as will be seen below.

The chaos south of the border had other ramifications in the North as well. Whiskey traders from the US did a brisk business on the British side; one of their posts was appropriately named Fort Whoop Up. There were also refugees fleeing the US army. The first Sioux party rode over the border in the 1860s, many of them displaying medals from the Queen of England, awarded to their forebears for services rendered in the War of 1812 – further proof of the hardships experienced over fifty years as these bands had been driven to the West. A second party of Sioux refugees was to come later following their historic victory at the battle of the Little Bighorn, and they too were admitted, though not permanently. But by that time, the end was near. In 1877, the US army adopted a policy of slaughtering the buffalo in order to reduce the tribes which, refusing the proferred reservations, were making a hopeless, last-ditch stand against the army. The buffalo, however, had already diminished to the point of scarcity and people were dying of starvation on both sides of the border. The last buffalo were seen at the Bow River in 1876 and they had long vanished from the eastern prairies.

In the midst of all these disasters, on the brink of the buffalo's demise, the Plains people on the Canadian side of the border signed the treaties which ended the free life forever. The treaty-making process stretched over six years, beginning at Red River in 1871 and ending at the Bow. These were all years of diminishing food supply which culminated in famine in the tipis of the Blackfoot. But it was not a long period, given the primitive communications of the day, the logistics of summoning the scattered bands and staging the meetings, and it is better described as done in haste. From the perspective of the Canadian government, speed was of the essence, for agreements with the resident nations were necessary if the Northwest was to be held for settlement attached to Canada, and that was the dream that had forged a nation from the separate colonies. In 1870, all of this stood at risk.

The press of US settlement threatened to turn northward at any time, while the restless bands on the Canadian side, their situation increasingly desperate, seemed poised to act in ways that could invite the attention of the US army. Against the chaos stood a tiny outpost at Red River, connected to eastern Canada only by the old canoe routes or through the United States, and a string of trading posts stretching to the west. In 1870, the Métis at Red River rose in rebellion. The new Canadian government raised an expeditionary force and got it to Red River by a combination of rail, lake steamer, and canoe transport, punctuated by forced marches through more than six hundred miles of rock, lake, muskeg, black flies, and mosquitoes. This force put down the rebellion in short order, and the same determination was brought to bear on the treaties. Treaty One was signed within a year of the rebellion, and the first seven, which covered the whole of the Prairies and some parts of the North, within a space of six years.

THE WESTERN TREATIES (1871–1877)

The treaties signed by the chiefs of the several nations and the Canadian government are the basis for continuing obligations assumed by the government, and they have an importance for Indian peoples today that other Canadians find hard to understand. Harold Cardinal, when president of the Indian Association of Alberta, said of the treaties that they had been "entered into with faith, with hope for a better life with honour."[8] The treaties are also the source of continuing disputes and recriminations over what had been promised, which promises had been broken, and so on. For these reasons, it is useful to see something of the process, including the inequality of the bargaining positions and the pitfalls in communication, although the legal niceties must be left to lawyers.

Basically, the government held most of the cards, despite its anxiety to get the agreements signed quickly. The US experience showed clearly that white men's wishes could not be resisted for long, and Red River confirmed it. The chiefs, beset on all sides by changes which threatened to destroy them, hesitated to press too far beyond what the government offered, and were even more restricted by not knowing what their future needs might be. In the case of farming, which was to be their livelihood, they were quite unable to assess the adequacy of the acreage or the farm implements that were offered. But they knew their plight was desperate. As the process got under way at Red River, Lieutenant-Governor Archibald received a message from Sweetgrass, one of the great Cree chiefs, transmitted by the Hudson's Bay officer at Fort Edmonton: "We heard our lands were sold and we did not like it; we don't want to sell our lands; it is our property and no one has a right to sell them. Our country is getting ruined of fur-bearing animals, hitherto our sole support, and now we are poor and want help – we want you to pity us. We want cattle, tools, agricultural implements and assistance in everything when we come to settle – our country is no longer able to support us."[9]

The government knew well enough that help was needed, but had already determined just what would be forthcoming. Among the many advantages it possessed was control over the process: it picked the meeting sites, summoned the bands, set the agenda and the terms – none of which was revealed in advance. The scarcity of competent translators further weakened the Indian position: many chiefs discovered, at some later time, that their assent had been based on a misunderstanding of the offer.

The negotiations were conducted with great formality on both sides. After 1873, when the North West Mounted Police was established, the Queen's interest in her subjects was attested to by the presence of scarlet uniforms, and by the flags and medals for distribution. Some chiefs appeared in traditional splendour, while others had already acquired western-style suits. The Commissioners spoke in flowery language, attempting to imitate the poetic gifts of their opposite numbers. Thus Governor Morris at Treaty Six: "I see the Queen's Councillors taking the Indian by the hand saying, 'We are brothers; we will lift you up, we will teach you if you are willing to learn, the cunning of the white man.' All along that road I see Indians gathering, I see gardens growing and houses building."[10]

Western treaty makers drew on a history going back to the Royal Proclamation of 1763, in which the British government "reserved" land for the Indian people and undertook to secure it for all future generations. This security rested on the Crown's retaining title (rendering impossible the otherwise inevitable loss of land through sale by individual owners, encouraged by white speculators) and while the method proved less than fully effective, the losses have been kept within bounds. Later agreements in the nineteenth century, when the land was filling up, began a policy of setting aside special tracts of land on which Indian people were encouraged to settle and become farmers, under the tutelage of white teachers, missionaries, and farm instructors. The most recent agreements, prior to the western treaties, had been signed with the Chippewa (Ojibwa) in the general area of Lake Superior and Lake Huron, only a decade or so before Confederation; these came to be known as the Robinson Treaties.

The terms offered in the western treaties essentially followed those of their predecessors. The government would provide a grant of land, the Queen's protection, a small per capita annuity (with higher amounts for chiefs and councillors), the basics for farming, and schools. The chiefs, in return, agreed to surrender the land and keep the peace. There was some bargaining at Treaty Three which got the annuity increased from three dollars a year to five dollars (where it remains to the present day, much eroded by inflation), and won some increase in the land grant. The greatest difficulty was encountered at Treaty Six on the North Saskatchewan, where the Crees, living in close proximity to the Métis who had fled Red River after the rebellion, had picked up some of their disaffection, reinforcing their own doubts and fears. They had stopped the geological survey the year before, and the second Riel rebellion was only nine years away. Chief Poundmaker, adopted son of Chief Crowfoot and widely respected in his own right, expressed his concern that the amount of land offered was not enough, noting that he himself did not know how to cultivate the ground or build a house. Some chiefs sided with him, while others were more accommodating. "Surely," urged Chief Starblanket (Ahtukakoop), "we Indians can learn the ways of living that made the white man strong,"[11] and Chiefs Mis-Ta-Wa-Sis and Big Child took this side. Treaty Six was rejected three times, but signed in the end with some improvement in terms, notably a fourfold increase in the size of the land grant (from 160 acres per family of five to 640 acres), and the "medicine chest" at the house of each agent, which in modern times was used to lever more money for health care.

Treaty Six was signed by a second group of chiefs at Fort Pitt, including Chief Sweetgrass, whose concerns had been expressed five years before. Now he accepted the government's terms but added an eloquent plea: "When I hold your hand and touch your heart, let us be as one; use your utmost to help me and my children so that they may prosper."[12]

Dissenting voices were raised at Treaty Seven in the year following, but by 1877 the Indian situation was deteriorating rapidly and Chief Crowfoot of the Blackfoot convinced the majority that a deal with the white men was the best course. And so the treaty was signed and the treaty-making process on the Prairies came to an end, having established the terms and entitlements that were to govern reserve life down to the present time and perhaps for years ahead.

The chiefs had done the best they could. Contemporary accounts – Governor Morris, in particular, left a full picture of events[13] – convey their essential dignity, seriousness of purpose, and recognition that their people's future rested on the help they could get in establishing a new life. Yet none of them was in a position to judge the adequacy of the government's terms. With respect to farming, for example, the treaties provided two hoes, one spade, and one scythe for each farming family; one plough for every ten families; five harrows for every twenty families; and for each band, one axe, three saws (of different kinds), files, a grindstone, an auger, carpenter's tools, seed, one yoke of oxen, one bull, and four cows.

Even by the standards of the 1870s, these provisions were minimal, shaped more by a wish to cut costs than by any real concern for the people or for what it might take to get them established in an occupation that only a few of them had practised.

Good intentions and genuine concern were not altogether absent. Lieutenant-Colonel Provencher, one of the Indian Commissioners, made clear his view that the government had a responsibility to instruct and civilize the people, not just to pay them a sum of money and leave them to be beggars once the hunting and fishing had gone. Governor Morris impresses us as a man who genuinely liked Indian people and wished to help them, but it was not in his power to improve the terms of the treaties. This is the heart of the matter, that the terms were set with a view to minimizing obligations in the light of commitments already made to the construction of a railway and other costly enterprises. Influential voices in the business community at Red River and back east were pressing for speed, and the treaties were, in fact, rushed through too quickly to establish what the needs of the people really were.

Some of the subsequent difficulty with the treaties is rooted in the flawed process: chiefs, for example, with only a day or two to consider the assistance being offered for a future they could barely envisage; misunderstandings that reflected the low quality of the translation; the flowery language and traditional courtesy of the chiefs, disguising real differences which would have been better acknowledged and discussed. A fundamental difficulty lay in words and concepts that were impossible to translate: land, for example. In the government's version of the agreement, which is the one recorded in the treaties, the chiefs agreed to surrender the land. But many of the signatories said subsequently that they had no idea they were giving up the land; they had, in fact, no concept of ownership. A statement attributed to Chief Crowfoot puts it thus: "We cannot sell the land that was put here by the Great Spirit ... it does not really belong to us. We will give you anything as a present but cannot give you the land."[14]

The chiefs who signed could neither verify that the written treaties were faithful to the verbal agreements nor that the wording meant the same to both parties. But their understanding and intentions have been preserved in an oral tradition, much studied by their present-day descendants. Chief Crowfoot's view of the land survives through this oral tradition, as does the understanding of many of the chiefs at the time that they would settle on the reserves but continue to hunt in surrounding woodlands. Indian leaders today feel that such oral testimony should be admitted to the discussion of treaty rights and that a broader interpretation of the treaties could greatly increase the money available for dealing with the problems of today.

The government has always resisted any but a literal reading, although what the treaties promised is plainly minimal. Judged by the standards of the 1870s, they might be seen as slightly more generous than the Robinson Treaties, but, in that case, the Ojibwa would go on living in accustomed ways, wresting a living from the lakes and forests where they would continue to live. But the people of the Plains had been severed from their past and would have to learn new occupations. Successful adjustment hinged wholly on the government's ability to fit them out and teach them. But aid for farming was not adequate (see below), which makes it difficult to believe that the treaties got it right, whatever the words say.

The chiefs who signed the treaties were acutely aware of their inability to define future needs. Chief Badger said at Treaty Six, "When we commence to settle down on the reserves that we select, it is there that we want your aid, when we cannot help ourselves and in case of troubles unforeseen in the future."[15] What did Chief Badger know of farming? Or Chief Mis-Ta-Wa-Sis, who put it this way: "We do not mean to ask for food every day but only in case of famine or calamity. What we speak of and do now will last as long a time as the sun shines and the river runs. We are looking forward to our children's children, for we are old and have but a few days to live."[16] They could but trust in the government to deal decently with them. As things turned out, the hoes and scythes which the treaties promised were soon obsolete, as were the wooden ploughs and the oxen, and for the next hundred years reserve agriculture floundered, as government continued to deny its legitimate needs. This is but one example of what makes a literal interpretation of the treaties untenable in any but a strict legal sense.

In the short-grass country, the thinning herds of buffalo had put pressure on other game, which was never abundant, and by the time the buffalo vanished the proud Blackfoot were eating gophers, badgers, and mice. Many died of starvation or fell victim to disease. After Treaty Seven was signed, the Blackfoot went south to Montana where a few buffalo herds could still be found, despite the onslaught of countless desperate bands and the US army's extermination policy. Two years later, the Blackfoot straggled back to the Bow River, most of them on foot since their horses had been sold to buy food. Hungry and ill, their wealth spent and the buffalo gone, the Blackfoot took up residence on their reserve.

Not all bands had such a traumatic introduction to reserve living. In the northern forest lands, which nobody wanted, it was not even required that they take up residence on their reserves. The people continued to trap and fish and trade their furs, and with the addition of treaty money and the annual ceremony at which it was dispersed, life went on as before until after World War II. Bands in or near the Park Belt, which stretches in a broad arc between the Plains and the Canadian Shield, also tended to have an easier transition, since hunting remained possible for many years. But animal populations were not unlimited, and even in the Park Belt, it would be necessary to get the farming started.

Captain Palliser had reported an interest in farming in the late 1850s and there was, in fact, a small base. The Saulteaux at Red River had taken it up during a time of scarcity in the 1830s and retained it as part of their sustenance.[17] It had been at the missionary's suggestion and was indirectly the product of the good relationship between Chief Peguis's band and the Selkirk settlers, going back a decade or so to the settlers' first terrible winter, which the Saulteaux helped them to survive. The Métis, too, provided an example, growing crops and raising livestock on their long, narrow river lots, not only at Red River but also west and north in Saskatchewan River country. In Manitoba, several places have been identified where Indians kept gardens "long before the Treaties,"[18] including the Roseau River area, Fort Alexander on the Winnipeg River, Fairford on Lake Winnipeg. Lac Ste Anne, north of Edmonton, was another site of early farming, thanks to an Ojibwa missionary from Ontario, Henry Steinhauer. Working at Norway House deep in the north country, Steinhauer was roused to action by rumours of the declining buffalo herds on the Plains and went west to help his people. At

Lac Ste Anne, he started a demonstration farm and school and spent the rest of his life in the area, where a farming community was firmly established.

In the years of scarcity that preceded the treaties, interest in gardens and farming had increased, and by the time the treaties were signed, it was widely recognized that farming would be the future. Many bands waited eagerly for equipment and instructors, while some managed to get started with whatever they could find. The Red Earth Crees, who had earlier fled the chaos on the Plains and settled in a marshy delta area where the Saskatchewan River flows into Lake Winnipeg, made a new life based on potato growing and cattle, which they acquired for themselves, becoming completely self-sufficient.[19] A recent history of the Key Band reveals that some members had farmed for years before they came to the reserve in the Qu'Appelle area. Among these were the Brass brothers, whose paternal lineage went back to a Hudson's Bay man from the Orkney Islands. An early report by the Indian agent describes this group as working hard at farming, though "quite a majority still cling to the hunt as their chief industry."[20]

The Blackfoot stood at the opposite end of the spectrum. Although some of the younger men took up farming readily enough, the larger number resisted, a stance made possible by the government's decision to issue rations in a bid to keep the Blackfoot loyal. It was a critical time, for trouble was brewing on the North Saskatchewan, where the Métis had settled after their defeat at Red River, and many of the young Cree warriors in that area were urging their leaders to join in rebellion and putting pressure on the Blackfoot as well. In the end, the Blackfoot stayed clear, largely due to Chief Crowfoot. This was a man whose name was known across the Plains, highly respected for his wisdom by other bands and by white officials alike. He and the missionary Father Lacombe had been good friends for many years, both of them delighting in discussion of the nature of the cosmos and mankind's place in it. From conversations with missionaries, Department men, and high-ranking officers in the Canadian Pacific Railway (CPR), whose right-of-way went through the Blackfoot reserve, Chief Crowfoot knew better than the young warriors how numerous the white men were. He also felt a debt to the North West Mounted Police for controlling the whiskey trade, and trusted the Queen to keep her promises.

The Blackfoot stayed out, but the Crees joined the rebellion. Poundmaker, another wise and much-loved chief, was unable to stop them; he served a year in prison when the rebellion was put down and died soon after. At this point, the options closed, not

only because the rebellion failed but also because, with the comple-
tion of the CPR, the settlers poured in. It was now apparent that the
free life was indeed a thing of the past, and that farming was the
only option left.

The story of farming is part of a larger plan for settling the people,
and will be told within that framework. This larger plan involved
missions, schools, farm instructors, and a small army of civil serv-
ants, all directed to the day when a nomadic people, now settled
on the land, would be absorbed into the main fabric of Canadian
life. How it all went wrong will occupy the balance of this chapter.

Of the two sides in the drama, the government had all the power:
it controlled the resources which went to assisting the transition and
determined what actions would be taken. It also had a nineteenth-
century world view which ranked aboriginal society rather low on
the scale and conferred a civilizing mission on government men who
had no understanding of what was involved in taking up a whole
new life. The government's plan was poorly designed for other
reasons as well, including parsimony.

On the other side, the conquered people started from a position
of weakness, yet still retained a basic pride in themselves and a wish
to preserve their culture. They had also to learn a new life, in which
certain aspects of that culture worked against adjustment. Something of the same problem could be seen at James Bay in modern
times when the Crees, still trappers and hunters, found themselves
increasingly caught up in the white man's world. A scholar at Ottawa's Saint Paul University explained their situation in the 1960s:
"The fact that the Cree are increasingly having to act in terms of the
non-Indian world does not mean that they are able to think in Euro-
Canadian terms. The opposite is the case, and here lies the root of
the problem."[21] So it was with the Plains Crees and the other nations
in the 1870s and 1880s. As they settled on the reserves, they brought
with them the values and practices by which they had always lived
and which defined their identity and ordered their society. These
could not easily be put by to fit the white man's plan, still less so
when the people did not understand the plan.

The values and practices of the Plains people were all shaped by
the hunt. The most basic element in the culture, a strong sense of
group identity, reflects the fact that the hunt was a group effort. It
had to be, for even the best hunter, if he went alone, would not
always be successful; individual survival depended on the survival
of the group. Various customs reinforced this group identity: the
deeply ingrained practice of sharing; the importance attached to
behaving in ways approved by society. In the white man's world,

these customs had less practical purpose and drastic changes in outlook were required. Here, the individual, as earner, is motivated by his own interest or that of his family. The qualities that conferred status in the old life – intelligence, skill, daring – were still valued in the new, but opportunities to use them were infrequent. The buffalo hunt was a thing of the past, as were life-threatening expeditions when food ran low in the dead of winter, and decisions made by leaders on which all their lives depended. On the reserves, the agent made the decisions; the simple farm tasks were soon learned, but did not lead to more challenging roles. Gift giving had been very important, earning status for its conformance to the sharing principle, but not individual wealth and accumulation; a nomadic society had little to store and less wish to carry things about. Horses, of which there could never be too many, were the one exception to this view of wealth. Finally, the hunting society had had a weak sense of the future, which was natural in a situation in which nothing much could be done about future needs. But a sense of the future was something that would be needed in the years ahead.

So it was that the new life involved many difficult adjustments. The difficulties should not be exaggerated, for many individuals did find their way from the outset, as will be shown, and the vast majority might have done so as well, had the regime been more sensibly designed to meet their needs. But the difficulties should be kept in mind as part of the larger problem – in particular, the declining power and importance of the group and all the practices that supported it.

In Ottawa, as in the more important capitals of the era, there really was no knowledge of how aboriginal societies functioned or of the strength of the values and practices that held these societies together. Nor was it understood that attachments to accustomed ways were just as strong in societies labelled primitive as they were in European and even British society. Old ways of thinking were seen as something easily changed, of the same order as adopting Western dress. This captures one basic weakness in the government's policies: an inability to see the Indian people as they really were and to deal sensibly with the problems. As it was, policy makers and administrators tended to see them as primitive and inferior, undeserving of respect, and probably incapable of attaining the higher culture of the white man. Such views shape the whole subsequent history of the western treaty nations.

Settlers and townspeople tended to similar opinions, although exceptions could be found in both the government and the larger society. One of these exceptions was an Irish colonel in the British Army, R.A. Butler, who made two trips of discovery across the Plains for the Canadian government – the first in 1870–71, from Fort Garry (now Winnipeg) to Rocky Mountain House southwest of Edmonton, resulted in a report which led to the establishment of the North West Mounted Police. Butler saw the strength in the Indian culture and admired the people because they lacked the white man's greed. His portrait of a typical individual shows something of the beliefs and customs that were so deeply ingrained in the Indian culture.

He holds all things in common with his tribe – the land, the bison, the river, the moose. He is starving and the rest of the tribe want food. Well, he kills a moose and to the last bit the coveted food is shared by all. There is but a scrap of beaver, a thin rabbit or a bit of sturgeon in the lodge; a stranger comes and he is hungry; give him his share and let him be first served and best attended to. If one child starves in an Indian camp you may know that in every lodge scarcity is universal and that every stomach is hungry ... The most curious anomaly among the race of man, the red man of America is passing away beneath our eyes into the infinite solitude. The possession of the same noble qualities that we affect to reverence among our nations makes us want to kill him. If he would be our slave, he might live; but as he won't be that, won't toil and delve and hew for us, and will persist in hunting, fishing and roaming over the beautiful prairie which the Great Spirit gave him; in a word, since he will be free – we will kill him.[22]

Butler admired what so many of his contemporaries found backward and out of step. Whites also tended to criticize the simplicity of the Indian people's wants, although this, too, was the way they had lived. Beyond what was necessary in the way of food, clothing, and shelter, they turned to family life and social pleasures, the beauty of nature and their spiritual heritage. Family values were strong in Indian society: children were cherished and old people respected. And the culture that they brought with them to the reserves helped them survive the difficult years ahead.

Reverence for the land was central to this culture, a sacred trust to be cherished and preserved for future generations. It was the wellspring of their religion, which, though scorned by most Christians, was yet a living thing which gave meaning to their lives and fixed their place in the cosmos. An old man who lived on after the treaties described the way his people had lived in these words: "They were wealthy because they had all they could possibly desire. They were happy because they were healthy, and had such a beautiful country. Kitchie Manitou took care of them in those days. He held them in the palm of his hand as if they were as frail as an eggshell; when there were storms and tempests and in the wintertime, He would cover them with His other hand and shield them from all harm."[23]

The settling-in process must also be seen in the context of other changes on the Prairies. When Butler made his journey in the early 1870s, the scattered bands and the Métis were still the only inhabitants, apart from a little settler colony at Red River and the traders at the posts. By the late 1880s, a thin line of settlement ran right along the CPR all the way to the Rockies and homesteaders, making their way north from the railroad, had been establishing farms near to or in the Park Belt, which seemed a less daunting location compared to the treeless Plains. Branch lines were under construction and wheat had been shipped for a decade. In the boom year of 1882, sixty thousand settlers arrived. Techniques and tools were evolving for farming the Plains – the steel plough, summer fallow, barbed wire. Small towns were springing up where posts or missions had stood or where there had been nothing but grass or scrub. Although the boom had tapered off by the late 1880s and the next was a decade away – waiting on the free land to fill in the American West and the development of early-maturing wheat – the lands which surrounded the reserves had been changed forever.

White settlement added another dimension to the Indian people's experience. Not merely confined to a tiny fraction of their domain, increasingly they lived as outcasts, separated from the society developing around them. Outcast status did not preclude shopping in the towns or working for white farmers or even having good relations with individual white people but overall acceptance was lacking. Settlers in general, says one historian, "often regarded the natives with open contempt and made no effort to socialize with them."[24]

As the new Dominion exercised its manifest destiny to settle the territories, the welfare of the Indian people hinged wholly on the government's ability to deal fairly with them and to provide the assistance that would make a new life possible. That ability, however, was limited by several factors, including the prevailing view that the culture was primitive and inferior and the people unlikely to adapt. The overriding interests of the settlers were another factor, as was the fact that in settling these nomadic people, the government was entering uncharted waters.

In southern Ontario, early in the century, the bands had been encouraged to farm and take up Christianity, but not as pressing matters; the recent Robinson Treaties were no help either, because the Ojibwa in northern Ontario could be left to their old pursuits, running their lives as they saw fit. In the West, change was urgent. The people had to learn farming and do it quickly in order to support themselves, and they would have to be "civilized" if there was to be any success with the farming. This was the way the government saw the problem; the longer-term goal tended towards vagueness. Officially, the goal was assimilation, and it seems to have centred on the children who would acquire the new knowledge and values they needed by going to school. But some adults were also seen as capable of adapting, which got them special treatment, as recounted below.

Given the importance placed on "civilizing," the Church was a natural choice as senior partner in the venture and it was given particular responsibility for the schools. But the Department of Indian Affairs was to be the lead player; its plan encompassed civilizing along with most aspects of life on the reserves. The essence of the plan was a system that would take control of the people's lives, manage their affairs, and show them how to become useful citizens.

Department headquarters in Ottawa was the hub of this highly centralized system. It was the place where policies were designed or changed and where decisions were taken on all matters, including some that might seem personal or unimportant: the need for passes to leave the reserve, for example, or permission to hold a dance. A network of agents had charge at the local level, each responsible for one or more reserves, and they were powerful figures in their own right, given the primitive communications of the day. These were the men who saw the farm programs implemented, enforced school attendance, allocated housing, and dealt with domestic disputes and a great many other matters. They wrote full reports to Ottawa on both the progress and the problems of their charges. Some agents were dedicated men who did the best they could within the limits of the system; some were political appointees, poorly educated and unsuited for the job; a few were rogues intent on profiting from their position.

The role assigned to the people for whose benefit the system was designed consisted largely of following instructions and refraining from making trouble. It was a demeaning situation for a people which had always managed its own affairs and taken pride in its many skills and ability to survive in difficult times. Their chiefs, now government-appointed, might have seemed less their own to the people than formerly; more importantly, they seldom had the power to help people in difficulty. That role fell increasingly to the agent. Many years later, in the 1970s and 1980s, when dependency came to be seen as a major problem on the western reserves, few Canadians would realize just how early the seeds had been sown.

The main components in the government's plan – schools and farming – are best understood with reference to the guiding principle that the desired changes would occur through the adoption of civilization. The concept of civilizing, as one tries to get at it through various statements made at the time, seems to have been an amalgam of Christianity, Western dress and deportment, following instructions, and working hard. One of hundreds of such statements that survive in the literature is taken from a US source, *The Congressional Record*, and refers to the settling of the tribes in that country. It is included here because it so neatly captures the several elements in the Department's plan – minor schooling, the Bible, morality, and hard work: "Put into the hands of their children the primer and the hoe and they will naturally, in time, take hold of the plough and as their minds become enlightened and expand the Bible will be their book and they will grow up in the habits of morality and industry, leave the chase to those whose minds are less cultivated and become useful members of society."[25] It proved less simple, however, notably in the case of the western reserves where the system attempted to elicit hard work, while overlooking the need for monetary incentives. Well into the twentieth century, although farming, schools, and missions have all disappointed expectations, the Department still insists that the plan will succeed if the people can just be made to work. In the 1920s, after forty years of effort towards this end, an agent wrote: "The real problem to solve for the present generation is to teach them to work. Manual work will do more than any other single agency to civilize them and to obliterate their nomadic and pleasure-loving habits."[26]

On the same theme, a directive from the Deputy Superintendant General of Indian Affairs, Duncan Campbell Scott, went out to all agents in 1921:

It is observed with alarm that the holding of dances by the Indians on their reserves is on the increase, and that these practices tend to disorganize the efforts which the Department is putting forth to make them self-supporting.

I have therefore to direct you to use your utmost endeavors to dissuade the Indians from excessive indulgence in the practice of dancing. You should suppress any dances which cause waste of time, interfere with occupations of Indians, unsettle them for serious work, injure their health or encourage them in sloth and idleness. You should dissuade and if possible prevent them from leaving their reserves for the purpose of attending fairs, exhibitions, etc. when their absence will result in their own farming and other interests being neglected.[27]

Today, any approach based on character and cultural transformation is entirely discredited. But it was imposed on the western bands and is much of the reason for the current plight of the Indian people. Not only did it fail to establish farming or make education seem worthwhile to the children: it also struck at the culture, which the Indian people needed to sustain them, and weakened their social structure, which was just as necessary to them in the new life as it had been in the old.

This is an episode in Canadian history which has been banished from the collective conscience – if it was ever present – and deserves to be revived in discussions of current strategies as an item for which compensation is owed. Thrust into a new situation, the Indian people needed support and encouragement, but what they got was a harsh regimen which belittled their customs and religion and banned their few pleasures. They needed to develop strength and initiative in the new life. Instead the system took charge.

MISSIONS AND SCHOOLS

The Church made its formal appearance in the 1820s, when a future Roman Catholic bishop, Joseph Provencher, was sent to Red River from Quebec. The Catholic Church had a constituency in the Selkirk settlers with a second one in the Métis, and support enough from the East to build St Boniface Cathedral, made famous by the American poet John Greenleaf Whittier, although he never saw it. The Anglicans arrived shortly thereafter. Their Church Missionary Society, represented by John West, began its work with a school that was to train Indian catechists, ministers, and schoolmasters who would, in turn, be sent further afield.

In the next stage, the major initiatives shifted to the North; James Evans, a Methodist, was at Norway House in the 1840s with his corps of Ojibwa assistants from Ontario, while the Oblate Fathers established their mission at Ile à la Crosse, a trading post in northern Saskatchewan. Not long after, Father Lacombe from Quebec made his headquarters at Lac Ste Anne, conducting an itinerant mission; although interested mainly in the Blackfoot, he converted mainly the Crees. The people of the northern forests are said to have been particularly receptive to missions at this time. Historian John Grant describes a sense of excitement among the people who travelled great distances, an expectation that their lives were about to change.[28] Yet none of this happened south of the park belt. By 1870, only a handful of missions were operating on the prairie, although most bands had been contacted across the vast reaches of the North and in British Columbia as well.

The missionaries came to the Prairies at a time when Indian people were beginning to sense threatening changes on all sides and feared for their future. Sometimes they perceived the missionaries as having come to help, sometimes as bearers of gifts that they didn't want. Some missionaries established a good rapport, as did Father Lacombe with Chief Crowfoot, or saw to it that the people's wishes were taken into account, while others saw their roles in a more authoritarian light, bringing a superior way of life as well as the true religion. One prime source of difficulty was the way the people lived; the constant moving about so hindered instruction and regular church services that for many missionaries, getting the people to settle down became the priority. Unfortunately, this gave them a preoccupation with farming and schools, neither of which appealed much to the people who, in any event, were looking for something else. As John Grant put it, in confronting a breakdown in the social order, the Indian people were seeking a new kind of cohesion and "they sought a religious solution as they had always been accustomed to do."[29] Another modern historian notes the missionaries' insistence that their followers give up their own forms of spirituality, along with their customs and language.[30]

Some missionaries were disappointed in the treaties, but all welcomed the opportunity to render services under the settled conditions of the new reserves. The Crees had asked for missionaries at Treaty Six and the churches, experiencing an upsurge of interest, set about increasing their presence. Emanuel College in Saskatchewan was founded for the training of Indian catechists and teachers, and by the 1890s missionaries were present on reserves wherever the population was large enough to justify them. The women's missionary societies sent boxes of old clothing (warmly welcomed by the destitute bands) and were critical of the authorities for their apparent unconcern. On the other hand, the missionaries lost ground with the Indian people over the treaties, which they tended to support, and similarly over their support of the suppression of the second Riel rebellion. The residential schools caused further alienation. The missionaries strongly favoured them because they increased their control over the educational process, but the schools were much disliked by the Indian people because it was through them that their children lost their own culture.

Christianity was embraced by an increasing number, although not, it is thought, with the enthusiasm earlier displayed by the northern people and "not without a degree of ambiguity," according to John Grant. His last word concerning the experience on the Prairies is as follows: "On many reserves and within many individuals, traditional and Christian ways co-existed without coalescing into a new outlook. Underneath the surface old resentments persisted, and indigenous rites such as the sun dance took on a harder edge in defiance of white and Christian ways than their counterparts elsewhere in Canada."[31]

Education, one of two key elements in the government's plan, began in earnest after the treaties. The churches were to have charge of it and the government would give some financial support. Day schools on the reserves were the first step, some with facilities for boarding the pupils. In his memoirs, Henry Stocken, an early missionary to the Blackfoot, writes of the fifty or so shacks and tipis near his school, and of his pupils being disturbed by the "tom-toms [as he called them] beating incessantly through the night."[32] But the government wanted large boarding schools, deliberately situated in remote locations far away from parents and unwanted influences. Beyond removal from distractions, the government had what one historian calls an ideological commitment to suppress the native culture as rapidly as possible and fashion a new generation of Indian children raised in isolation from their parents, in the image of the white man.[33]

This was a further element of harshness in the system devised for the West for no such grandiose goal had obtained in Ontario. Education there was voluntary and consisted of day schools, which was what the parents wanted, so that the children could have a traditional education as well as formal schooling. This pattern held through the first half of the nineteenth century and was not much changed when the government began to press for the residential, "industrial" schools it had admired in the US. Of the fourteen such schools operating in Canada by 1890, only four were in Ontario and only two preceded Confederation.[34] These same schools had been much criticized in the US, but the Canadian government held firm to its belief in them. However poorly they may have worked elsewhere, they would do the job in the West.

The residential schools were never numerous enough to carry the whole burden of education, nor were they all bad. In the better ones, the headmaster and the staff were sympathetic to Indian culture, parental visits were encouraged, beginners were taught in their native tongue, and the whole atmosphere was friendly and welcoming. Here, learning did take place. Some students went on to higher grades; a sprinkling went to college and then usually joined the missions. Blue Quills in northern Alberta and Lebret in Saskatchewan were two such schools, remembered with much affection by their graduates. In modern times, the fact that treaty Indians in northern Manitoba were more literate than the Métis has been attributed to the residential schools. [35]

But the dark side remains: schools with poorly qualified teachers who cared little for the pupils; a harsh philosophy permeating classrooms and dormitories, making the children feel inferior and ashamed of Indian ways. In the worst cases, native languages were forbidden; young children were taught in English which they didn't understand, parental visits were forbidden, and heavy demands were made on the children for housekeeping, gardening, and other chores.

Even the good schools tended to work poorly for most young people because, in the end, they came back to the reserve with no real opportunity to make a living or any roots in their own culture. The dilemma has been explained in recent times with reference to the Crees at James Bay. The children went off to boarding school at an age when they were beginning to learn the skills used in their society and acquire its values of cooperation, generosity, and self-reliance. They would spend the next six to twelve years in classrooms where competitiveness, something that had no part in Cree life, was promoted and rewarded. Many came back unable to speak the Cree language, in conflict with their parents, and with severe problems of identity. [36]

This kind of suffering was imposed unwittingly in the nineteenth century, since education had not yet come to be seen as it is now, as a process that performs much the same function in all societies: transmission of the values and beliefs of that society and preparation of its youth for the work that is done. In traditional Indian society, education took place in the context of everyday life. The children watched while tasks were performed and learned by example; the adults had a vast fund of stories which told the children who they were, what was right and wrong, and how they should behave. [37] When the people came to live on the reserves, many of the old skills had lost meaning and much of the educational function was gone. But the will to preserve and pass on the culture remained strong.

The white man's schools were another matter. Their aim was to prepare the children for a new way of life, make them give up accustomed beliefs, take white people as their models, and aspire to live as much like them as possible. This was neither realistic nor well executed. Quite apart from the children's natural affection for their parents, the white people they met were mostly teachers who were often unsympathetic and sometimes oppressive. It took an unusual child to recognize that education might be worth having and unusual fortitude to survive the experience. In good schools and rare cases, such children were to be found; some spark was struck that carried the individual through. But most children saw their lives as patterned on their parents', to be passed on the reserves where education didn't matter.

As with so much else, the failure of the schools is very much a product of the times: a combination of unrealistic goals, a low view of Indian people, and considerable hostility towards them. A Manitoba source quotes teachers who credited Indian children with limited reasoning ability but acutely developed "animal faculties."[38] The same study cites an inspector of Indian agencies, who pronounces that "little can be done for him [the adult Indian]. He can be taught to do a little farming and stock raising and to dress in a civilized manner, but that is all ... The child again, who goes to a day school learns little and what little he learns is soon forgotten while his tastes are fashioned at home and his inherited aversion to toil is in no way combatted."[39] These sentiments convey something of what the Indian people – adults and children – were up against.

It is interesting to contrast the school experience with the way syllabics were absorbed by the Crees. The written form of the language was devised by James Evans at Norway House in the 1840s and immediately picked up by the Cree people. Trappers wrote messages on birchbark and left notes in cabins. By such practical means, skill in the use of syllabics spread, in part as the people themselves taught one another, and with such rapidity that the Crees achieved near-universal literacy within ten years over an area stretching from James Bay to the far Northwest.[40] Education, it seems, is not an inherently difficult process, but the Canadian government made it so through low expectations and failure to see that the children needed a reason for learning.

The white culture had little meaning for Indian children as it was conveyed to them or as it affected their lives. Even with day schools, the education process was damaging to families because it cut adults off from their accustomed parental tasks. This was part of the larger trauma in the early years and the sense of loss persisted, while the benefits to the children, which might have compensated for the loss, failed to materialize. Except in the best residential schools, the children moved slowly through the grades, emerging with some nominal standing but basically schooled only in the "three Rs," with some farming or trades instruction for the boys and homemaking for the girls.

Worse was to come. After the turn of the century, the government became increasingly concerned with the cost of Indian education, which was seen as high relative to the value received from education expenditures. Most school leavers, it was observed, were going back to the reserves; this was called "retrograding," which meant returning to pagan ways. It was also observed, more callously, that some fifty percent of the children did not live to reap the benefits of education.[41] That is one estimate of the death rate, caused mainly by tuberculosis and other infectious diseases. Indian children were particularly vulnerable and the residential schools were particularly unsafe, thanks to over-crowding and poor sanitation. Thus, the government came to see the goal of immediate assimilation as misdirected. If the schools could not produce instant white people, it would be better to shift the goal. This the government did in 1910, announcing the new goal to be "to fit the Indian for civilized life in his own environment."[42]

Cost cutting produced some benefits, for it greatly enlarged the role of day schools, which gave the pupils the continuing support of their parents and thus a more solid sense of their identity and history. On the other hand, when the assimilationist objective was jettisoned, the incentive which might have raised educational standards went with it. Given a policy based on a grudging concession to educate the children in the cheapest possible way, the schooling stuck in a state of backwardness, which "ensured that Indian education would remain minimal through to the mid-twentieth century, while the white child's education became more extensive."[43] In 1921, less than half the Indian children in the Prairie provinces were enrolled in any school. Many did not attend until age eight or ten. Grants were available to grade eight graduates for going to high school or trade schools, but only on condition that they passed grade eight by age fourteen; there were few applicants.

In 1938, the schools on the Blackfoot Reserve were described as providing elementary literacy in English, a Christian outlook, and familiarity with the techniques of civilized living – which is to say, such things as housekeeping (considerable emphasis was placed on toothbrushes).[44] After eleven years in school, the children had nominally completed grade eight; in fact, few school leavers had even the most elementary knowledge of subjects commonly taught in village schools. What they had was considered adequate for living on the reserves.

No moves were made to improve the educational system until after World War II, which means that the backwardness persisted for more than seventy years. The consequences for the Indian people were profound. Low levels of education barred them from all but the lowest-paying jobs, which not only kept them poor but perpetuated stereotypes of incompetence and lowered their self-esteem. It was lack of education, as much as anything else, that maintained their isolation on the reserves. And in modern times, when jobs in rural areas had all but disappeared, these same poorly educated people were forced to try their luck in the cities where they were at an even greater disadvantage.

Education is the most serious of the promises broken under the treaties. It was not for minimal literacy that the great chiefs had pressed for education at Treaty Six; they recognized it as a prime requirement in the new life. Parents themselves, though sometimes hostile when their children were taken away, knew that education was needed. The tragedy is the educational system they got, which in no way fitted them for Canadian society. It was a cheap and cheerless package judged good enough for an unimportant minority.

INTRODUCTION TO FARMING

Getting the farming established was the second main element in the government's plan. Although the implements and cattle that were promised were slow in coming, it was clear that there was widespread interest on the reserves. By 1878, the John Smith Band had 120 acres under crops, and many bands had done as well. But the difficulties were enormous. Consider the band on Pasqua Reserve, which broke thirty pieces of virgin prairie for planting without the aid of draft animals; with no way to feed themselves while at this work, they had been forced to eat their dogs. Chief Pasqua journeyed to Regina to ask the lieutenant-governor for help: seed, cattle to work the land, and provisions to keep his people going; he received only a small dole of provisions, nothing else.[45]

Difficulties of this kind persisted. Meanwhile, the new farmers faced the same hostile climate that frequently defeated the better-equipped settlers. Farming had no long history on the open plains, even in the United States, and the innovations that would improve the success rate – better implements, summer fallowing, early-ripening wheat – had yet to emerge. Many harvests were lost to frost and, especially on the reserves, through want of animal power and implements to get them in. People on the reserves also suffered more from illness caused by a combination of poor diet and susceptibility to disease.

Nevertheless, farming went ahead. Agents from various parts of the territories reported that "the Indians began their agricultural enterprise with considerable energy and curiosity."[46] Officials in a position to observe the operations judged that setbacks were due not to want of character or training, as many believe to this day, but to the economic and climatic conditions that made it a high-risk enterprise for Indians and settlers alike. The Cowessess Band in the Fort Qu'Appelle area had a notable number of individual farmers, which may have reflected their long association with the Hudson's Bay Company as employees and hunters. The chief of Day Star's Band in the Touchwood Hills area sold seed potatoes and wheat to the agent and received a silver medal from the governor-general for his magnificent garden. The refugee Dakota, who had done a little farming on their American reserve, planted gardens and raised cattle and ponies in western Manitoba. They are said to have been "eager to learn new ways of doing things, either by taking instruction or by experimenting."[47] One of their chiefs planted test crops and ranked among the earliest farmers in the West to plant the newly developed Red Fife wheat.

In the late 1880s, "farmers in the Treaty 4 area were among the first in the Northwest to experiment with summer fallowing" – an effective technique for moisture retention. In 1890, the first prize for wheat was won by reserve farms, both at Prince Albert and Regina. On Cowessess, Louis O'Soup's field of wheat was said to be no different from a white farmer's and he won prizes at the Broadview Fair.[48] An inspector at one of the Dakota reserves declared the wheat crops to be "as fine as any I had seen among the white settlers," and the farmers "a very nice lot of Indians [who] seem to be industrious and therefore are deserving of encouragement."[49]

This promising beginning does not fit the popular image of hunters who were unable to adapt to farming. It also raises a new question as to why the farming ultimately failed, having made a good start. But answers are not long in coming for, as early as the late 1880s, little more than a decade after the last treaty was signed, Indian farm policy moved into a new phase. This new policy, together with the continuing scarcity of equipment and working capital, defeated the efforts of the farmers themselves.

The new policy aimed at creating a kind of peasant agriculture, making the reserves quite separate from the commercial farming which surrounded them. Introduced by Hayter Reed, superintendent in the Department, it began with a survey which divided the reserves into lots of forty acres which were allotted to individual band members. Reed's vision was that "a single acre of wheat, part of another in root crops and vegetables, a cow or two could provide for the farmer and his family."[50] The forty-acre farm contrasts with the basic quarter-section (160 acres) which launched most settlers, who then went on to acquire more land as fast as profits from farming permitted.

So daft a plan demands explanation. Cost saving would have been one element, for the small acreage and emphasis on root crops greatly reduced the need for machinery. But there is more than a hint of ideology as well. Superintendent Reed, who was no farmer, had a special feeling for root crops, believing that their cultivation would teach the Indian farmers to be diligent and attentive. "I've always advocated growing as many root crops as possible, but Indians have to be humoured a good deal in such matters; and as soon as they begin to make some little progress they become fired with an ambition to grow larger quantities of wheat and other cereals [rather than] roots which require working and weeding at the very time they like to be off hunting."[51] This view is consistent with Superintendent Reed's belief in immutable laws of social evolution which would require Indian farmers to repeat the evolution of agriculture over the centuries – impossible to arrive, full-blown, as modern wheat farmers in a single generation. He also believed them incapable of operating commercial farms. His complaint that the Indians were too ambitious does not exactly fit his larger view of Indian capabilities, still less the general view that the Indian was lazy, but such inconsistencies seemed to bother no one. Duncan Campbell Scott, who was a senior administrator by World War I, then superintendent-general through the 1920s, saw civilizing as a slow process; one of his beliefs was that Indian people "harboured primitive instincts that would take generations to eradicate."[52]

Indians farmers protested the new policy, and many angry agents and instructors took their side; some agents defied orders and were fired for their pains. The policy went ahead nevertheless, fatally changing the course of reserve agriculture. Historian Sarah Carter says that the Indian farmers had been tending in the same direction as the white farmers around them, focusing on wheat and machinery and large acreage. This was, in fact, the only way to make money on the Plains. But the new policy required the Indian farmers "to step aside and function in isolation from the rest of western Canadian society."[53]

The 1890s saw further restrictions on farming, and new powers for agents and resident instructors on the reserves. Chief among the restrictions was the permit system: the piece of paper which the Indian farmer had to have in order to sell his grain or other produce, or to buy stock or implements. This requirement was to last for more than forty years. An account of Poundmaker Reserve in the 1920s describes the permit system as a device for control; if an agent did not like an individual or was displeased for some reason, he could refuse or dely his permit indefinitely.[54] Cash transactions also had to go. Indian farmers were to be paid in "chits" which could be exchanged at the store, and this chit system did not entirely disappear until the 1950s. Even the business of purchasing a horse was affected. The Indians of Saskatchewan passed a resolution requesting permission to inspect the horses which the government was buying for them,[55] and this was in the 1930s.

The permit system was condemned by many settlers who "were incapable of imagining themselves having to operate under such strictures,"[56] but the government paid no heed and the more enthusiastic agents could make the system even worse. W.A. Markle, who had charge of several "go-ahead" Dakota bands in the 1890s, was rigorous in his enforcement of the ban on credit "In this way," said he, "I hope to assist the Indians to spend their gains from farming to best advantage."[57] He expropriated cattle which the Dakota had purchased and hired an instructor, whose main duty was to search out offenders in the matter of alcohol purchase. During the ten years in which he pursued this objective at Oak River, fewer than five convictions were obtained in a population of more than five hundred; meanwhile, the farming withered.

Many Indian farmers gave up in this decade, including some of the most successful. Louis O'Soup transferred to a Manitoba band, where he made his living by hunting.[58] Many turned to casual wage work, mostly on neighbouring farms, because it paid more than they could earn from the plots or because they couldn't stand the restrictions. Some historians blame the permit system; I tend to agree with Sarah Carter that the low returns were more important, but it hardly matters: the real point is the loss of agriculture as an economic base, the frustration for enterprising people, the discouragement, and continuing poverty.

There remains the special case of reserve farmers who did prosper under the system. Their success was, in essence, another aspect of control, for the grants or loans needed to make money out of farming were available to a select few, handpicked by the agent. This might seem to be the most baffling part of the system since, when farmers who received grants or loans, got ahead, the logical course would have been to make capital more accessible. But the government didn't reason that way. The problem, as seen by officialdom, was not one of communicating the art of farming and seeing to capital needs; rather, it was to select from the population those rare individuals who had the capacity to be farmers and to act like white men. Those who got loans were usually sons of chiefs, young men who had done well at school or who had shown other evidence of acculturation. One such was Victor Sunderland, a lay reader from

Red River who had taken up residence on a Saskatchewan reserve. An agent's report to Ottawa in 1903 describes him as follows: "Chief White Owl died recently. The leading and most progressive members of the band are now Victor Sunderland and his sons, all of whom speak English and aspire to live like white men."[59] Victor Sunderland did become a successful farmer, as did others like him, because the qualities admired by the agents got them the land and equipment necessary for farming on the scale of successful white farmers.

The agent's power with respect to loans rested on the special status of reserve land; with title being vested in the Crown, it could not be used as collateral to obtain bank loans. The objective, a worthy one, had been to protect the land against unscrupulous dealers, and its unfortunate consequences could have been overcome by a government loans program aimed at establishing farmers in general. Such, however, was not the aim of farm policy and so the loans were restricted to a favoured few, leaving the rest to their small plots.

That character, as perceived by the agent, was the key to successful farming fits with the emphasis on character dealt with earlier. Similarly, the perception that character was missing in the large majority of Indian people is the key to the government's philosophy and the basis for its obsession with making people work. These beliefs, which explain the basic shape of the farm program, were rooted in theories that passed for knowledge at that time, at least in some quarters. But there was useful knowledge in the 1890s that could have been drawn on – for example, that farmers in modern countries were motivated by the expectation of returns, just like businessmen. The profit motive was generally recognized as a driving force, and had been proclaimed as such in Adam Smith's *The Wealth of Nations*, published exactly one hundred years before the signing of Treaty Six at Fort Carleton & Fort Pitt. Yet, the government's farm plan saw to it that small farmers would earn very little and expected them to work hard, if only for a winter's supply of potatoes.

Another serious consequence of the new farm policy was the loss of whatever freedom the people had retained, to this point, in the running of their own affairs. Those who signed the early treaties had had fifteen to twenty years on the reserves, during which time they had perceived opportunities, taken decisions, assumed risks, and thus learned to make their way in a new world. The Dakota had used this freedom to retain something of the old ways, such as leadership based on consensus and guidance from elders and the sharing of labour and products, benefits and responsibilities. If, as seems likely, the various combinations of adaptation and retention were widely dispersed, this could have laid the basis for cohesive as well as prosperous societies.

As the years went by, Indian people and the authorities were increasingly at cross purposes. The people had come to feel they had been poorly treated. That the promise to establish them in farming had been broken was obvious whenever they passed the crops on neighbouring farms. The hoes and scythes granted by the treaties were still used on the reserves long after the settlers had moved to steam-driven ploughs and mechanical harvesting equipment. There was little benefit in sending the children to school. As Louis O'Soup remarked in 1910, "For many years we have put our children into school and there is not one yet that has enough education to make a living."[60] Indian people also felt unwelcome in the towns. And the more lost and isolated they felt, the more they clung to Indian beliefs and ways, and the more the Department saw them as ungrateful and rebellious.

By the early years of the twentieth century, the Department itself was feeling discouraged. At the time when the government was retrenching on the schools, similar doubts were being expressed about whether the Indian would ever be a farmer. To general public and government alike, it began to appear that too much land had been tied up in the reserves, and so the Indian Act was amended and a sympathetic ear lent to requests for surrender of reserve lands that were not in use. Before, during, and after World War I, an enormous acreage passed to white men. Sometimes it was made to seem that the Indians themselves would benefit. One such case was Coté Reserve in Saskatchewan, where some severed land was to be used as a townsite, and the Department stressed the benefits to the people in being near to an "active, prosperous railway town with a well-established market, since they had to learn to make their living in the same way as other settlers."[61] It was a curious argument, since few of the residents had much of anything to sell and the likelihood of town employers hiring them must have been very close to zero. The next chapter includes a short stop at Coté in the 1950s, by which time the harm experienced by the Coté people was decidedly more visible than the benefits.

The land surrenders are tangible evidence that the government had given up on farming as the industry which could put an economic foundation under the Prairie reserves. While its own policies had been the chief architect of failure, such things are never admitted, and mainstream society in the West has always found it more acceptable to put the failure on the Indian side, as a natural consequence of their nomadic past. But the facts prove otherwise.

The people did try to make their way in the kind of farming that was offered to them. That was what defeated them: a system as poorly designed to make them farmers as the schools were to educate their children.

In the United States, a similar policy of subsistence farming was relentlessly pursued – we may, in fact, have copied it. Economist Douglas Hurt recently published a study which also finds the policy at fault and the consequences dire: "Subsistence agriculture meant continued segregation and poverty. Only by developing their farming practices to participate in a market economy could the Indians have acquired the wealth and education and status that would have enabled them to move freely and equally among whites."[62]

Moving briefly to the 1920s, life on the reserve may be described as little changed. In their biography of John Tootoosis, an activist in Indian organizations, authors Goodwill and Sluman say of the people on Poundmaker Reserve "grey was the colour of their lives and silence their shield."[63] The commissioner in Regina still held all the power and was, at this time, actively persuading people to sell off reserve land; his success in these matters drew praise from superiors. But a rare failure is worth recounting. At issue were five sections (more than 3,000 acres) used for haying, that the agent had leased to a white farmer. Deciding to put up a fight, John Tootoosis (the father of the activist) consulted a lawyer, who said the transaction was legal. But when he was asked whether it would help to fence the land, the lawyer replied "good idea," and offered to defend the Indians in court. The agent, furious, ordered the fencing stopped, whereupon the Poundmaker delegation went to the commissioner in Regina. This worthy admitted defeat, but saved face with a parting shot: "You can put the fence up but you won't take care of it and it will soon fall apart. The people at Mistawasis tried the same thing and now the wire is lying on the ground. You will make money if you lease it but not get a thing for the land if you fence it. You will just waste it."[64] The shot had little power to wound, for the men had all heard such sentiments many times. Tootoosis Sr later likened the wonderful feeling of this victory to what his ancestors must have felt after a raid or a battle.

This little tale suggests how far the Department had moved from its original mandate to help the people get established as farmers and future citizens. As early as the 1890s, the harsh views of Agent Markle and Superintendent Reed were taking hold, although some of their employees out in the field opposed them. Later, as the reign of repressive policy lengthened, Indian welfare seemed even less important as a goal; career paths were charted on keeping costs low and serving the interests of white farmers. In the 1930s, the people's struggle to survive became still more difficult. John Tootoosis (the son) speaks of men completely defeated, not so much by drought and poverty as by the system. Quoting a character invented by author and activist Reverend Edward Ahenakew: "for myself I would rather starve than go beg for such a trifling thing as a permit to sell one load of hay."[65]

In retrospect, failure to establish the farming underlies the whole subsequent history of the Prairie reserves. Rejected by their neighbours in the early days because they were different, rough-looking, and poor, the people retained much the same appearance because their condition remained unchanged. Later, as the casual wage work on which they depended began to dry up in the mid-twentieth century, the government had to abandon all pretence that farming was moving towards the day when it could support the people. And so poorly were they living that the government was forced to bring in welfare, which spread rapidly to cover a large majority of the population.

This is not to say that farming could have supported the present reserve population. No more could farming support the white population, not even that portion which was born and raised on the farm. But farming should have been the initial base for the reserve economy, where men learned how to farm in the manner of their neighbours, as promised under the treaties. As they moved up the income scale, the Indian family's situation and outlook would have encouraged children to stay in school and lowered the barriers against them in the towns. Increasing numbers would have chosen to leave farming as the years passed; but their chances, too, would have been better because of self-confidence, education, and better relationships with whites. Ironically, the stated goal of government policy in the early farm years was assimilation, but its implementation ensured continued separateness and poverty.

CONTRAST WITH EXPERIENCE
IN EASTERN CANADA

The frustration and misery of the next hundred years flow directly from the cataclysmic nature of the changes experienced in the West and the wrong-headedness of the government's plans to settle the survivors. Caught up in a harsh system which kept them poor and dependent, the former wide-ranging hunters had also to live in close proximity with white settlers and townsfolk who made them feel inferior. What with white agents, farm instructors, teachers, employers, storekeepers, and neighbours, the Indian people were daily exposed to the prejudices of the dominant society.

Some historians believe that those in authority had expected a rather short period of adjustment to reserve life. It is certainly possible, for the age was one of unbounded confidence combined with limited knowledge which masked all difficulties. Yet something the government might have pondered, and apparently didn't, was the earlier and very different experience of settling the bands in eastern Canada.

The earliest white settlement in what is now Quebec occurred two hundred and fifty years before Confederation. This is a key point of difference in itself, for the earliest white men depended heavily on the Indian. If the latter were not always seen as equals, they were highly valued as military allies and essential working partners in the fur trade. The seventeenth century saw some of the Algonkian people living in settlements established by the Jesuits; these were people who had farmed before, and the settlements were in thinly populated country where farmers could pursue the old hunting life as a sideline for many years to come. No coercion was involved; the people ate well and were able to retain much of their culture. All of this contrasts sharply with settlement in the West.

"The Algonkian and Iroquois Nations neither feared nor felt inferior to the arriving Europeans," according to historians.[66] When the Iroquois Confederacy aligned itself with the British in the mid-seventeenth century, many gifts were sent by the British monarch to Mohawk chiefs, including a Bible from Queen Anne which is still in their possession. Both in the colonial wars between Britain and France and again in the American War of Independence, Indian nations on both sides were able to see themselves as equal to the European. Joseph Brant, who led his people over the border to British territory after the American victory, is said to have been "as at home in British drawing rooms and with American colonists as he was in Indian villages; he could deal equally well with all three."[67]

Joseph Brant and his people received grants of land on the Grand River in Upper Canada where they settled down to farm. Even here, although gradually surrounded by settlers, time was on their side, for agricultural technology was simple in the early nineteenth century and changed but slowly. No great gulf emerged between the Indian farmers and their neighbours; such a gulf was present from the beginning in the West, and it grew with the years.

Another difference in the eastern experience was that opportunities still existed for the skills possessed by the Indian people. The great canoes which left Montreal in the spring, traversing half a continent and returning laden with furs, were the keystone of that city's economy, competing with the British company on Hudson Bay. And when the fur trade declined, other opportunities appeared.

On Kahnewake reserve, located then, as now, on the St Lawrence River near the Lachine Rapids, the men had been voyageurs to the West for more than fifty years, but turned to river piloting, bringing the boats and barges through the rapids to the port in Montreal.[68] When the Grand Trunk Railroad began building the Victoria Bridge, the river men, delivering building supplies, would climb the piers for the view and were spotted by the foreman, who noted their indifference to heights. Thus, many became high-steel workers, a career still practised today. Over the years, the Kahnewake men have worked on both sides of the border and earned well; their culture has remained intact and they have maintained a pattern of family life that had proved satisfactory in voyageur days.

Kahnewake's is not, of course, a typical experience, but it does point to a world where Indians could be viewed as prospective employees and valued for their skills. This contrasts with the Canadian West where men from Indian nations were not even hired to help build the railroads. The Canadian society of earlier years appears to have been more accepting of the Indian people who lived in their midst, albeit on the reserves. The various governments that were involved had never decreed assimilation as an objective and the Indian people had had a hundred years or more to become accustomed to a white society which grew slowly around them. They were able to support themselves either by farming or wage work; they sent their children to school and brought them up in the Indian culture.

The western experience falls in a wholly different category. It was an era infused with white men's dreams of money – of modest amounts to be made by settlers and vast fortunes to be won in commercial enterprises. From this perspective, the Indian people were an obstacle to be got out of the way and their well-being was left mainly to the government and, to a lesser extent, to the Church. It was also a time when Western nations viewed their own culture as the pinnacle towards which others should strive; the harm that could be done by suppressing an indigenous culture had yet to be recognized. Thus, the Canadian government charted an impossible course. It set out to make the people over so that they would think and act like white people, and this meant denying their culture, along with the right to manage their own affairs. It soon proved impossible, under this equation, to provide them with a livelihood. The result was poverty and a loss of self-respect and community cohesion. Even the caring qualities which Colonel Butler had admired were difficult to maintain on the reserves, where the agent had a different agenda, practised favouritism, and ignored suffering.

White society worried no more than the federal government did, although Indian death rates remained high through the settlement period. As one historian put it, there was reason to believe that "the Indian would follow the buffalo into oblivion."[69] This same historian states that susceptibility to disease was reinforced by the change from meat to bannock as the principal element in their diet, and goes on to record "the callous disregard for poor living conditions and continued toll from disease" which characterized officialdom and the population at large. In the settlers' view, Indian people had always lived in poverty; the squalor on the reserves was their accustomed state and their shacks were seen as a step up from tipis.

This first stage in the saga draws to a close in the years running up to World War I, with growing doubts about the Indian people's future. Many officials believed that, with rare exceptions, they could not adapt and that the exceptions would be absorbed into the larger society. In reality, it was the system which largely governed the ability to adapt, and on absorption the officials were wrong. The better farmers tended to stay on the reserve. These were the years when programs were cut and lands sold off, as Canadian society turned its back on a people who failed to take advantage of the opportunities provided. And the years which followed brought few changes. One could say that the first fifty years of the twentieth century passed in a holding pattern: the schooling and the farming stuck in backwardness, with the Department as untroubled as the public was indifferent.

The next chapter takes us on to the years after World War II, an era of rapid change for the reserve economy, but change in the wrong direction. New disasters and adjustments are in store. Meanwhile, the present chapter ends with a closer look at the Blackfoot in the settling-in period. This nation was selected chiefly for the richness of historical sources, and is in several respects atypical; many nations had better land and many worked harder at farming. Nevertheless, the common elements are there: the power vested in the Department, wrong-headed farm policies, isolation from mainstream society, and the failure to make a future for the children. It all serves as background to the new catastrophes at mid-twentieth century.

THE BLACKFOOT TAKE UP FARMING

A nation with a proud history and a difficult adjustment to reserve living, the Blackfoot and their confederates, the Blood and the Piegan, were long-time residents of the Plains with a history stretching back for millenia. Their attachment to the land was, and is, profound. But the short-grass country is less than ideal for farming and, in the nineteenth century, it posed every hazard imaginable. Not least among these were the Department men who ruled their lives.

Farming held no appeal for the Blackfoot. Brave in battle, skillful and cunning as hunters and horse stealers, their legends were replete with bold deeds from the past and their chiefs renowned for wisdom. Who had not heard of their wealth in horses and the abundance of their food, guns, and blankets? They had made their way back from Montana, their last rendezvous with the buffalo, at a time when farming was well underway on the reserves to the east, yet their own view of farming remained, as a later observer put it, one of "humiliating and arduous work, to grovel in the dirt when one was accustomed to riding over it on a fast buffalo horse."[70]

The Blackfoot were starving when they took up life on their reserve and the government issued rations – a regular distribution of flour, beef, and tea. Chief Crowfoot's biographer, Hugh Dempsey, describes the people waiting daily in the line-ups, with Department employees, rude and belligerent, "treating the Blackfoot as if they were dirt under their feet."[71] The rations took the edge off a hunger which might otherwise have impelled the people towards farming; but the government feared to put it to a test lest these fierce warriors upset the settlement so recently achieved and throw their support to the Crees and Métis on the North Saskatchewan, also disaffected. Rations were maintained throughout the troubled years leading up to the second Riel rebellion, after which some of the younger members did take up farming; but, for reasons that are less clear, the rations continued on until 1901, a full twenty-five years after Treaty Seven was signed.

Interest in farming did increase in the interim, largely because of the considerable success of their Piegan neighbours with potato growing. The Blackfoot were motivated in part by their wish for the goods which could be had by selling potatoes, but the real drive stemmed from the humiliation they had endured in being unable to match the gifts they received from their Piegan visitors. Potato growing became the rage – clear proof, had the Department been looking, that Indian people were motivated by wants and desires like anybody else. Both the Piegan and the Blackfoot grew potatoes in order to sell them. Unfortunately, successful potato growing lasted only a few years before the price fell, eliminating the profit. Interest declined sharply.

In the 1890s, the Department added cattle. Distribution was limited mainly to the owners of large herds of horses, some of which were exchanged for the cattle; this was a departmental device for keeping costs down. There was a larger benefit, however, because it established a herding industry which provided wage work for non-owners. Wheat was brought in at about the same time, but fared poorly. The industrious Piegan worked hard for fifteen years at wheat growing but had little success, mainly because of early frosts.

Farming was also hampered by the restrictions of the farm plan and government frugality. Missionary Stocken comments on their equipment: "Indians saw the settlers plowing the land and reaping fair harvests but they themselves had nothing more than a borrowed plow with which to work."[72] He went on to say that neither the government nor the Church was prepared to face the heavy costs that "real farming" would entail. On the neighbouring Blood Reserve – then, as now, the largest in Canada – the farmers complained that one instructor was not enough.

Thus, the Blackfoot struggled on into the twentieth century, still on rations. In a way, the rations preserved a kind of continuity, for the Department's employees distributed their sustenance much as the chiefs in former times had handed round the spoils of the hunt. Only a handful of men had got a toe-hold in farming. Many more had gone over to wage work or, when coal outcrops were discovered on the reserve, to digging coal and peddling it in the district. Hugh Dempsey tells some early success stories. There was a Blood chief, for example, who took a hay contract, borrowed equipment which he quickly paid off, and competed with white ranchers; there was a Piegan who opened a stopping house on the stagecoach route.[73] Some students returning from school, especially sons of chiefs, got into farming at levels comparable to their white neighbours, but the balance fell heavily the other way; in 1900, the band was described as living well below the standard of the poorest whites.

A new era dawned in 1901 with the arrival of a new agent, W.A. Markle, who had followed the Blackfoot saga from his post in Manitoba, where the Dakota and the Saulteaux had settled down to farming and sent their children to school. In short order, Markle cut out the rations, got the farmers onto individual plots, brought in more cattle and wheat, and presented a plan to raise capital. With Blackfoot consent, he proceeded to sell off part of the reserve, and used the proceeds to pay for roads and heavy equipment, fences, houses, and barns, and a loan fund through which individuals could purchase equipment. A second land sale produced a trust fund, the interest on which was to pay for instructors and the wages of equipment operators, and provide help for the needy. Missionary Stocken was overcome with admiration for the plan.

Unfortunately, it had some serious flaws. While solving the chronic shortage of capital which held Indian agriculture back, it introduced a kind of farming that in no way resembled the white man's, whether on the Prairies or in any other place. Four paid instructors made all the decisions on planting and harvesting, supervised the operations, and did the bookkeeping. In the fall, the big machines moved through, taking off the crops on all the farmers' plots; the cattle were removed to the hands of a professional stockman. It might have made some sense, viewed as a first step and linked to learning, with the Blackfoot moving either into management positions or to full-fledged individual operations as they got the experience. But there was no long-term objective, nor was it a true farm. It was simply a farm operation, run by white men, which took care of most of the work on the individual plots and kept the farmers from learning anything about machinery, costs, profits, productivity, or whatever else was necessary for being a farmer.

More than thirty years later, when Lucien and Jane Hanks came to stay with the Blackfoot in 1938, the farmers were seeding plots of forty acres, although white farmers in the district needed 640 acres to make money.[74] By this time, farming had become even more paternalistic: farmers were given the seed grain and paid a wage by the Department to plough and sow. Even the relation between effort and reward was gone: returns in cash were doled out as the agent saw fit.

The Hanks couple sensed a pervasive hostility towards departmental officials. They thought this might be attributable to a profound dissatisfaction with the situation along with an element of blame, for the people had taken up farming and done as the Department directed, but had acquired none of the prosperity of their neighbours. When it was put to the agent that Blackfoot farming lagged behind, the response was quick and unembarrassed: quite simply, the Blackfoot had failed to take advantage of their opportunities.

Nothing could more clearly reveal the closed minds of the white men who ran the western reserves or the depth of their ignorance about farming. The Blackfoot had been slotted into a system which bore no relation to true farming and this must have damaged them as individuals, while ruling out any form of economic advance.

In later years, the land sales were criticized as a reflection of pressure from settlers, once an empty land began to fill up. The settlers' demands doubtless were a factor, as was Markle's interest in his own career, for he must have looked a winner, having sparked farming in a way that cost the government nothing. Neither of these factors bore much relation to Blackfoot welfare, and there was yet another objectionable feature in the way the money from the land sales – Blackfoot money – got spent.

The Hanks couple documented how the substantial income from the trust fund was used during their stay. The money went on rations (which had been re-established), rent-free housing, medical care, old-age relief, furniture, a horse and wagon for each farm family, and much else besides. Some of the larger items on the list, such as housing, medical care, and old-age relief, were provided to all other Canadian bands out of the Department's budget, paid for by taxpayers. There was no need for the Blackfoot to use their money in this way and it could have been used to better purpose, given that, far from being rich in real terms, the Blackfoot were impoverished. This was documented as well. Most of their income went on groceries; the people moved to log shacks in the winter because their houses were too cold; clothing was insufficient and furniture more so; some families had no beds.

The worst abuse was the money spent on establishing a type of farming invented by the Department, which neither taught the business nor paid a living wage. As the Hanks couple put it, the Department had made a major mistake in failing to use the trust fund to capitalize individual enterprises and establish the farming as it was practised elsewhere in North America. They also offered some comparisons with reservations they knew on the American Plains, all of them distinctly unfavourable to the Blackfoot in Alberta. As well as enjoying a higher standard of living, the Blackfoot south of the border owned stores and service enterprises of various kinds, including filling stations and car-repair shops. Such car-related services were hardly relevant to their northern counterparts who, for the most part, still travelled by wagon. Thus the Hanks couple had found them, on the brink of an agricultural revolution; but they would never be able to seize the gains or even keep what farming they had.

To end on a brighter note, the picture painted by Jane and Lucien Hanks is less bleak than its economic dimension would suggest. There is pride in being Indian and in adhering to the ways of one's ancestors. "As a devotee of Indian ways one gives up the ambivalent position of trying to become a replica of the whites who themselves deny the possibility."[75] The Blackfoot attend movies and play "snooky" in the billiard parlour. Some individual whites are friendly and the Ukrainian farmers, shunned by other whites, are good neighbours. There are some hard-working individuals among them who have managed to achieve a "fairly comfortable income" working in the mines or for white farmers. To do so, they have given up the folkways for "comforts." For most people, sociability is a major part of life. Houses are built in clusters which often accomodate groups of relatives; many families pitch a tent at the mine in winter, some because the man works there but others for the simple reason that they enjoy living in the centre of activity. Warm relationships are maintained with people on other reserves. The Hanks couple recorded that they tended to move in groups: "As though following inter-island trade routes through a sea of white culture, the wagons travel frequently from reserve to reserve."[76]

CHAPTER THREE

New Adjustments
(1945–1975)

When World War II ended, Prairie farmers set about buying more land and big machines, changing the whole scale of Prairie farming. Making money now hinged on volume production, so small farmers, unable to expand, grew gradually poorer, their numbers slowly diminishing over the years, their land passing to the big operators. Reserve farming was harder hit. The small number of people who had achieved efficient scale kept pace because they continued to get advances from the Department, while a sprinkling of veterans had gratuities which gave them a good start; but the great majority were left far behind.

A 1964 survey at Mistawasis tells the story.[1] Here were two farmers with a full line of equipment, running operations on the same scale as better farmers in the district. A further five farmers, their sons, were associated with them. After that came seven "independents" – so called because they owned a tractor and perhaps one or two other pieces of equipment – and a similar number of share-croppers who owned nothing. Nobody in the last two categories could have made more than a few hundred dollars. To complete the picture, two-thirds of the cropland was not even farmed by the men of Mistawasis; it had been leased for a pittance, and on the agent's urging, to district farmers.

It was not what Chief Mis-Ta-Wa-Sis had envisaged for his people. He was one of the Cree chiefs who signed Treaty Six at Fort Carleton, having opposed the dissidents – Big Bear and Poundmaker – and supported the government's view that his people would take up farming. Once settled on the reserve, he worked hard at extracting help from the Department and farming did go forward, although here, as elsewhere, it lagged behind the district. In the 1920s, many were still farming on a subsistence basis. Yet forty years later, when the survey was made, it came out that the farmers themselves remembered the 1920s as a good time, a time when farming moved ahead. Several of the older farmers preserved the memory that the white farmers were still using horses then, and perhaps it was the feeling that they had all been in the same business that made the 1920s look good.

By no stretch of the imagination could they now be seen in this way, and Mistawasis was not an isolated case. It was the same story across the three provinces, and the sorry state of reserve agriculture was the inevitable outcome of the Department's policy. Launched in the early days on the premise that only a few men were worth helping, the policy had ensured that only these men would succeed, for only the Department could supply the capital that farming required. Not until the 1960s was there a loan fund accessible to the small farmers, and even then, the maximum loan was five hundred dollars, although white farmers were borrowing thousands from their banks.

So it was that the Department's expectations proved accurate: the small farmers could not learn to farm in the manner of their white neighbours. Facing reality, the Department counselled leasing, advising those who looked to them for guidance that "at least you will get something." But vastly more was lost. Two-thirds of the cropland at Mistawasis went to enhance the operations of neighbouring white farmers, and the larger picture across the Prairies was much the same. There was also the loss of occupation, one that had provided a sense of purpose as well as a small income, and marked off the days with useful things to do.

Some may think this a sentimental view, for clearly the day of the small farmer had passed, whatever the Department did in the sixties. It is certainly the case that farming could not have supported whole reserves in modern times, for technological change ensured that there were larger farms and fewer farmers; but the leasing was not inevitable. Given a different government policy, the lost acreage could have been used, in combination with technical and financial aid, to establish a good number of farmers with efficient scale and district-level incomes. While this solution would not have covered everybody, it would have improved the lot of many families and seen that their children were better educated and able to move out of farming when the time came. It might even have swung the public around to a recognition that Indian people prospered like anybody else, when given half a chance.

An interesting sidelight on the influence of government policy comes through in another sixties study which traced the ancestry of leading families on a Saskatchewan reserve.[2] It happened to be the reserve of Victor Sunderland, the agent's favourite, encountered in chapter 2. A "leading family" was defined as having a certain level of income, a large farm, and good contacts in the Department. The study found only three such families, and all of them had a family head or wife of the head descended from Victor Sunderland. It is a telling comment on the nature of opportunity over half a century in the closed world of the reserves.

As reserve farming declined through the fifties and sixties, so too did the demand for wage workers on white farms. It was a second major blow to the reserve economy, for wage work had been an important source of income in the days of the hired hand for small farmers and non-farmers alike. Demand was also drying up for many of the jobs the men had found in construction and on the roads. During this "time of hardship," as it was called at Maple River (see below), the people got by on whatever they could, working in the beet fields, begging at the mission, scouring the district for work.

The worsening circumstances of the fifties and sixties have never been recognized by the Canadian public which tends to see a straight line of unrelieved poverty. But the postwar era does mark a real downturn, for the simple reason that mechanization cut out much of the casual employment on which the reserves had lived since the 1880s. And how were the new jobless to find employment, when they had only a grade school education or less? The Department had few ideas beyond an arrangement made with the sugar-beet growers. It was hard work for low pay – other Canadian workers would not touch it – but the men from Mistawasis helped to make up the contingents from Shellbrook Agency that were bussed to the beet fields in Alberta for a few weeks' work, the most that some would have in the year. Sometimes, whole families were moved to the beet fields for the brief harvest season. Indian poverty can hardly have been touched by this arrangement, but it was all that was offered. The onus fell on individuals to keep searching, even for a few days' work, travelling, if necessary, to distant places where jobs were rumoured to be available.

In the larger perspective, it can be seen that the reserves were victims of the same economic forces that were driving white farmers out and depopulating the small towns. But the hardship experienced by the Indian people was of a different order because they had nowhere to go. Their education levels were too low for any but the casual jobs which were now disappearing, and they weren't wanted in the cities and towns where young people and failed farmers went if they were white. It was the end of an era which had begun seventy to eighty years earlier with the distribution of hoes and scythes, and the end of the plan to have the people supporting themselves by farming. Yet so critical a turn in a long-term policy prompted no searching questions in Parliament, no studies or conferences. If there was any real concern at the time, it has left no discernible trace.

Reserve conditions worsened as white prosperity increased. Alice Kehoe, an American who had studied the Dakota in the western states, was shocked by the backwardness of their counterparts in Manitoba and Saskatchewan, where she continued her studies in the 1950s. Among others, she visited the people on the Dakota reserves whose early enthusiasm for farming was recorded in chapter 2. Kehoe describes them as "encapsulated on their reserves," having a "reservation culture"; one reserve is characterized as "a veritable moat of submarginal agriculture."[3] Their principal contacts were all made through the agent. Kehoe found they were good at finding work in the bush and that they excelled at firefighting, a situation which she likened to a Plains war party, a short-term activity demanding bravery and endurance. But the really telling comparison was with the stream of young white people going to the cities, for the young people on reserves didn't have the basic grade-ten education for semi-skilled urban jobs.

By the 1960s, some individuals were finding their feet in this new world. In the course of long-term hydro projects in northern Manitoba, two brothers from Fairford Reserve in the Interlake Region won a contract to erect steel transmission towers which would run the lines down to Winnipeg. Having worked as crew members themselves, they picked a team from the reserve, all men they knew to be good workers. They won the contract and successfully completed it.[4] Subcontracting might have been the formula for significant inroads in the construction industry, but it was never easy for men from the reserves to make the necessary contacts or get the job experience that was needed for a start. These were difficulties that the Department could have helped them to surmount by actively sponsoring subcontracting as a means of increasing employment, but it never raised its sights beyond the sugar-beet fields.

Another success story from this era concerns the band at The Pas, whose good fortune it was to have both entrepreneurial talent and the only gravel deposit in the area at a time of extensive road building. The band started a business hauling gravel, which prospered and expanded into general trucking, and ultimately became the stepping stone to a full-scale shopping centre on the reserve, conveniently located across the river from the town. There were individuals who made it through to higher education, taking up careers in education and the Church; but, again, the numbers are not large. Alice Kehoe tells of a man she met whose experience might be more typical. He is described as "highly intelligent, meditative, well read, fluent," yet he worked for many years at Churchill as a common labourer and was never able to get anything better. In the end, he returned to his Saskatchewan reserve, openly hostile and profoundly distrustful of the entire white world.

The larger picture is unaffected by individual success or failure, for it is dominated by the precarious reserve economy, which by now had collapsed. Farming had failed and wage work, the only alternative, was fast following suit. The people would have to find new ways to support themselves, but, already handicapped by poor education, they were rapidly becoming more so as education and skill levels in the mainstream labour force moved steadily upwards. Some were further handicapped by an attitude and outlook that was completely out of tune with mid-twentieth-century Canada and these, too, would be coming to the cities.

The northern forest lands also experienced worsening circumstances. The forest dwellers – Cree and Chipewyan, for the most part – still followed a traditional way of life in the 1950s, living in small family groups, spread out through the forest for most of the year, and coming together at the post for the annual provisioning and sale of furs. This event included an appearance by the agent, who checked the register for births and deaths and distributed the treaty money – a highlight of the gathering. But the agent was not otherwise a factor in their lives. These people had been fortunate in that they had retained their independence, an ancient way of life, and their culture; as for their poverty, they had always been poor and did not think of themselves as such.

What set change in motion, oddly enough, was family allowance – a gift from far-away Ottawa. Because it was a poor society, in which the returns from trapping were often little more than what was paid back to the trader for supplies advanced, the family allowance of five dollars a month for each child was a significant amount. Coupled with the requirement that the children attend school, the family allowance program brought the women and children into the settlements, where the province quickly built schools. This, in turn, brought in most of the men, for few were willing to endure the hardships of a winter in the bush without their families. Thus, a national program, designed with southern Canadian families in mind, effectively ended a way of life in the North.

Village residence combines poorly with trapping. While some men still managed to make the journey to distant areas where the fur was good, the trip was expensive and most of them switched to short journeys based on the settlements, whose surrounding areas were inevitably over-trapped. Yields fell and incomes with them. In the 1950s and 1960s, when fur prices followed suit, the value of the fur harvest in Saskatchewan's northern region barely exceeded the money coming in from family allowance. When the trappers' expenses were deducted, the fur in fact brought in less.

The new economy required difficult adjustments. Most trappers were earning less than they used to and often their wives controlled more money. In the old life, the people hadn't needed much money; now, many things had to be bought. Now, too, they lived at close quarters with others as a permanent arrangement, not for just a few weeks in the year. The loss of traditional functions was hard on both marriage partners and, in particular, their role in teaching the children: not many of them, in these times, would need to know about the patterns of animal behaviour, the curing of pelts, or the preparation of food that they no longer ate. In effect, the old family partnership in which each member had a role to play dissolved. As one scholar put it, "Village life not only destroyed the economic base, but relegated the family hunting team to the cultural dustbin."[5]

In the larger communities, life was further disrupted by the advent of government agencies to deliver services. Staffed by whites, they offered little employment for the long-term residents, while taking over the management of their affairs and introducing set roles: white officials and their families on one side, native people on the other. Ironically, at a time when colonial powers elsewhere were booking passage home, a colonial society was establishing itself in Canada's northlands.

The former trappers did no better in the mining industry. This had been an important employer in northern Manitoba since the 1920s and set up in northern Saskatchewan in the 1950s to extract uranium ore in the wilderness around Lake Athabaska, where a few hundred Chipewyan scratched out a living. The Manitoba study which reported on the Fairford crew also found a mining company which hired Indian workers, had sensible policies allowing for adjustment difficulties, and encouraged the men to train for higher-level jobs. The authors of the study saw in such examples the way employment could be found for a large potential workforce in northern Manitoba, "a workforce used to the rigours of work in a severe climate and to the solitude of physical isolation."[6] It was an eminently rational argument, given the costly bonuses that were used to attract men from the South and the high turn-over which persisted nevertheless and further raised costs. However, white society, including the mining industry, saw it otherwise.

A more forthright attack on the industry's hiring policies, published in a 1969 bulletin of the Canadian mining industry, helps to convey how Canadians viewed the problem of unemployed Indian people at that time: "Most mining men have worked in other parts of the world and have seen indigenous people working at various stages of employment, whereas in the Canadian mining industry the Indian is blamed for not coming forward and for his poor attitude to work."[7]

The practice of blaming the Indian is of long standing and by no means limited to the mining industry. The account of the pulp-mill operation at Maple River shows why men tended to hang back when work at the mill involved working alongside whites, enduring their jibes and hostility, as well as the no-win situation of being foreman. Bunkhouse life has been particularly hard on the men from the reserves who, unlike their white co-workers, were forced to endure taunts and humiliations on a daily basis. Pushed too far, many have simply taken off for home, providing further evidence to reinforce the belief that the Indian has poor work habits.

Another, perhaps more critical factor at work in the mining industry has been society's belief that the mines were there to provide jobs for white workers from the South. This belief recalls the early days on the Prairies, when homesteads were being established and the whole of the West was wanted for white farmers and their families; the land set aside for the reserves was resented. So, too, in the decades which followed World War II, the massive exodus from Prairie farms made jobs a big issue in the western provinces and the jobs in northern mines were viewed as the special preserve of the white man.

When the Leaf Rapids mine opened in 1970, the Manitoba government made a commitment to get some native people employed. It may indeed have acted on this commitment; but a Métis businessman who was there describes a predominantly white community whose small native component stood completely apart. They were not wanted, they told the visitor, either at the mines or in the schools.[8] To the same era belongs the murder of a young Indian woman at The Pas, and an apparent cover-up, revealed eighteen years later, in which much of the town must have participated.

Manitoba Hydro was another big employer in the 1960s and 1970s. Several thousand white workers made their way into a remote wilderness where Indian and Métis people lived in poverty. Some native people did find work on the crews and the odd subcontractor was employed, but Hydro had no policy to hire them and many were too shy or lacking in confidence to apply. The unions raised further barriers, requiring all hiring to be done through hiring halls in distant Winnipeg. The Manpower office in Winnipeg is said to have processed hundreds of applicants from overseas who joined the unions and went on the North. If that is so, the wish to save jobs for southern Canadians becomes less convincing as a reason for excluding native people than a deep-seated wish to keep them out.

Another clue is found in the report of the prestigious Committee on Manitoba's Economic Future (COMEF), published in 1963. A section on northern Manitoba deals briefly with the presence of native people and finds "no evidence of racial discrimination on the part of major employers." Then follows the Committee's own view that "industrial concerns in this area should not be expected to employ native labour which is not as productive as white labour ... It is difficult enough to persuade large investors to put money in resource development in the north without expecting them to assume the added cost of solving the welfare problems of the native population."[9]

Reports like this don't get written in modern times, so only by going back to them is it possible to see the real barriers erected by society. The report suggests a majority society that is entirely caught up in problems of economic growth for the benefit of its own members; a society in which the Indian people are a nuisance, but not an obligation. This may also help to explain the seeming complacency of the guardian Department – why, for example, it could see the sugar-beet fields or a northern fur-enhancement program as adequate responses to a massive need for employment. Since the Department took its cue from public opinion, there *was* no place for Indian people beyond these fringes.

By 1960, the western reserves had been home to the people for eighty-five years or more, but they were less able to support themselves than they had been before World War I. The COMEF Report estimated that a total of 650 registered Indians were employed in Manitoba, out of a population of 16,000. Later in the decade, the Hawthorne Report, commissioned by the Department, supplied data from a sample of reserves across the country. The Prairie provinces were represented by eight reserves, one of which, with a hundred percent on welfare, had the lowest income in Canada. The rest were all below average. On six of these reserves, eighty to ninety-seven percent of the men worked fewer than six months of the year.[10]

In North and South alike, Indian people were living under appalling conditions. Journalist Heather Robertson writes of a band in southern Manitoba – one of those which made a good start in farming before the treaties were signed.

[The reserve] has only 55 homes: these are houses and shacks and 40 families are without shelter altogether. People are forced to double up and sometimes triple up with relatives and friends. A house inadequate for a family of five holds 15 people ... The shacks are uninhabitable – no insulation, no floor, no furniture, often no windows – but people live in them because nothing else is available. A shack which, at best, could contain three or four people, holds seven or ten ...

The houses have too many people for furniture. There is room for no more than two or three beds, a table, a couple of chairs. Mattresses are spread on the floor. Most of the inhabitants sleep, eat and watch television on the floor. They sleep in their clothes, wearing coats or parkas in winter to keep warm. They huddle together, three or four to a mattress, often just on the bare boards ... The Indians can do nothing about the situation except put up with it.

The Indians [on this reserve] are sick. Eight members of the band were admitted to hospital with tuberculosis in 1965 ... A health survey showed that no baby under one year old was immunized. The infant mortality rate ... is one of the highest for any community in Canada. Between 70 and 98 percent of the preschool children are not inoculated against any disease, including small pox ... Pneumonia, bronchitis, colds, sinus trouble and intestinal infections are chronic and general ... the unavoidable result of cheap, badly heated homes, overcrowding, bad food and poor sanitation.[11]

These people did not want for health services. The federal health department paid all the bills – doctors, home-nurse calls, hospital care – and the people spent "an extraordinary amount of time in a hospital." On the other hand, there was apparently no money to spend on the housing, sanitation, and other aspects of the environment. The river where the people had been getting their water was polluted, so water had to be hauled by truck from a neighbouring town. There was never enough water for baths in a family of ten or for clean clothes; there was no proper storage to keep the drinking water safe; there was no garbage-disposal system and toilet facilities were still at the outhouse stage.

Much the same conditions could be found in the northern settlements, with their flimsy, overcrowded shacks, polluted water, and unsanitary waste disposal. The Saskatchewan air ambulances flew out with people made sick by the conditions of everyday life. From Manitoba came reports of limping toddlers, who could be "seen all over the north": parents refused to sign consent forms for operations because their children were kept in Winnipeg hospitals for months on end while the parents received no news.[12] At the same time, since death rates decreased and birth rates remained high, the population was growing rapidly, putting further strain on housing and raising the spectre of still more undereducated people who would be looking for employment down the line. The reserves, plainly, lacked the resources to tackle the problems, while the off-reserve option fitted poorly with remote locations and the clear message from employers that Indian people weren't wanted.

This central dilemma is highlighted in Jean Lagassé's pioneering study of Manitoba's Indian and Métis communities in the late 1950s.[13] What most struck Lagassé was how many of these were situated in places that lacked any conceivable way for people to make a living. Taken aback by the poverty and hopeless circumstances, he concluded that the people would have to get employment in neighbouring communities, or be relocated to places where jobs were available. Checking the neighbouring communities, he found a few treaty men who had jobs but were unable to rent houses; there were families on the reserves that wouldn't move to villages nearby for fear of being unable to call upon the Department for help, should they find themselves in need. He talked to village councils which opposed renting to Indian people and sometimes took action to get them out of town. The councils also acted out of fear, since it would fall to them to provide "relief" should the breadwinner cease to be employed. One village official declared: "We do not have any Indian problem because we know how to deal with it."[14]

In fairness, it must be said that these communities were poor themselves and relief costs were then fully borne by local taxpayers. The residents, being poor, tended to resent what they saw as special treatment for registered Indians, and these were the communities that were likely to be near the reserves in all the poorer parts of the provinces. They were not prime territory for finding jobs.

Lagassé tried another tack with his idea for relocation. He canvassed local councils, the provincial government which had hired him, the federal Department of Indian Affairs, political figures, and local businesses, but found very little support for the idea. He concluded, with regret, that "the belief that an Indian's place is on the reserve is still very strong among the Canadian people."[15]

THE EMERGING WELFARE SOCIETY

Despite their poverty through the ninety years since the treaties, Indian people had been basically self-supporting. Apart from a few bands which got rations in the early days, income support had been limited to the treaty payments, set at five dollars per year and never increased; "food relief," which went only to disabled adults and the aged; and, for families, an entitlement to housing, which was not always honoured. Even with worsening circumstances after World War II, the system made no provision for families whose principal earner had no job or earned very little. So it was that, for many families, both North and South, family allowance and the old age pension became the main sources of income.

Some signs of an awakening national conscience came with a new decade, the 1960s, beginning with a special parliamentary committee, whose hearings had brought out some uncomfortable facts concerning life on the reserves. Attention was further focused as poverty and racial discrimination became hot issues south of the border. The Third World conditions on the reserves in Canada were becoming an embarrassment to the government and to a department which was unused to criticism; but the circumstances did, in fact, reflect badly on the government's stewardship. Provinces in the West were becoming uneasy; by the early 1960s, they had extended provincial welfare to registered Indians with reimbursement from the federal government.

Thus pushed, and lacking the will to tackle the knot of problems surrounding mass unemployment on the reserves, the Department converted its old food relief program to social assistance, broadened eligibility, and gradually extended coverage to take in the worst cases of need.

Once begun, social assistance expanded rapidly to become a major source of income for the reserves, reflecting the backlog of families which had been living far below any statistically devised poverty lines. The number of recipients was further raised by the shrinkage in rural labour markets, which had been more or less continuous from the 1950s on, and by the abandonment of activities that hardly covered expenses. Checking traplines at minus forty degrees, for example, was not a worthwhile activity in a poor fur area or when fur prices were low, now that an alternative was available. Thus, expenditures on social assistance mounted rapidly, increasing fourfold by the early 1970s.

By 1972, seventy-eight percent of the reserve population in Manitoba were receiving social assistance, seventy-six percent in Saskatchewan, and seventy-three percent in Alberta.[16] The statistics relate to total population and so include payments on behalf of children and non-working wives, as well as payments to people working for part of the year and drawing assistance the rest of the time. Nevertheless, they still show a very high level of dependency, which is borne out by scraps of information on employment such as the Hawthorne surveys, which found a majority of men on the western reserves working fewer than six months of the year and, on some reserves, fewer than two months. Other corroborative evidence is found by comparing the social-assistance population for Ontario reserves, which was then only twenty-five percent.

Having thus solved the income problem, the Department stepped up its housing program, although limited budgets and the backlog of need prevented rapid progress. The Department also increased its small budget for economic development, experimented with new programs, and commissioned an academic team (H.B. Hawthorne and colleagues) to provide some new ideas. But none of this would make much difference. Not until the 1980s would an economic program be given some teeth, which means that social assistance has been the dominant factor on the western reserves for more than twenty-five years, and its dominance is only now beginning to be challenged.

The emergence of a welfare society marked a further decline into dependency, for the people had managed, hitherto, working at whatever jobs they could find, hunting and gathering much of their food, helping one another through various turns of fortune. These activities had given them a certain autonomy and preserved their self-respect. But the growing welfare presence went against the grain. A poverty income was one thing – Indian people were used to that – but a man's role as provider was valued as it is in any society and men unable to support their families felt diminished. Social assistance reinforced feelings of inadequacy and hopelessness that had been building since the treaties.

It also increased resentment for what the people saw as poor treatment. They had not asked for handouts; what they wanted was a chance to work, to support themselves as they had always done, and it was this chance that they saw being taken from them. The white people were deliberately keeping them from jobs and giving them this money that they couldn't turn down, but which was humiliating to accept. In the 1950s, Lagassé had described how Indian people felt the hostility of white people and the assignment of inferiority, and how they also felt hostility and resentment for the wrongs done to them. Such feelings could only have grown in the 1960s, when work was harder to find and dependence intensified.

Social assistance brought new problems, including further damage to the Indian family. This stemmed, in part, from a policy which made it difficult for a man to qualify for assistance while it was paid automatically to mothers on their own. When a man earned very little, his family might be financially better off without him, which could tip the scales in troubled marriages already stressed by poverty and fear of the future. And the deeply troubled young men who found themselves unable to act as heads of families had their counterpart in young women raising children on their own, for Indian society not only set great store by children but placed no stigma on illegitimacy. The Canadian census for 1971 showed that twenty-five percent of Indian households were headed by women, as against fourteen percent for all households; later surveys in Prairie cities put the figure much higher – fifty-three percent of native households in Winnipeg, for example, in 1981. [17]

The costs were high in human terms; they included men being deprived of their parental role, an important one in Indian society; women raising children in difficult circumstances; and children growing up in alien cities, cut off from the extended family, the homey atmosphere, and the culture that were all part of life on the reserve. The fault, of course, did not lie with social assistance alone, but welfare became the key piece in a system which had refused to tackle the basic problem of access to employment and make a place for Indian society within the Canadian mosaic.

Social assistance was soon followed by provincial child-care workers, who tended to see the overcrowded houses and poor sanitation, but missed the love that was there, the support from the culture, and the strength in the extended family. The tolerance with which the rest of Canada viewed conditions on the reserves was not for these modern missionaries, and judges in provincial courts agreed with them. The children were to be "saved," which meant taking them away, placing them in non-Indian foster homes, or getting them adopted by non-Indian families. The statistics are shocking. In 1980, when these practices were losing favour with the authorities, registered Indian children made up twenty-two percent of all children in care in Alberta, thirty-two percent in Manitoba, and forty-six percent in Saskatchewan. [18]

The 1966 Hawthorne Report described the child-welfare services as "varying from unsatisfactory to appalling." [19] The enforced separations were damaging for the children, many of whom in later life were unable to find a place in either culture; it was also hard on the parents and such an affront to Indian society that, years later, when bands began to administer the services themselves, many of them made it their first priority to gain control of the child-welfare services. The damage to the society remains. Patrick Johnson, an authority in the field, believes that by weakening the Indian family, the child-care system contributed to the disproportionately high rates of juvenile delinquency and incarceration that exist today.

The intrusion into child rearing is the strongest possible evidence of the low view that Canadian society had of the Indian, but it was only one of many pressures on the Indian family. Generational conflict had been present from the first days on the reserves, when children were set on a course which was different from that of their parents, so that many lost their culture without finding a new identity. But the potential for conflict expanded in the 1960s as more parents lost control of their lives and as grandparents, who had always helped, assumed a larger role in parenting. Their part had worked well in the context of a whole culture, one to which all adults subscribed and all children aspired to learn; but it was a wholly different situation when grandparents, with little education and a traditional outlook, had charge of children who were bussed to schools in the towns, where they were expected to blend in with and acquire the values and outlooks of the majority society. These children were pulled both ways, and parental models might support the traditional culture, or the schools, or neither. A departmental survey, published in 1980, declared that "the strength and the stability of family units seems to be eroding,"[20] and went on to cite divorce rates, illegitimacy, children in care, adoptions, and juvenile delinquency. But by 1980, the process had been ongoing for years, not to say decades. The statement seemed long overdue and clearly required action; instead, it passed without a ripple.

Not by coincidence, the era of social assistance has been marked by a mounting burden of social problems. The incidence has varied from place to place and should not be exaggerated, for their culture has remained a source of strength to untold numbers of individuals and families, as have the Christian churches. Yet a growing number of people appeared to draw support from neither one nor the other. "Many Indian people," writes Bradley Bird, "are left in a state of limbo, unsure of past practices, unaware of current requirements."[21] He went on to point out that the loss of language, religion, and way of life is something that, in Canada, has been experienced only by native Indian people.

Problems also stemmed from what was retained. Many people, sometimes called "traditionalists," held fast to the world view of the hunter-gatherer, unable to think in terms of tomorrow, much less of the years ahead. Taking each day as it comes, they have had a particularly hard road, attempting to deal with schools, jobs, and eventually with life in the cities. It might seem odd that an agency so bent on intrusion could let a hundred years go by without recognizing the seriousness of the problem. Yet, immigrants to Canada were recognized as a group that needed help in integrating, and money was found for that purpose.

Problems such as delinquency, suicide, and alcohol abuse are plainly related to the underlying situation, but they have many dimensions. These become clear in the case of alcohol abuse, the source of so much misunderstanding and stereotyping. A 1962 study by the Ontario Drug and Alcohol Addiction Foundation concluded that men on the northern reserves (an environment closely resembling that of northern Manitoba) drank to forget the anxieties and frustrations of reserve life – a world without meaning.[22] In the western forests, where there was frequent contact with white people, the reasons seemed to centre more on exclusion from jobs and resentment of the low opinion whites had of them. Another author associates alcohol abuse with the absence of employment and the resulting despair, seeing it as "a symptom of the powerlessness of native people denied the right of self determination."[23] Others have stressed drinking as a social activity or a continuation of the happy-go-lucky days of the past. These several explanations are not mutually exclusive, but rather seem to capture different kinds of drinking. People may drink for different reasons at different times, one person's pattern may differ from another's, and all these variants may coexist on the same reserve, much as strong families coexist with broken ones, or as people steeped in their culture live alongside the lost and alienated.

The author of the Crowe Lake study outlined below, adds that it is misleading to examine drinking among Indians without reference to similar patterns among whites. He is speaking from observations made in a particular town, where "if differences exist with respect to the use of alcohol, they lie primarily in the fact that whites drink considerably more and more steadily."[24] The reason, he suspected, was that whites could better afford it.

What does mark the 1960s is the emergence of alcohol as a serious problem, linked to other social ills. Manitoba estimates suggest that fifty to sixty percent of the health problems of Indian people were alcohol-related, as were seventy percent of suicides and eighty-three percent of sudden deaths.[25] Alcohol is also associated with the growing numbers in jails and prisons, family breakdowns, and much else besides; but it seems better treated as a symptom than as a cause. There is a malaise in the Indian society of this era; its origins stretch back to settlement days, but are exacerbated under the new stresses and conflicts of the welfare society. Behind the media reports of violence and self-destruction lies the difficult history of a people who lost their independence long ago and now suffer new humiliations.

Some reserves have been little afflicted by social problems, while others have had a long history of disaffected individuals and families who are only weakly attached to the community. Such people spilled over into the cities in the 1960s and many of them were "traditionalists," uniquely ill-equipped for city life. In one of the early urban studies, they are described as never having been acculturated, and author Edgar Dosman attributed their fringe status in society to departmental policy, which was content to see a few move up the ladder, while ignoring everybody else.[26]

An even darker side to reserve life is exposed by R.W. Dunning, respected anthropologist, in a study of an Ontario band for which he invented the term "collection."[27] The term denotes a community that failed to function as a society. It contained individuals wresting a living from the environment; but there was no transmission of culture and only minimal controls to guide behaviour. Individuals were prone to psychological disorders; most children did poorly in school and those who did well moved away. The people depended heavily on social assistance and on the Department to solve their problems. Clearly, this is an extreme case, but it might have some application in the western provinces, describing the situation of individuals in cases where the local community, for whatever reason, was unable to supply direction and support.

All in all, the emergence of the welfare society marked a new downturn in the fortunes of the western reserves. The money was badly needed, but it did nothing to relieve other problems – indeed, it made them worse. What was required was education and skills, and the strength and confidence to combat discrimination in the labour market and assert the right to a livelihood; social assistance merely reinforced a long-standing dependency. The primary reasons for the Indians' "caste-like position in Canadian society," says Dunning, "are the government policies that create and maintain a relationship of perpetual dependency."[28] Many others have said essentially the same thing, including a 1984 House of Commons Committee report, which will be considered in chapter 5.

RELATIONSHIPS WITH CANADIAN SOCIETY

The mid-twentieth century saw changes in a neglected corner of Canadian society that made a bad situation worse, but this was not an issue that could arouse mainstream Canada. Although they won attention briefly in the 1960s, the new miseries were accepted as if they stemmed from a law of nature that was unaffected by the actions of individuals and government. Here, one comes up against the widely held view that Indian people have a certain place in Canadian society and it will not be much changed, whatever government may do. It is a factor of considerable importance, because it allows government to muddle along indefinitely.

This view that Indian people have a particular place can best be seen in circumstances where the two societies, white and Indian, live as close neighbours, having daily contact. Studies have been conducted in many such communities, and the profiles that follow draw on three of them. They show, for example, that Indian people get little work in the towns; more revealing are the ready explanations for their exclusion. They show children who go to a town school but remain separate, an indigestible group; some grade eight children in a reserve school reveal their determination not to go to high school in the town, knowing what it is like. The third study probes the origins of social breakdown and finds one reason in people who cling to the past, failing to make needed adjustments; equally, it finds another in the Department's indifference to these people's welfare. This same indifference is characteristic of the townspeople.

Maple River (1960s-1970s)

This account is based on a book by Swedish anthropologist Yngve Lithman, who spent three years on this Manitoba reserve.[29] Maple River (a disguised name) sits on the very edge of the farm belt, more part of the forests which stretch north to Hudson Bay. The Saulteaux people, who have lived there since they signed Treaty One, saw the farming started, but most of the land was unsuitable and, as the years went by, they depended more on trapping, hunting, berry picking, and wage work of various kinds. These carried them through to the 1920s, when they found themselves with a paper mill on their doorstep, as well as a company town, both built on land severed from the reserve.

For the next twenty years, the men got work in the mill and related bush operations. This was the most prosperous time that Maple River has ever known, but it ended with World War II, when the men were squeezed out of the mill. Although the pulpwood operation lasted another ten years, the whole time from the loss of the mill employment onwards is remembered as a time of hardship. Entire families went south to the beetfields, picked berries, took on odd jobs, and whatever else they could find. There was hunger and begging at the mission. The pulpwood operation ended in the fifties. It had been run mainly by Indian subcontractors with big camps employing many men, and they were put out of business by the union, which wanted the jobs for white men. When that went, the reserve economy was in shreds. Maple River, a community of about twenty-five hundred people, came to depend on transfer payments and government works projects.

At first, the Swedish visitor found it puzzling that the people of Maple River (and other reserves in the region) stayed in their impoverished communities. But the longer he lived with them, the more reasonable their behaviour seemed to be. Lithman's book records day-to-day life in Maple River in the early 1970s; recollections of past experience and views of the present situation, all of it in an analytic framework that brings out the forces at work. Some of the highlights are presented here.

Employment.   None of the Maple River people were employed in the town, which is only a ten-minute drive from the reserve, or in any of the other towns within easy driving distance. The few who were employed at the mill had lowly positions. Interviews with company managers produced two explanations. First would come the assertion that the company stood ready to hire anyone who could do the job, a stance which seemed to blame the Indian people for the scarcity of applications from the reserve. Next came a litany of Indian shortcomings, which covered not only their low education and lack of skills but also their wish for special treatment, such as being allowed to work together with other Indian employees, not being made foreman, and so on.

Interviews with men on the reserve who had worked at the mill conveyed an entirely different picture. As they saw it, work at the mill was made next to intolerable by the slights and humiliations which had to be endured. "You always feel you have to watch yourself. The white guys will always keep an eye on you. If you make a mistake they will raise hell. They will be interested in what you bring in your lunch bag, as if you didn't eat the same things they do. They'll ask you all sorts of screwy things about a reserve but they'll never come and visit you. They behave as if you were an animal."[30] As to becoming foreman, an Indian foreman giving orders to a white man is just asking for trouble. One man tells his story: "I was appointed foreman but ... I never should have taken it. All the white guys started to raise all kinds of trouble and there was no way I could keep things going right. I could never get them to do what I wanted and they were always back-biting and trying to make a fool out of me. I couldn't take that kind of shit so I resigned as foreman."[31]

The men's wish, and they felt it strongly, was simply to be seen, each individual, as a worker. Many white workers, however, felt an equal need to vent their views on Indian inadequacies. In a conflict situation, the Indian culture tends to favour withdrawal, which meant that if there was any hope of scraping by without the job, they would leave it. This is the reason so few men from Maple River were working at the mill.

In the bush camps, where some all-Indian crews were back in operation at the time of the study, they were often assigned to areas already cut over. The boss, when interviewed, had a ready explanation: "First, one has to think of the white guys, with families and cars and houses to pay for and so on. The Indian guys, well, they are taken care of by Indian Affairs anyway."[32]

Ethnic labelling.   Living side by side, using the same stores and services in the company town, with their children in the same high school, Indian and white people led entirely separate lives. The author describes at some length how the one viewed the other, using various spokespersons. The two examples included here make clear the nature of the relationship. In the white's view, "Indians have poor life styles with violence and alcoholism a prominent part. They are unreliable. They live on welfare and do not try to better themselves. Indians do not live up to the essential demands that society puts on everybody, such as neatness, punctuality, etc. The Indian department takes care of the Indians and gives them all sorts of money. Indians are dirty."[33] In the Indians' view, "white people exploit Indians. White people cannot be trusted. If you trust them they will cheat you. Whites will never give any credit to what an Indian does. The white's deception has caused our poverty. White people look down on Indians and laugh at our clothes and our homes and our cars. They think we are savages and heathens."[34] Ethnic labelling tells each group to keep apart.

The high school.   Maple River had its own school for lower grades, but high-school students were bussed into town. It was a traumatic experience for the first-year students who, having met with prejudice all their lives, had not previously had to deal with it on their own. They soon found that teachers treated Indian students differently: less was expected of them and less given to them in the way of time and encouragement.

The school system was marked by ethnic stereotyping. The expectation that Indian students would do poorly had the result that no special measures were taken to ease their adjustment to high school or to redress shortfalls in their academic background. Some teachers said that special measures would not be fair to the white students. This response may be seen as unwillingness to admit prejudice against the Indian students, but it hardly affects the result, which is that Indian children did not get the extra help they needed. The Indian students' own view of the situation was that most of their teachers were bigots.

Non-acceptance by fellow students was another part of the high-school experience. Apart from sports, interaction was minimal; none of the school organizations included Indian students. The mixing of the races in sports consisted of an Indian team against an all-white team, an event where feelings always ran high and much ill will was generated. Often, the white team felt it necessary to stock up with outsiders to improve their chances of winning.

Indian students, asked for their views on white people, would give such responses as "some are okay," or, "a lot wouldn't trust you with anything." Daily encounters with teachers, other students, and the whole education process in general added up to a lot of discouragement; between low grades and the difficulty of seeing any real benefits from finishing high school, it is not surprising that the drop-out rate rose sharply in grades nine and ten. Interviews with several of the Department's supervisors elicited a single response: they were unworried.

Analysis.   As an outsider, the Swedish visitor was not bound to take for granted a system that assigns Indian people to a separate sphere. A key element in the study is his explanation of how the system works. It begins with a proposition – namely, that Indian people are competent, capable of meeting the requirements for mill worker, high-school student, etc. The question then becomes one of explaining their failure in these roles. To give a very brief summary, the answer lies with white society, which exercises a two-fold power: first, to block access, as at the mill, and second, to deny that Indian people can perform adequately, as when someone says, "Indian students are bound to fail," and, "Mill workers will quit; why hire them?" Thus are Indian people kept from joining white society to any significant degree.

The usual explanation for racial separation finds the Indian people at fault; it is their deficiency or failure, or their preference for keeping to themselves. But here in Maple River, the people were daily demonstrating that they could take part in the mill or attend an integrated high school; as to preferring to live in poverty, nothing could be further from the mark. These people know the pleasant streets and houses in the milltown, and have watched the good life on television; they do want these things for themselves. They have also heard the message, "Get an education; take a job; work hard; you can get what you want." But white society sends out a second message which comes through with greater force: "Indian students don't belong in classes with whites, the men shouldn't be working alongside white men, and those who do will hear that their real place is on the reserve." The basic stumbling block for the Indian, says Lithman, has always been white society.

Migration. In the early seventies, roughly a third of the Maple River band was living off-reserve – further evidence, in the observer's view, of the desire to improve their situation. But it wasn't migration in the usual sense of a permanent move, with a growing attachment to mainstream society. As it seemed to Lithman, migration was more a flow in both directions, with family A packing up for the city as family B, which had been there for a while, was driving back to the reserve. Young people seemed to spend a lot of time in Winnipeg, but tended to come back to the reserve when they married.

The migration pattern says a lot about the city experience. Although some of the people from Maple River held "fairly stable" jobs, a large number were casual workers, picking up what they could get. As far as Lithman could tell, it was seldom the case that living in the city involved a change in one's perception of oneself or one's place in society or prospects. Since expectations were low to begin with, and since the city confirmed them, the most natural outcome was a return to the reserve, which did not rule out another sally at some future time. It was a world with a solid centre in Maple River, but including Winnipeg and Brandon on the periphery.

Crowe Lake, Ontario (1960s–1970s)

This profile, drawn from a study by David Stymeist,[35] is included because the relationships it describes for northern Ontario apply equally in the Prairie provinces.

Crowe Lake (also a disguised name) is the administrative centre for services to Indian bands scattered over a large area of north-western Ontario. The town came into being with the building of the National Transcontinental Railway in 1909–12 and was settled with much assistance from new immigrants, giving it a rich ethnic mixture. Its two main industries, the railroad and forestry, went into decline after World War II and it was the expansion of government services that provided a new economic base. Both the federal and provincial governments have offices there; with district headquarters for Indian Affairs and the Indian hospital together representing a third of the jobs with major employers, it could be said that looking after Indian people has become a leading industry in Crowe Lake.

At the time of the study, the modest prosperity of the town stood in sharp contrast to the "extreme deprivation" of the Indian people coming in from the bush. Not many of them were living in the town, but they could be seen on the streets daily, coming in for the stores, going to school, trying to get jobs through the agencies, seeking treatment at the hospital, or visiting patients there. They could also be seen in the courtrooms and the jails, at the movies, and in certain beverage rooms and restaurants. Another striking contrast was that between the Indians' contribution to the town's modest prosperity and the low status assigned to them. As in northern Saskatchewan in the sixties, there was a keen sense of rank and place. Agencies performed the services as required and, as clients, the Indian people had cordial dealings with whites; they were not, however, accepted simply as human beings, in the same category as the white people. Nor were there many jobs for them, apart from low-paying work at the hospital for women and firefighting for men. The men in the firefighting crews stationed at Crowe Lake stayed in a camp outside the town, and only got their pay when they were on the plane going home.

Some, but not all stores and restaurants served Indian people; in the beverage rooms, which were the most frequent point of contact between the two races, each tended to sit separately in order to avoid trouble. When fights did break out, they usually escalated quickly. A lone Indian male attacked on the street was helpless, for most white men saw it as a mistake for him to seek help from the police. Although a white man might well be found guilty of assault if charged, the Indian who laid the charge would be in serious trouble. "In a sense, the Indian enters a strange and hostile territory when he or she comes into town and cannot rely on friends or relatives for support."[36] Virtually all whites in town were united in their opposition to the Indians. Offering insults was a favourite pastime; but, as Stymeist explains, "for an Indian to respond in kind would mean arrest or hospitalization, so he is forced to adopt passive strategies, ignoring the provocation and walking on. Even that was not always allowed."[37]

The justice system seemed to mete out heavier penalties to Indian offenders. For example, an Indian man and wife arrested for fighting were asked by the judge what they were doing in town, and whether they had jobs there. The answer was no, to which the judge replied, "Well, if you would stay out of places you don't belong, none of this would happen to you. Fifty dollars or thirty days."[38]

Indian children came to understand how the world worked at an early age. In an essay written at school on the reserve, one child declared, "I am not going to high school when I finish grade 8. I hate to go to high school because I heard about it. The White Boys that go to high school get drunk and try to beat people up. Why?"[39] Another wrote, "What I am going to do when I finish grade 8 is quit school because I have lots of things to do at home and I hate to go to high school because I hate to get into trouble. I like to stay home."[40]

A hostility extending to the entire Indian population was the subject of particular interest to Stymeist and he offers several interpretations, all useful in the context of the Prairie provinces. The first is that despite the numerous ethnic groups in Crowe Lake, Indian people were placed in a separate category, not so much as a different culture as a different, and inferior, race. This was particularly noticeable in the case of recently arrived groups such as Chinese, Pakistanis, and West Indians; all these, while seen as culturally different, were apparently accorded white status. Hostility was reserved for the different race, members of which could be characterized as dirty, lazy, drunken, or living on welfare: "I don't care what they do for or to Indians. Nothing that they do will do any good and it's a waste of time and money to think that anything around here will ever change."[41] Many whites were violently hostile and "fiercely denied the humanity of native people."[42]

The second explanation goes back to the early years of the century when men came from many parts of the world to work on the railroads, but men from the reserves were not hired. Thus began the economic segregation which left the people without the means to support themselves and led to the host of organizations needed to take care of them in the 1970s. Stymeist describes the mechanisms of exclusion. One is informal, as when Canadian National was hiring and news spread by word of mouth; unwanted people didn't hear about the jobs. Similarly, word spread that an Indian man working at the hospital wanted to rent a house; he was unable to find one, although a house did get rented before he quit his job, unwilling to live in town without his family. The second mechanism is violence and intimidation, played out in the beverage rooms, on the streets, even in the schools, so that Indian children are deterred from going to high school because it means going into the town.

It is a strange place, Crowe Lake, with so much hostility directed at this single ethnic group. The hostility includes refusal of employment, yet blame is heaped on Indian people for not pulling their weight. The visibility of the services they get is a problem, says Stymeist, for it seems to the whites that Indian people are excessively willing to accept things for free. "What do Indians give in return?" is their question. In this way, a whole edifice is built on racial prejudice. Initially, the white society excluded Indian people from participating in the economy; later, it found them at fault for being destitute and needing services which the taxpayers were expected to provide. All the major elements in the relationship between Indian and White at Crowe Lake – exclusion, hostility, contempt, fear, blame – have been experienced in the West.

Coté Reserve and the Neighbouring Town
(late 1950s)

The changes experienced at mid-twentieth century involved much adaptation on the part of individuals and communities. Some managed better than others, as might be expected. This piece focuses on a reserve that went through a very bad time, drawing much publicity and leading to the study which is still a fruitful source of insight.[43] Authors Shimpo and Williamson attach particular importance to the phenomenon of living between two cultures, which describes a considerable segment of the population which has still not come to terms with the twentieth century.

Coté is situated in east-central Saskatchewan, settled by a band of Saulteaux people who, in the early 1900s, were pressured to surrender a large portion of their land. Part of the severed land became the town of Kamsack. Band and town were necessarily close neighbours thereafter, although it was a purely commercial relationship, consisting of Indian people shopping in the town. This relationship took a turn for the worse in the 1950s, when jobs which Indian people depended on were disappearing while dependency increased and social problems multiplied. But Kamsack saw the problem as too many Indian people coming into town and behaving in ways that distressed the residents. So said the petition that went off to the minister of Citizenship and Immigration in Ottawa, with much more in the same vein "The aimless lives of Indian people lead them to loitering in the streets from early morning till late at night. They spend most of their money including relief money on liquor and court fines."[44]

The first question seemed to be: why Coté? Most Saskatchewan reserves had the same problem of unemployed men with long days to get through; others were situated as close to a town. The authors sifted through their conversations and interviews, which covered many dimensions of life on the reserve, and gradually their attention focused on the amount of day-to-day tension which all band members seemed to endure. These tensions were judged to be rooted in the past, so the authors embarked on a historical reconstruction, drawing on memories of band members, departmental records, and their own knowledge of how people and communities function. Something that seemed significant about early days on the reserve was the split between band members who adapted (learned English, took up farming, got along with the agent) and those who did not (the "traditionalists"). The latter gave every appearance of compliance, but were, in fact, living a double life. The agent was deceived. The records make frequent reference to a "good and obedient people," while the oral history makes clear that many people were only going through the motions when the agent was around. Unobserved, they continued to find their identity in the group, speak the Saulteaux language, live each day as it came, and preserve everything they could of the old life.

Dual behaviour patterns of this kind have been identified in many cases of colonial conquest and they tend to be counter-productive, particularly when the traditional economy has been destroyed. Accommodation of some kind is necessary to survival, and that includes adjustments in world view which enable people to make their way in new circumstances. The traditionalists at Coté were people who could not make that adjustment; others like them might be found on most reserves, in varying degree. In the Coté study, they are described as having rejected all aspects of the white man's culture.

To live thus removed from the world around them, yet still having to deal with that world, was the source of endless conflict through the years and has perhaps worsened in modern times. One example would be traditionalist parents whose children are attracted to white society in early school years and so fail to become rooted in their own culture. On growing older, these children would find themselves rejected by white society but without a group identity of their own, lacking emotional security and facing the scorn that their elders felt for Indians who wished to live as white men. These were people caught between two worlds, neither of which could "fulfill their need for stability and self-respect."[45] The authors believed that each generation of school leavers had members who were alienated from their parents, so that it became a society where many individuals were isolated and alienated, and many forms of withdrawal could prevail. The situation worsened in the 1950s when jobs became hard to find, while social assistance, which followed, lowered people's self-respect and increased feelings of inadequacy. There were more failed marriages, more children being brought up by grandparents, who were frequently traditionalist and hostile to the white man's ways. The consequences of living between two cultures took on new forms. An extreme example is taken from the Saulteaux method of child rearing, which was based on example and trial and error and eschewed instructions and commands. In this tradition, some Coté parents were unable to forbid young daughters from going into town, although they knew very well what would happen. As to the drinking which so aroused the people of Kamsack, the authors had a wide variety of causal factors to choose from. They tended to focus on the loss of function – as worker, parent, etc. – but particular emphasis was given to drinking as a way of relieving tensions, allowing the expression of aggressive feelings in a form that is ex-cused. In their summation, the authors describe drinking as the result of "social and economic deprivation and isolation; of strains, ambivalences and frustrations ... of absence of adequate opportunity for constructive self-expression."[46]

Finally, why Coté? The causal factors supplied by the authors tend to be couched in general terms and would apply to many western reserves; but, specific to Coté, they offer the proximity of the town, the lack of cohesion in the band – "an atomistic people" – and a certain failure in leadership. The leaders were seen as men who found ways to get on, but failed to find help for the floundering traditionalists. Explanations for unrest and social breakdown with wider application illuminate the experience of many, perhaps most Prairie reserves. First place is given to the nature of the change from a hunting to a settled society: it was too sudden, too radical, too damaging to the social equilibrium. Time was needed for adjust-ments, but the Saulteaux had to accept new ideas, indeed a wholly new approach to living, in a situation of weakness, with the result that many individuals were unable to cope in a positive way, while they retained much that would make the adjustment more difficult. The second factor emphasized by the authors is the government's failure to establish an economy, a necessary base for any society. The authors also felt that the people could have been helped to take a longer view – to think in terms of the future – and that the gov-ernment, as guardian, should have provided that help. Thirdly, the authors faulted Canadian society for allowing the Indian people to remain physically and socially isolated from the 1870s on. Deploring the fact that Indian people did not act in a responsible way, white society did not itself behave in ways that reflected its higher values. What Indian people have seen are the restriction of jobs to white people; massive indifference to Indian poverty; foot dragging on long-standing claims under the treaties and on claims for damage inflicted by companies and governments; shady land deals; and programs ostensibly for their benefit which fail to address their problems. The authors concluded that too large a section of Canadian society has given up on Indian people.

CITY LIGHTS

Prior to 1960, people of the western reserves had little experience with cities. Although they foraged far and wide in search of employment, they mainly got it on farms or roads, on construction projects or in the forest industry. Barely ten percent of Manitoba's treaty population was living off-reserve, less than that in the other two provinces. But, as farm and other rural jobs evaporated and reserve conditions worsened, the cities were the last hope and the exodus began. By the mid-1970s, roughly twenty percent were living off-reserve in Alberta, twenty-five percent in Manitoba, and almost thirty percent in Saskatchewan. The migrants concentrated in the five major cities which, although no more welcoming than the smaller centres, did offer some prospect of jobs.

The exodus included students and job-seekers – people with a purpose – and others who were more influenced by the wish to escape personal problems or who just drifted into the city with no clear plan, seeking change or excitement. Differences would also be found in the matter of qualifications: the few with degrees and diplomas or experience in the trades, the many at the lower end of the education spectrum whose work experience was likely to be casual labour. Push would seem to have been a stronger factor than pull, for the city was known to be unfriendly, even dangerous, the job prospects chancey, and separation from friends and family hard to bear. But "push" factors were present in abundance: the absence of jobs and the deep distate that proud men felt for welfare, the boredom felt by young people, the wretched living conditions. With population growing faster than the Department's housing budget, two and sometimes three families were being crowded into a single house, and the waiting lists for housing were increasing all the time.

A probing view of the migrant experience in the early 1960s is supplied by Edgar Dosman.[47] The setting is Saskatoon, a small city whose attractions included a housing boom – possibly a source of jobs – and the absence of outward signs of prejudice. For most of the migrants, however, the barriers to be surmounted proved too high. With an Indian-Métis population of roughly four thousand, the study found only twenty-five families that qualified for the category of "settled comfortably." Most of these were headed by men with steady jobs and a good education who came from the better-off reserve families and usually worked in government agencies. A smaller number were found in semi-skilled jobs, and there were even a few labourers, who managed to qualify by working long hours and having the determination to succeed. Although their income levels varied, all these families had in common a commitment to the city and a tendency to live in rather better neighbourhoods.

The second category, labelled "welfare," was the largest and fastest growing, but hardly settled at all. Many in this group were traditionalists, still caught in the time warp of the hunter-gatherer society, unable even to think in the terms required to climb the white man's ladder. Few, if any, had held regular employment, and they would manage in the city on the same combination of short-term jobs when they could get them, and welfare, they hoped, when they couldn't. In the city, they lived in real poverty, with a high degree of personal disorganization, but also with much social interaction and community spirit. Indeed, their social life was vibrant, with parties that lasted all night and much time spent in beer parlours (men only, in those days), where they had an easy association with white men. Rather frequently, they could be found back on the reserve, which they saw as less demanding than the city, but also less interesting.

The author's third group consisted of people caught in the middle, without the advantages of the affluent, but similarly work-oriented. These people had come to the city to get ahead, not to live on skid row, but lacked most of the necessary qualifications. They got jobs with low wages and intermittent employment, weathered layoffs, and were sometimes reduced to welfare; they were never free of the worry of financial collapse. The survey found them living in dilapidated homes in or near slums, with their children in the worst schools. It is this group that suffered most. Not only did they live in poverty when they had come with hope but they lived with constant anxiety, anticipating and experiencing unemployment, evictions, or trouble with teachers; dealing with discrimination, with salesmen and repairmen who frequently cheated them, and with the ever-present fear of sinking back to welfare. They felt alone, separated from friends and family on the reserve and without support systems in the city. Through it all, they had to maintain the sense of self-respect and inner strength that defined them as human beings. It is this group that was least well served by the system. The Placement Office worked hard on behalf of migrants with a good education, usually from well-off families on the reserve; it helped them to get housing and also jobs, often in the government. The Department was also able to help the "welfare" group, insofar as their needs could be met by money. Oddly, however, the third group, which had the values and behaviour that the Department so prized – the wish for a better life and a willingness to work hard for it – slipped completely through the net. Typically, the Department dispatched them to the Manpower office, which as quickly sent them on to unskilled labouring jobs, if such were available. In Regina, journalist Larry Krotz describes men and boys standing in line at dawn, ready to ride in a van to a construction yard and unload eighty-pound sacks of cement all day for minimum wage.[48] The jobs might last a month, a week, a day, and as long as the family could live with uncertainty and insufficient income, it could manage to stay in the city.

The experience of Indian people in Regina was more turbulent than that described by Dosman for Saskatoon. Regina being the natural destination of a high percentage of reserves in the province, as well as of the Métis, its native component quickly rose to the fifteen to twenty-five percent range, the highest for any city in Canada. At that time (the mid-1970s), Regina was a city with racial tensions. The hostility that so many white men harboured found expression in the bar scene and brawls became commonplace, with mostly native offenders going to jail or laying charges of police brutality. Eventually, the city took action, establishing a race-relations council (the first in Canada) which investigated complaints; gradually, racial clashes were brought under control. But other problems, as elsewhere, were more intractable. Most newcomers, as Krotz saw it, were only very slightly prepared for urban life. They got jobs that didn't last, lived in the worst housing, and had troubles with landlords. A later survey placed eighty percent of Regina's Indian population below the poverty line – ninety-two percent in the case of single parents – and the 1970s can hardly have been better.[49] Like other poor families, Indian families tended to frequent moves, and probably more so than most because reserve ties remained strong. The reserves drew them back when things got too bad in the city, only to push them out again with the sheer hopelessness of the prospect. Some schools in Winnipeg reported a complete change in the names of their Indian pupils between closing in the spring and opening in the fall.

Something else that marked the movement to the cities was the disproportionate number of women. In the age group twenty-five to forty-four years, women in Regina outnumbered the men by almost two to one; single-parent families (mainly mother-led) outnumbered the two-parent families by eight percentage points.[50] These statistics seem to reflect two divergent aspects of family life on the reserve. On the one hand, girls as a group tended to do rather better at school and by the 1970s, when Krotz was there, some were finishing high school in the city and taking courses. Some were getting jobs, although mainly in Indian organizations or agencies that worked with Indian people. On the other hand, the pressures and frustrations of reserve life that weakened families put many women in the position of raising children on their own, and these, too, felt the pull of the city where the children might have a better chance.

The great tragedy of the exodus from the reserves is that so few managed to benefit, even in the second generation. The parents knew that education was important, saw it failing to take hold on the reserve, and hoped that city schools could work the needed magic. But the schools were unprepared, government and civic authorities uncommitted. Larry Krotz interviewed twenty-six junior high-school students in Winnipeg, of whom fewer than half spoke English at home and more than half had attended five or more schools.[51] The children encountered unsympathetic teachers and hostile fellow students; experienced the same feeling of being bound to fail that dogged them in village schools. Parents, overwhelmed by problems, could do little to help. So it was that the children left school early; in grades seven, eight, and nine, the drop-out rates climbed rapidly.

The movement to the cities, was further evidence that Indian policy had failed, but while it may be seen as a positive response, its success rate was very low. Too few had the necessary qualifications; too many found themselves in the same state of dependency they had tried to escape, while losing much that had made life worthwhile on the reserves. In the next chapter, which covers roughly the same span of years, attention turns to the government's role in all this: the lack of employment and deep social problems on the reserves; the exclusion practised by mainstream employers and white society generally; the resulting movement to and limited success in the cities.

CHAPTER FOUR

The Government's Role: Some Perspectives

NEW TIMES, NEW PROGRAMS

The last chapter traced the worsening circumstances in the 1950s and the advent of welfare in the next decade. The sugar-beet fields were opened to Indian employment, but not the mines or the hydro projects, or much of anything else that could replace the rapidly disappearing jobs in rural areas. The Indian family bore the brunt of new pressures and social problems multiplied. Some turned to the cities, a last desperate hope, and within a decade, these numbered in the thousands. A solution for the few, it was a new struggle in worse circumstances for the many.

Social assistance had been brought in at a time when the Department was the subject of searing criticism, and it was portrayed as a stopgap measure while longer-term solutions were explored. The need for new policies was obvious enough, and this section traces the various attempts to find them. The most ambitious of the new directions was a basic change in education policy, designed to break the pattern of failure in the schools.

This change had, in fact, begun in the mid-fifties and was in part a response to representations from parents who felt very strongly that their children had to get a better education. The new plan was to get the children into provincial systems by bussing them to town and village schools, which were now accessible by road in all but the most remote northern areas. The parents could see the difficulties, which the Department apparently did not; but, balancing pros and cons, they approved the change. The local school boards agreed readily enough, since the Department would pay all costs; for the poorer municipalities, it was a bonanza. Thus, with agreement from all parties concerned, a major change-over was affected in less than a decade.

On the face of it, the plan was plausible enough. The federal schools were decidedly second class or worse, their facilities and equipment minimal, the quality of the teachers tending to be low. There was also a worrisome weakness in the motivation of the students. While this clearly had several causes, the Department put it down to the absence of stimulation which, it argued, would be provided by the better-motivated white students in the integrated schools. After a decade of bussing, however, the results fell far short of expectations. In Manitoba, for example, although elementary-school completions rose to fifty-three percent (the provincial average was only sixty-six percent), the drop-out rates rose sharply thereafter, highly correlated with age sixteen,[1] which was the cut-off age for family allowance. When the allowance ceased, its requirement that the child attend school was rendered null and void. The same Manitoba statistics at the grade-twelve level showed only twelve and a half percent of Indian students remaining, whereas the provincial average was almost fifty percent. These were crucial differences from the standpoint of the students' prospects for employment and other aspects of their adult lives.

From the parents' standpoint, it was not good enough. Any improvement was overshadowed by the slow pace of change and the distance yet to go, and the parents' support for integrated schooling declined. It was clear to them that the new policy was not providing an equal education and seemed unlikely to do so. They also knew why. Whether or not their children told them what the schools were like, they knew well enough from their own experience with white people.

The schools were a piece of Canadian society and could not help but reflect the attitudes towards Indian people that were standard for the times. What the children were up against was earlier described for Maple River: white teachers who made them feel backward and unwelcome, white children who didn't mix with them, much less transmit the motivation which the Department had so confidently envisaged. The school plan rested on a false premise; it would have been better to recognize the differences between white and Indian students and provide remedies for the obstacles. But the Department soldiered on.

National studies in the 1960s found a certain pattern of failure among Indian school children, centring on grades one and four. "An Indian child who enters school at age 7, fails grades one and four, is of legal age to leave school at grade 6. Most continue on to grade 8 but then do not want to continue because they are discouraged, 'feel silly with all those younger kids' and don't anticipate they will feel comfortable socially in a high school environment."[2] Nationally, only twelve percent of Indian students were in their proper age-grade at that time; the average was 2.5 years behind the non-Indian average at the end of grade eight.

As noted earlier, Indian children also reacted to being a separate category of people held in low regard. They continued to see the schools as having no purpose for them, because their lives were defined by the way their parents lived. The competitive environment was alien, diametrically opposed to the one in which they had been raised. And the long bus rides – the Stonies, among others, rode sixty miles – worried parents and wearied the travellers. Even the goal of better teachers proved elusive, often because the teachers themselves were unsympathetic or hostile, and in the poorer districts because standards for teachers, as for everything else, fell far below provincial norms.

With so many factors against integrated schooling, it is now hard to understand why it engendered such high hopes in the Department in the first place. Changing the schools did not change the crowded houses in which the children lived, nor their feelings of being different. High-school graduates were not very numerous on the reserves and the kind of jobs they saw the adults in did not encourage children to put their faith in schooling. As Harold Cardinal pointed out, "Education cannot operate in isolation from the people. Unless it is accompanied by adult achievement, it will have little meaning or appeal to the student."[3] The experiment with bussing was, in fact, a repeat of the mistake the Department had made in the 1880s, when it believed that the schools, operating in isolation from the environment, could put Indian children on the white man's road. More than that, according to a recent departmental paper, it had the same unrealistic objective. Integrated schooling was intended not merely to improve school programs and broaden education opportunities: "Above all, it was thought that the economic and social assimilation of Indians could be brought about by this means."[4]

Meanwhile, parental dissatisfaction mounted. Indian parents had been willing initially to submit their children to this hard-knocks education because they believed the advantages outweighed the disadvantages, but it was the parents who blew the whistle in the end. Seeing that the integrated schools weren't working, they came to feel that their own schools could do it better. By the mid-1960s, parents were holding meetings in many parts of the West, and Indian organizations had become involved in a major way, all of them struggling with the question of what education should do. It was, they knew, the key to their future. One group of parents made headlines by occupying a school – Blue Quills residential school in northern Alberta, one of the few that had always had a good rapport with the people – in answer to the Department's decision to close it. When the Department was forced to back down, the group went on to establish the Blue Quills Native Education Centre.

By this time, control over schools was becoming a leading item on the list of demands nationwide; parents were thinking about what Indian education should be. Before long, there was a policy, a statement of Indian views on education, prepared by the National Indian Brotherhood and presented to the minister for Indian Affairs in 1972. It is probably unfamiliar to most Canadians, despite the passage of nearly twenty years since it was written, and is worth quoting at some length for that reason.

STATEMENT OF THE INDIAN PHILOSOPHY OF EDUCATION[5]

In Indian tradition, each adult is personally responsible for each child, to see that he learns all he needs to know in order to live a good life. As our fathers had a clear idea of what made a good man and a good life in their society, so we modern Indians want our children to learn that happiness and satisfaction which come from:

• pride in one's self
• understanding one's fellow men, and
• living in harmony with nature.

These are lessons which are necessary for survival in this twentieth century.

• Pride encourages us to recognize and use our talents, as well as to master the skills needed to make a living;
• Understanding our fellow men will enable us to meet other Canadians on an equal footing, respecting cultural differences while pooling resources for the common good;
• Living in harmony with nature will ensure preservation of the balance between man and his environment which is necessary for the future of our planet, as well as fostering the climate in which Indian Wisdom has always flourished.

We want education to give our children the knowledge to understand and be proud of themselves and the knowledge to understand the world around them.

The time has come for a radical change in Indian education. Our aim is to make education relevant to the philosophy and needs of the Indian people. We want education to give our children a strong sense of identity, with confidence in their personal worth and ability. We believe in education:

- as a preparation for total living;
- as a means of free choice of where to live and work;
- as a means of enabling us to participate fully in our own social, economic, political and educational advancement.

In 1972, the Department agreed to Indian control of education as a basic principle. The way was now clear for bands to set up their own schools and run them their own way, with the Department defraying the costs with funds that had gone to local school boards. Most bands chose provincial curricula, with added cultural content. And while the move to band schools was not as rapid as many had anticipated, it had begun and would continue. It marked the first important step toward Indian control of their own affairs since the treaties were signed in the 1870s.

Another breakthrough in the 1960s was the easing of restrictions that had defined reserve life since the 1880s. Agents were phased out, the last one departing in 1969. Chiefs and councils, hitherto appointed by the agent, could now be elected by members, although some bands preferred to stick with the old system of hereditary chiefs. Band councils were beginning to administer certain services: not only education but housing, roadbuilding, sewer and water installations, and so on. When CMHC funding became available, some inroads were made in the housing backlog, and higher-quality housing began to appear.

None of these changes had much to do with the reserve economy, now in near-terminal condition. Economic policy had never been the Department's strong suit, and the results could be seen in the high percentage of people now on welfare or living in the city. Much ground was lost in the sixties, literally as well as figuratively, as the land that had supported many families passed to white farmers. This loss was directly attributable to a departmental policy that countenanced farm loans of five hundred dollars and counselled farmers to lease. Somewhat later, in the 1970s, Indian farmers themselves took action by establishing their own associations and attracting support from the three provincial governments. Special agencies were set up and staffed with experts of various kinds who worked closely with the farmers; in this way reserve farmers finally got the combination of credit and technical advice that had been their basic need since the 1880s. It was not a major advance from the standpoint of employment, but it made the farm base stronger, and raised incomes for the farmers.

The Department, meanwhile, has been casting around for something that might work and was gravitating towards economic-development techniques used in the Third World. It was attracted to cooperatives, which were part of the anti-poverty arsenal in those days, but its support for them went mainly to the Northwest Territories, which puts them outside this account. A second program, known as "community development" (CD), had wider application. This was an approach or technique which had made a deep impression on Jean Lagassé when he visited the Inuit of Greenland.[6] Somewhat similar to cooperatives, although lacking the business base, CD worked on the principle of group action. However it might get started, the basic unit was a group of people who had come together with a view to solving problems; the government's role was to assist them, although the assistance could be, and often was, of a minimal nature. Mainly, it took the form of a resource person (the French term *animateur* spread across Canada) on whom the group could call for advice and guidance as it went about its tasks of defining problems, setting priorities, exploring the resources available, and choosing solutions. There was a certain logic to CD for people who had had their lives arranged through several generations, but there was also a fundamental flaw which placed limits on its effectiveness – namely, the lack of money.

Because the CD programs had no money to speak of, the projects were necessarily of a minor nature. To give one example, there was a village in northern Saskatchewan where population had far outstripped the resource base and work was as rare as money; the CD project, which was provincially funded, had been to erect street signs on what were mainly footpaths through the bush. It sticks in the mind. That there were benefits for members of the group that went beyond community improvement is not in question, but it could be seen as an unduly slow way to help people who wanted work and a better life.

In any event, the CD officers (mainly young college students or graduates) got hired and sent off to the reserves. But CD was essentially a long-term approach – the Inuit in Greenland who inspired Lagassé had pursued it for three generations – and the time which the Department could give to CD turned out to be quite short. The young *animateurs* were critical of the conditions on the reserves and some of them thought they had a mandate to stir things up, so there were clashes with the authorities in the everyday course of doing their job. Much unwanted publicity was generated and, after a three-year trial, the Department called it quits.

So brief an episode might not seem worth recording, but it illustrates the kind of thinking which kept more sensible solutions from emerging. The problem, after all, was the basic need for employment. These people had been able to support themselves as long as there was work that matched their qualifications and employers willing to hire them. They had been made destitute by changes in the world beyond the reserve and by the Department's failure to see that they got educated, trained, and hired, or that they got access to capital for farming or business. Instead of addressing real problems, the Department turned to what was essentially a Third World technique; even at that, it failed to notice that CD in the Third World was not simply a matter of the organizational and decision-making skills that CD schemes in Canada seemed to focus on. In the Third World, CD was associated with village wells and small-scale agricultural or fishing projects that did raise living standards in a way that tended to conform with people's aspirations.

But the western reserves were not in the Third World, however much they might look like it, and the aspirations of Indian people were, not unnaturally, shaped by the wealth of the country in which they lived. By turning to Third World solutions, the Department revealed its continuing obsession with "backwardness" and its devotion to the principle that solutions must not occasion hardship for employers or loss of investment in resource industries. This principle was, doubtless, thrust upon the Department by the larger society which held it as an article of faith. The Manitoba report cited earlier, which declared that big business must not be put under pressure to hire Indian people, came out in the early 1960s, within a year or two of the Department's decision to go for community development.

The CD episode must have been bewildering for the people on the reserves, but they did not come away empty-handed. They saw their all-powerful Department viewed as a negative factor by the young *animateurs* and they learned something about extracting resources from the bureaucracy. The band councils, which had not had the authority to participate in CD, would soon be pushing their own wants directly.

Another event of the 1960s was the Hawthorne Report, an assessment which had been requested by the Department and which made major recommendations for change.[7] Produced by a team of academics, the Report was a ringing condemnation of the Department's policies and *modus operandi*. Economic development, it said, got an inadequate share of a budget that was itself inadequate. Too much emphasis was placed on "suitable" economic activities such as fishing, trapping, and guiding, low-income industries that were forced to support an ever-growing population. Too much money went on make-work projects and too much money and manpower on accounts and records. Amassed in the several studies done for the report and in other academic studies of the same era, the evidence was indisputable. Indian organizations were emphasizing the same points. Economic development, said a Federation of Saskatchewan Indians policy paper, was "very much the poor relation, in terms of money, if not of words, and the funds which did get assigned to economic development tended to be spent on studies and research."[8]

The poor marks from Hawthorne and other critics had little impact on the Canadian conscience, although the government paid enough attention to establish a new loans program, grandly called the Indian Economic Development Fund, in 1970. Even earlier, however, before Hawthorne, government policy had taken a new direction with the decision to involve two additional departments, Manpower and Regional Economic Expansion, thus breaking the long monopoly held by the Department of Indian Affairs and adding new resources. Both newcomers appeared to hold much promise, but particularly the newly created Department of Manpower (now the Canadian Employment and Immigration Commission – CEIC), which was given charge of the critical task of getting Indian people trained for the kind of jobs the economy now offered.

If ever a decision seemed right in the long history of government rule, this was surely the one: at last, a plan to open doors to employment in the mainstream economy. And, from this time forward, manpower courses remained a major element in Indian economic policy. By the early 1970s, they were absorbing more than two thousand registered Indians per year in the Prairie provinces alone, and the cost, nationally, considerably exceeded what the Department allocated for economic development.[9] And yet, for all the millions spent, a quarter-century of manpower courses has not made much of a difference.

The poor results are evident in the continuing high levels of Indian unemployment and in the low regard the Indian people have for these courses, often expressed by their leaders. Their basic objection has been that the courses don't lead to jobs. Statistics on course outcomes might seem to suggest otherwise, but these statistics have only recently been published and their interpretation raises questions.[10] A little knowledge of how the courses work supports the Indian viewpoint.

To begin with, they are classroom courses – the same courses available to Canadians in every walk of life, covering a variety of occupations, but of limited application in the trades (where apprenticeship is required) and omitting most skills where training is usually done on the job. Classroom training works best in a limited range of occupations, many of which have high educational requirements and are therefore unavailable, as a rule, to native people. Classroom training also poses special difficulties for the undereducated, including native people, who tend to associate it with earlier failure in school. And finally, classroom training leads to a certificate for those who complete the course successfully, but leaves many further hurdles between certificate and job. These include employers with racial prejudice or a low opinion of manpower courses and, in the trades, the requirement for apprenticeship, which means that the successful trainee has still to find an employer who will take him on as an apprentice, and must often get union approval as well.

Visible lack of success in the job market has been a major source of discouragement for course takers, amply abetted by the stress and strain of coping with the city. Drop-out rates in the courses have been very high. Kinew Housing in Winnipeg had four hundred native people on its payroll over a six-year period, of whom "large numbers had dropped out of or failed Manpower courses and only two had a trades diploma." The manager states that native people didn't take the courses seriously because they know they wouldn't get a job. In his words, "it is not unusual to meet native people who have been trained 10 or 12 times at various trades and never held a real job."[11]

Half or more of the training dollar went on upgrading education and basic "job-readiness" training. Such things were needed but, in an unstructured system, didn't necessarily do much good. A grade nine English course was not much use by itself, yet nothing in the system encouraged step-by-step progress through to skill courses and jobs. Statistics for all students, white and Indian, show that only fifty percent of those in upgrading courses completed them, while only twenty-five percent went on to acquire a skill; the rates might well be lower for the Indian students.

This, in a nutshell, is the classroom system through which the money earmarked for training registered Indians has been channelled for twenty-five years. Some course takers have benefitted, of course – perhaps women in particular, because office skills are well suited to classroom instruction – but the point is that the benefits have been minute compared to the vast sums spent and the enormous need for jobs. Men from the reserves were processed through the courses as if the courses were an end in themselves; only a trickle went on to jobs. In their briefs to the government, Indian organizations emphasized the frustration and anxiety associated with taking courses that led nowhere and added to what they called "the turmoil in Indian lives."[12]

Not until the mid-eighties and the advent of the Nielson Task Force would the Indian organizations find some high-level support, and even that proved unable to bring change. Still, it is of interest that the Neilson Task Force found the government "heavily overspending" on these same manpower courses, citing the "large numbers" who failed to get jobs and noting that fully a third of the students took courses in "surplus occupations." It recommended that the upgrading and job-readiness training be phased out altogether.[13]

Complaints by Indian organizations were often coupled with a request to increase the availability of employer-centred training, which they believed would serve their people better by linking training to employment and opening up a considerable range of skills which weren't covered by manpower courses. The Northern Alberta Development Council made this same point in a 1981 report that assessed the prospects for native people in the light of anticipated oil and gas development. The gains, it concluded, would be limited, partly due to low education levels and partly to the limited scope of the manpower courses. Based on consultation with industry, the report states that the major job opportunities would be for skills where industry does its own training; heavy-equipment operator was one example cited. However, the native people obtaining training would, for the most part, be found in the government manpower courses.[14]

Again, the question arises: why should the government have insisted on keeping policies that plainly weren't working? One answer would be the same reluctance to burden employers that had marked the Indian Affairs programs, as well as a similar indifference to results. Then again, the training system was classroom-oriented for everybody, and many non-Indians were not particularly well served either. The system was, in fact, closely modelled on that of the United States, a country which also lacked a strong tradition of employer training and was similarly caught up in the 1960s enthusiasm for pouring government money into one good cause or another. However that may be, it worked a particular hardship on native people because they lacked access to the large volume of training that was done by employers, notably in the trades, and because lower education levels tended to keep them out of the technology-oriented courses which worked well in the classroom. Indian people were thus more dependent on manpower courses than other Canadians, but were getting less out of them.

This would seem to be an argument for special treatment. But the whole concept of special treatment was anathema to the Manpower department, whose officials have always declared that Indian people have the same chance as anybody else; that they take the same courses and get the same services in the Manpower offices. It is a philosophy that strongly influenced the White Paper on Indian Policy, a milestone at the end of the 1960s.

Nevertheless, the Manpower department did make one exception worth mentioning because it was highly successful, although miniscule in terms of cost. This was the program "outreach," which delivers employment services in remote communities, using native officers. A federal task force found that in areas where outreach operated, the regular Manpower offices dealt more aggressively with employers to get native people placed, and it recommended that regular Manpower offices be phased out and replaced with outreach in the North.[15] Needless to say, this did not happen.

Special treatment or services never penetrated the training area, which was where most of the money was spent and which was so critically important to getting the reserves off welfare. Special-treatment models were available, for example Native Metals in Regina, a firm started by a local steel company, the province, and the provincial power company for the specific purpose of providing training and employment for native people. Once trained, the people got placed in the steel company or elsewhere in the economy. It worked well, and the operation continued for many years. Others like it came into being in various places; but taken all together, measured by money spent and individuals exposed to training, these efforts were a mere drop in the bucket compared to the federal manpower courses.

As Indian people saw themselves, they were not so much losing out in the job market as being left outside the competition. Their organizations had made training one of the highest priorities and pressed hard for a system that would work better for them. The government paid no attention. It seems almost sinister that the government held firm to the system and to the principle that there was to be no special treatment, despite all the evidence that Indian people were not benefitting from the manpower courses. In time, a certain cynicism developed, manifest in the saying, "Indians go on courses, white people get jobs".[16]

A second case of Indian people being lumped into national programs irrespective of the program's suitability is found in the make-work programs, also under the ægis of the Manpower department, which began in the early 1970s. They were launched, nationally, as a response to high unemployment and were extended to the reserves for the same reason. At their peak, towards the end of the decade – in the wake of media attention to mercury pollution and related unrest at the Grassy Narrows and White Dog reserves in western Ontario – federal spending on make-work programs in the native sector reached $34.5 million, which is almost certainly more than it spent on economic development.[17] Although subsequently cut back, make-work in the 1980s was still a large enough component in the government's strategy to draw the fire of Erik Nielson, who pointed to the lack of fit between the problem on the reserves (long-term unemployment) and the remedy (short-term jobs).[18]

The projects were short term and labour intensive, so that many people got work for a few weeks or months; roads got built or improved, and facilities of various kinds were added. But benefits of a more lasting nature did not flow, despite the millions that were spent, while individuals and communities experienced damage of various kinds: for example, the fostering of a short-term outlook and the belief that the people would be taken care of – already a serious problem which called out for redress, not encouragement. The projects also worked to ill effect on local efforts to establish businesses, for the project wages were high by community standards and often competed with legitimate ventures.[19] But the greatest harm lay in the high levels of frustration imposed on a people which, like anybody else, wanted jobs that lasted and paid a decent wage. A recent study of that era describes a northern Ontario band that was forced to participate in programs it did not like because they were the only alternative to welfare. The authors saw the band's participation, which was half-hearted and without long-term commitment or expectations, as a form of dependency, which in turn was largely responsible for the alcohol and other problems that so plagued the reserves.[20]

None of this seemed to worry the Department of Indian Affairs whose own make-work programs supplemented those of the Manpower department, although results have fallen short of expectations. According to an evaluation in the Alberta region, the program had been implemented with high hopes that participants would be weaned off welfare and acquire the skills that would carry them on to other jobs. The document brings out some of the reasons for disappointment, including the brief duration of the jobs and the fact that training had no part in the program.[21]

The second federal agency to be pulled into Indian economic programming was the Department of Regional Economic Expansion (DREE),[22] and it had an early success. This occurred in the special circumstances of oil development in northern Alberta, where large companies were moving into an area where native people lived in unemployment and poverty. DREE made a deal, putting in the infrastructure the companies needed, while exacting their cooperation in getting native people hired as trainees. The government saw to it that the people received counselling and a certain amount of job-readiness training, as well as jobs building roads, air strips, and industrial parks. Employer-based training was possible here because the big companies were working in tandem with the government and their interests coincided. In this way, development was forced off its usual course of bypassing native communities, and the benefits are visible in the Lesser Slave Lake area today.

More typically, DREE operated in areas designated for the weakness of the economy, rather than its potential. Although the formula that had worked with the oil companies could still, on a reduced scale, have found some applications, regional programming took a sharp turn in the 1970s to centre on government services. Interest shifted from improving economic opportunity to coordinating activities of the several departments and other levels of government involved, while Indian communities in designated areas got roads and buildings, short-term employment, and still more manpower courses. One program from the earlier era that did survive was "Special Arda," which made small loans to native people, provided advice and encouragement along with the loans, and dealt with people in a friendly, helpful way. Like "outreach" in the Manpower department, it has been well liked by Indian people and has provided genuine help; yet the real money has always gone to programs which seem mainly to create jobs for bureaucrats.

From the mid-1960s on, the Canadian government made much of the broader departmental base involved in Indian economic programs, although all it really meant was that Indian people got a piece of the national programs. They would have been better served by programs specially designed to meet their particular needs. As it was, they got roads and other useful things, but in an unfocused way, without a larger objective. They got manpower courses and make-work projects, but none of this addressed the basic need to improve employability or to put pressure on private companies both to train and hire Indian people. The cost was enormous. How it all looked to the Indian people has been summed up as follows:

The Canadian government has no strategy for development aimed at Indian people. It responds, sporadically, to ad hoc pressures where a first class opportunity for development appears, but there is nothing within the system which assures one step taken somewhere will be repeated somewhere else. Endless baseline studies lie gathering dust, with no action stemming from them. There is no coherent overall policy for reserve agriculture and no determined and systematic search for new employment opportunities on and off the reserve that has been communicated to the Indian people.[23]

THE SASKATCHEWAN PLAN

Lest the Department seem uniquely ill equipped to find solutions, it is worth a glance back to a major initiative that began in the late 1940s, launched by the newly elected Cooperative Commonwealth Federation government in Saskatchewan. The target area was the northern third of the province, which at that time was truly remote, lacking roads, tourists, pulp mills, or uranium mines, and which had a small native population living in historic poverty. These people were not the sole focus of the plan, but improving their lives was an important goal, and the programs drew applause from other parts of Canada and distant countries as well.

The planners' vision was a generous one in which modern health services led the way – a first in Canada for native people. Where the northern third of the province had been served with a single mission hospital at Ile à la Crosse, now came a series of outpost health centres and an air-ambulance service which put city hospitals in reach of every northern resident. Every settlement got a school, many of them extremely remote. Roads got built, linking some of the lakes to southern markets for their fish and laying the basis for a tourist industry. High-production lakes got a government air service which flew the fish directly to Chicago, raising the fisherman's price. There was a fur-conservation program which brought back the beaver from near extinction and, beaver being the most valuable pelt, trapper income in beaver-rich areas got a strong boost. Cooperatives were a key piece in the attack on native poverty.

All in all, it was a program of some magnitude, going well beyond what adjacent provinces were doing, or the Indian Affairs department, for that matter. It may not come through in this encapsulated account, but in those days, northern Saskatchewan was a place that got visited by people who were interested in the programs, many of them from international agencies and the Third World. Despite such encouragement, however, the situation of the target population was slow to improve, and fifteen or so years on, the provincial government called for a study to determine why the promised better life proved so elusive.[24] The question retains a certain interest today, for here was a plan that failed, despite a genuine wish to help the people and a major commitment of resources.

One reason was simply the "moving target" effect. As economic programs struggled to raise income, the number of people kept increasing – the rate of increase was, in fact, higher than in all but seven countries in the United Nations statistics. It was the inevitable result of naturally high birth rates suddenly joined to modern health services, which cut the death rate by over fifty percent and infant mortality by more than that.

A second reason was that the economic programs were firmly centred on industries which, however pushed or prodded, had only a limited ability to generate income. The cooperatives – one major thrust – provide a good example. A business owned by members, the co-op is intended to improve member incomes through getting higher prices (the fishermen's co-ops) or, in the case of co-op stores, by offering lower prices to member shoppers. Such changes are possible and can be important, but the greatest difficulty is encountered in generating enough improvement to accommodate all members and to sustain this improvement over a long period of time. Saskatchewan's northern fishery is a case in point. Here, a major effort was made, for the co-ops were strongly supported by a government marketing agency which opened important new markets so that both the catch and its value increased in a very significant way. The difficulty was that these benefits flowed chiefly to communities where the fish stocks were large and the human population small. The more typical situation was that of Ile à la Crosse, one of the larger settlements and, incidentally, one of the oldest in the province. I was there myself in the early 1960s, gathering data concerning the economics of fishing, and found the number of licenses issued to be twice what the lake could support. It was the only way that a semblance of economic activity could be preserved, although few families could live on the earnings.

Both fish and fur programs had other benefits; the participation involved was valuable in itself, the people got skills of various kinds and the satisfaction of working in their own organizations. It was the economic side that failed to meet expectations.

The research for the Hawthorne Report was underway at this time and the findings, soon to be published, would condemn the Department for failing to look beyond the traditional industries. To find the same myopia in progressive Saskatchewan shows just how widespread the feeling was that native people, at least for the present, would continue to support themselves from the old industries, however overpopulated. Such views may be seen as not necessarily based on race *per se*, but rather on the peoples' unreadiness for modern jobs and their wish to stay in the settlements. But a great mistake was made, nevertheless, in failing to recognize the economic reality: that there was an upper limit on the income that trapping and fishing could generate. Had that reality been faced in the 1960s, closer attention would have been paid to the schools. In Saskatchewan's northern region, the children continued to leave school early and the boys went into traditional industries, which became more and more overpopulated. The real problem, which remained unaddressed, was early drop-out, and high on the list of causes were the children's expectations. They did not prepare themselves for jobs which they did not expect to get.

The North in that era was a segregated society in which all roles were defined by race. When the first uranium mine began operations in 1953, it was plainly intended to provide employment for white men, just as the government's Fish Marketing Service, launched in the same year, was intended to meet the needs of Indian and Métis fishermen. The larger settlements experienced an influx of white workers from the South to run the business and agencies, most of which touched, one way or another, on the affairs of Indian and Métis people. These newcomers tended to replicate a southern way of life as well as they could, and to maintain a certain separation from the people they met as clients. On the job, many of them were idealistic and kindly disposed, but socially, few were inclined to cross the line. For Indian people, seeing whites on a daily basis, whether in their offices or simply in passing on the streets or paths, is one of the things that marks the northern experience off from the southern reserves. The feeling of inferiority this engendered was not missed by the children in the schools. Could they really aspire to these jobs that the white people had? And if not, was there any point to school? A study in the 1960s compared the aspirations of students at two levels, grade two and grade six. Boys in the first group were overwhelmingly in favour of airplane piloting as the occupation of choice; the second, more realistically, leaned heavily towards trapping and fishing.

In retrospect, it can be seen that major economic gains were not in the cards for native people because they had been put in a special category. The Saskatchewan government had had a twofold objective: to force the pace of economic development in the North, *and* to improve the lives of the native residents. But the two were not as closely linked as they might appear, for the development aspect was aimed primarily at the South. Northern resources would be brought into use to spur new industries and jobs in southern Saskatchewan, banishing the ghosts of drought and depression which still haunted the survivors. The vision for native people, however, was entirely different. Their part in the new industries would be relatively minor, and so their benefits would come through improved services and help for the traditional industries. The same thinking has characterized the Department throughout its history. Failing to see the people as having potential like anybody else, it failed to open opportunities for their advancement, which had the further result that their children saw no point in school. In this way, the problem of people ill equipped to support themselves has been passed from generation to generation.

HELP FOR CITY PEOPLE

Through all the years that Indian people have been coming into western cities, a second stream, comprising different races and cultures, has been coming in as immigrants. This second stream has faced difficulties too, especially its poorest members, yet immigrants as a group have had the critical advantage of coming from commercial cultures. Language differences and local customs have been less of a barrier for them, for what they have had is a good sense of employer expectations (or how to start a business), and this has set them on a course to acquiring whatever else they might need to earn a living. To have grown up with pride in race and culture gives them a good sense of themselves, and many, if not most of them, could count on help from compatriots or co-religionists already established in the city. Often associations were formed for this very purpose, while government offices stood open to give any additional help that might be needed.

How different was the situation of the refugees from the reserves, most of whom arrived in a very unready state, of which low education and job-skill levels were only the smaller portion. Part of the baggage they brought with them was the knowledge that they weren't wanted, and the daily reminders they got, as they searched for jobs and housing, reinforced their own expectations of failure. Unlike the immigrants, moreover, these newcomers had no well-established ethnic community to turn to, for too few Indian families had attained an "established" status. For this reason, and in the absence of public support, attempts to put organizations in place have not been very successful.

A case in point is "Neeginan," back in the 1960s. This was a group in Winnipeg, native and non-native, which proposed to deal with some of the people's needs by creating an Indian community in the city.[25] It was to start with a major housing project which would include small businesses as well, and provide places where people from different parts of the city could come to feel at home and share problems. Such a culture-based community would have been an enormous support to individuals and families dealing with the alien city, and the organizers worked hard to bring it about; but federal money was needed and the federal government turned it down. The reason it gave was that Neeginan would become a ghetto. Yet the people were already living in ghetto-type housing on ghetto-level incomes, without the friendliness and support that their own community could have provided.

Indian people dealt with the city in two main ways, one of which was by helping each other. Newcomers could always find a place to stay and were welcome to stay indefinitely. This is part of the sharing tradition. However, while sharing of this kind provided invaluable moral and financial support, it fell short of providing a foothold because the families already in the city were seldom better off than the newcomers. A second way of coping was by going home as often as possible. Back on the reserve, with friends and family, food that they liked, jokes and story telling, feeling at ease – this was what sustained them through the stresses of city life, and kept pulling them back to the reserve.

The government's stance in all this has been somewhat anomalous. Since the reserves were overpopulated from the standpoint of earning opportunities, the cities were the logical salvation, about the only one in sight, and the government might have been expected to push the urban solution for all it was worth. Moreover, since the ill-prepared state in which the migrants arrived stemmed directly from a system that had neither educated them nor prepared them for jobs, a certain sense of responsibility might also have been expected. But neither consideration applied. Far from seeing a solution or feeling responsible, the Department pursued its historic role of serving those who least needed help. Its off-reserve housing program has been described as being "designed to assist stable and upwardly mobile people to purchase a house."[26] Its placement services worked hard for high-school and university graduates, while the undereducated and marginally employable were dispatched to the Canada Manpower offices, which had no special services for Indian people, despite their handicaps. These people were sent on to employers in a hit-or-miss way, without any attempt to separate the work-oriented from those who might quit the next day. The

Canada Manpower offices have been much criticized by sympathetic employers on this point, while other employers have had their prejudices against Indian people confirmed. After twelve months' residence in the city, the hard-to-place migrants could be passed on to city welfare agencies.

Consultant Bill Hanson said of the assimilation process that "white society deals with winners and forgets about the losers."[27] This statement, made in the 1980s, referred to the traditionalist people in the city who had clearly failed to get the kind of help they needed. But Hanson's summing up would apply equally to the poorly qualified who came seeking work and whose plight was highlighted by Edgar Dosman, as described in chapter 3. These people needed help mastering basic life skills – banking and job applications, relationships with teachers, house agents, and repairmen, and dealing with prejudice – yet nothing in the system met these needs, just as nothing was available for upgrading their qualifications, getting them into better jobs, or even easing their anxiety. As to the winners, Dosman had brought out the contrast between the Department's efforts to hire the better-qualified people and its callous indifference to everybody else, and called it a failure "to generate a creative response to urbanization."[28] The policy is all the more inequitable in that the better qualified usually owed their positions to help which their families had received from the Department perhaps a generation or two before. A "creative" response, said Dosman, would have got at the needs of the others, so long neglected: for life skills, real training, support and encouragement for people battling poverty and discrimination. Instead, needs of every kind went unattended, as if they could be dealt with by the welfare cheque.

What did concern the Department was the so-called "twelve-month rule," which defined the length of time during which registered Indians in the city could qualify as the Department's responsibility; thereafter, they were to deal with the municipalities and the provinces, just like anybody else. From the standpoint of the clients, this does not seem to have made much difference, since the type of service they got either as federal wards or from other governments was pretty much the same. In what was surely the key dimension of improved employability and greater independence, none of the agencies had much to offer people from the reserves. They all worked best in a situation with a simple and clearly defined legal obligation: welfare, emergency housing, case-worker services, and so on, although the case workers were stretched too thin to provide the amount of support that was needed. Nor were the skills the people required to be found in the Canada Manpower repertoire. Meanwhile, the everyday pressures which eroded whatever confidence they might have brought with them fell beyond the reach of the system altogether.

Despite the need for employability and independence, the services provided in the city reinforced client status. It was the same kind of service that the Indian people had had on the reserves, where white people made the decisions, and it would do as little for them. Its patch-up nature is well captured in an extreme case in Winnipeg, where twenty-two agencies were working with a single family: the father and one son were in jail, two children were in treatment homes, another was seeing the school psychologist, and the mother and four children were on welfare, still living in abject poverty, despondent, and angry.[29] The amount spent on this family ($130,000; the amount would be more than twice that today) contrasts with the absence of funds to help parents become self-supporting, get control of their lives, and bring up their children without the need for social workers. The part played by the federal government seems particularly deficient, since it was the failed economy on the reserves that drove the people out, together with a housing budget that made living conditions intolerable. The people made an assault on the city to prove their worth as self-supporting individuals, only to experience failure or near failure once again.

Urbanization reaped high casualties. The young men who couldn't get jobs found various outlets for their anger, with many running afoul of the law. Their prospects sank even lower when they emerged from jails and prisons. Work-oriented families reduced to welfare were casualties as well, likewise the women caught up in prostitution and the bar scene and the mothers who lost their children to the streets. The cities were perhaps hardest on the children. Often from troubled homes, cut off from the friendliness of the reserve, they encountered the same hostility among teachers and fellow students that had been the norm in village schools. Many were scarred, quit school early, and began adult life not much better equipped than their parents. But progress, of a kind, lay ahead. Twenty-five years after the migration to the cities began, the manager of Kinew Housing in Winnipeg told me that the new generation of native children was different. "They're tough," he said.

CONFLICT OF INTEREST:
THE CASE OF HYDRO PROJECTS
IN MANITOBA (1960s–1970s)

Western bands have traditionally looked to the Department as their protector and viewed provincial governments as untrustworthy. It is one of the reasons they have always resisted any move to do away with special status. The following episodes show something of the provincial governments' willingness to ignore Indian interests; they also show, unfortunately, a certain negligence on the part of the federal guardian.

The first incident concerns Chemawawin, a Cree/Métis community on Cedar Lake in northern Manitoba. Chemawawin is destined to disappear under the floodwaters as Manitoba Hydro completes the Squaw Rapids Dam, a key piece in the works that are to bring cheap power to the South.[30] The Crees and Métis had been drawn to this site in the mid-nineteenth century, primarily by the quality of the fishing, but it was a good place for muskrat trapping as well, with lots of duck and moose for hunting. Even the land was suitable for gardening and the people, keen gardeners, grew fine potatoes, while a small sawmill operation provided seasonal work for some of the men. Thus, a broad-based endowment made possible a succession of activities which extended through the year, leaving time enough for visiting, ball playing, and dancing.

If the people were poor in terms of dollar income, by their own standards and in comparison with most northern bands they lived very well. This they knew, and saw themselves as fortunate. They were proud of their community, and they loved the beautiful lake, the forests, and their tiny houses which were dotted through the trees, separate and private the way they liked to live. But the Grand Rapids Dam would end this happy life: fifteen years before Thomas Berger spoke out against the harm that could come to native people if the Alaska pipeline were built,[31] it would not have occurred to anyone to halt construction for the sake of a few native people. The way the relocation was handled, however, could be seen as harsh and uncaring, even in the 1960s.

For reasons it didn't explain, the Department brought its relocation plan to the people at the very last moment. So little time remained before the waters would rise over their homes that the site selected by the Department could not be viewed, although it, too, was on Cedar Lake, less than a day's journey away. Instead, departmental officials painted a rosy picture of the place, for they needed the people's consent; the new site had been well chosen, they said, because the new homes could be hooked up to Hydro. Appliances they could buy would be waiting on the dock, and with stoves and washing machines, they could begin a better life. In a short time, there would be a road; the people would be getting cars and driving into Grand Rapids. The Chemawawin people, bewildered yet trusting, devastated by the loss of their community and the need to move out so quickly, approved the choice.

Their new home was a terrible disappointment, nothing more than a rocky ridge, barren and dusty. For people who loved trees, this was bad enough, but soon they found the thin, sandy soils unsuitable for gardening and the fishing poor. Some fishermen managed to adapt by buying big boats and motors which could take them back to their old fishing grounds at the north end of the lake, but few could afford the investment. The trapping proved poor as well and was gradually abandoned. Given also that the sawmill operation had been left behind, the move deprived the community of most of its cash income; with little game and no gardening, the people were unable to feed themselves, as they had at Chemawawin. Before long, most of the band was on welfare. They did get the appliances, as promised, and in due course were hooked up to Hydro. The road also materialized and a few people managed to buy cars, which made it possible to drive to the liquor store in Grand Rapids. None of these things served to compensate them for what they had lost. They missed the old life, filled with things to do and changing with each passing season. They had been independent, they had taken pleasure in their beautiful homeland, known the pride of accomplishment, and had thought well of themselves. The new location left them with little to do and dependent upon government cheques. Once energetic and busy, the people became bored and resentful of the way they had been treated. The new community was a profoundly unhappy place.

Twenty-five years later, in 1989, the band's chief made an appeal over CBC radio. The new community, now called Easterville, is still an unhappy place. Ninety percent of its families are on welfare and drugs are a problem, as well as alcohol; disaffected teenagers worry everyone. "Street kids of the unpaved roads," the CBC script called them; they spend their time in pool halls, partying, and watching videos. The parents see themselves as better off for having known a good life, but their lives are spoiled by bitterness.

The second incident dates from stage two of Manitoba Hydro's plan, which would see the Churchill River diverted into the Nelson, thus increasing the flow through the generating stations. It would also see higher and fluctuating water levels at five Indian communities – Norway House, Cross Lake, Nelson House, Split Lake, and York Landing – spoiling fisheries, damaging habitats, and converting shorelines to reedy swamps, so that boats would have to be hauled several hundred feet through the mud. Manitoba Hydro was slow to collect the information for estimating probable damage and by the time it was passed to the bands, construction was well under way. Formal meetings to determine compensation, which pitted the two governments and Manitoba Hydro against a committee of chiefs elected by the bands, also went slowly, while construction proceeded and indeed ended with no agreement signed. At that point, Manitoba Hydro, anxious to start the turbines, applied such pressure that the several parties managed to conclude an agreement in the space of a week. This was later ratified by the bands with sixty-five percent in favour.

The 1977 Northern Flood Agreement contained several good features, including the establishment of a task force to advise on how native people might be brought into employment in future Hydro projects and operations.[32] Out of this came the JenPeg program, financed by the two governments and Hydro, which launched apprenticeship training and jobs for native people in the trades as pipefitters, electricians, welders, crane operators, etc. The Agreement also provided guidelines for monitoring water levels and ecological effects of the diversion project, along with a commitment to pay compensation for damages. Finally, it contained a curious clause which can only be explained by Hydro's impatience, committing both governments to "eradicate mass unemployment and poverty" on the five reserves.

Over the next thirteen years, a familiar scenario unfolded. Low-income communities saw fishing and other earnings sharply reduced, while the number of families on welfare rose steadily. The other signatories were slow to pay compensation. Manitoba Hydro made an initial payment of $10.5 million to fishermen and trappers in the five communities. It may seem a large sum, but 11,000 people lived in those communities; assuming that there were 2,000 eligible families, it would work out to roughly $5,000 per family – hardly enough to improve the long-run prospects for very many. By 1984, one hundred and fifty disputes had been submitted to arbitration, most of them having to do with lost income or environmental damage; none had been settled. Only one of the five bands had received the provincial Crown land that had been promised. At this point, the federal government announced a $57 million sewer and water program which it construed as a special measure, although it was an ongoing program; the five bands had simply been moved ahead in the queue. How little was done, as more years went by, may be judged by the situation at Nelson House, as revealed in 1989 at Manitoba's Aboriginal Justice Inquiry. A fisheries officer testified to the lowered catches, the presence of mercury in the fish, and the high mercury levels that had been found in some of the people –

high enough, in his opinion, to pose a possible threat to their health.[33]

Another act in the drama opened in June 1990, with an offer from the two governments to give $253 million to the five communities in exchange for tearing up the original Flood Agreement. The offer seems surprising, given that the governments had spent more than a decade fending off claims and, apart from the JenPeg program, doing so little to implement the "poverty" clause. Indeed, the clause itself arouses suspicion: did the governments fear that the communities would take legal action to get this pioneering provision enforced? Statements to the press stressed the difficulties it posed. A high official in the Department stated: "We had our best minds working for years trying to figure out how to implement the clause, with little success ... It was just too imprecise."[34] It was a poor response. A good start had been made with the JenPeg apprentice program, and the five bands must all have had a backlog of projects awaiting funds: enriched classes, adult education, courses for house builders combined with energy-efficient housing, to cite a few. To plead failure before making a serious start makes little sense, still less to place the blame on imprecise wording. The "best minds" should have talked to the bands.

Another disheartening feature of the offer is that it was not $253 million in hard cash: $50 million only, or an average of $10 million per band, would go into an economic-development fund, while the balance would come in a package of programs covering job training, education, resource management, infrastructure, and employment. One suspects that, like the sewer and water program, much of the preferred settlement was already available under existing programs, without counting it as part of a settlement. One also suspects the influence of a federal task force which, six years earlier, had estimated the cost of implementing the Flood Agreement and put it at $500 million. Compensation for damages has yet to be paid, as this account is being written. All in all, it seems a sorry response to real losses in poor communities and, once again, raises questions concerning the government's role as the people's guardian.

This section was included primarily to draw attention to the potential for conflict in the Department's position. On the one hand, it has entire responsibility for the management of Indian affairs, including protection of the lands and furthering the well-being of the people. On the other hand, it is a government department, staffed by bureaucrats; its expenditures are reviewed by Treasury Board and any new policies require government approval. Is there a clue here, concerning the long years of ineffective and failed policies? It seems fair to state that the real failure lies with the Canadian public, which has not demanded a more creditable performance, yet one may still find that the Department has too complacently accepted decades of failed policies as the best that could be done.

Part of the trouble is inherent in bureaucracy, which tends anywhere to have a life of its own, with such goals as promotion and career paths, or the avoidance of criticism and inner dissension, assuming greater importance than the welfare of the clients. For such reasons, old policies will seem safer, no matter how little they accomplish, and so are kept on long after a clearer vision would see the need for radical change. Expenditure of public funds is another potent source of conflict. How can the good bureaucrats make a case for awards and settlements that vastly exceed what Treasury Board is likely to approve? Who, in fact, other than the people most directly affected, would applaud fair settlements for harm inflicted in remote places, on people whose member of Parliament is unlikely to raise the case in the House and who, in any event, barely count as citizens in the eyes of most Canadians? It will be seen, too, in the concluding section of this chapter, that the Department has only limited powers to set policy.

There remains the concern that even within these constraints the Department should have the power to ignore its responsibility toward its charges to the extent revealed at Chemawawin. It may be the worst case on record, but it is not the only one of its kind, and it is difficult to think of any reason, other than the obvious: that the obligation to protect its charges has not always weighed very heavily on the Department. All this serves to underline the profound weakness in the situation of Indian people.

POLICY VACUUM

Despite new programs, the 1960s marked no great advance over what had gone before; more money was thrown at the problem, but little of it was spent in a useful way. One reason, among others, seems to be the government's long-standing failure to define what the goal was, to give policy coherence and direction. The original goal, assimilation, had been quietly dropped in the early years of the century, and, while vague statements are encountered in later years, it proved impossible to find a clear statement of what the Indian people could expect to have or be, once the tutelage had stretched over a long enough period. It appears that for many years the Department has been performing a caretaker role with no vision of the future, and clearly, it was caught off guard by the agricultural revolution in the 1950s and the collapsing demand for unskilled labour. Other than social assistance, the Department found it difficult to respond. Then, in the sixties, policy development went on hold, awaiting the recommendations of the Hawthorne Commission which had been appointed for this purpose; when it came in 1966, the Report pleased no one.

The Hawthorne Report is best remembered for its concept of "Citizens Plus." Indian people would get the assistance they needed to become full participants as citizens of provinces and of Canada, while at the same time retaining the special privileges they had. There would be money for development on the reserves and the people would be free to choose – to go or stay. But the thrust seemed all towards going: there would be massive help for training and resettlement, while services would be delivered in the ordinary way by provinces. Indian people felt profoundly threatened by this concept, and the Department rejected it as well.

The policy gap stretched on, through a change in government in 1968 and a wholly new approach to Indian policy, contained in a 1969 White Paper entitled, "Statement of the Government of Canada on Indian Policy," then through a further hiatus in the aftermath of the White Paper, as its effects worked their way through the system. When in 1976 the new policy was finally announced, it was not particularly helpful, but it is best to deal first with the White Paper episode for the light it sheds on the place of Indian people in Canadian society.

The White Paper (1969)

The Department faced escalating problems in the 1960s and a level of public criticism that was quite unprecedented.[35] It had sought answers from a team of academics, but its own charges rejected them, while other critics maintained that the Department itself was the problem and that Hawthorne should have said so. Then came a new government bent on revising the Indian Act, and producing a White Paper that so shocked the Indian community that it dominated the landscape for a decade or more.

The revision process began with consultations during which the newly formed Indian organizations, with remarkable unanimity, made their priorities known. Surprisingly (from a general-public perspective), these were not cast in terms of economic development or access to jobs, but centred on the wish to preserve themselves as a people. This they saw as requiring (i) the continuing security of the reserve lands and of the rights deriving from the treaties; (ii) the settlement of outstanding issues, including treaty promises unfulfilled and compensation for lands sold off or damaged; and (iii) removal of restrictions under the Migratory Birds Act. The strength of the feeling for these historic rights is conveyed by Harold Cardinal, then president of the Indian Association of Alberta: "The treaties represent an Indian magna charta, entered into with faith, with hope for a better life with honour. We have survived for over a century on little but that hope."[36] And what would be had from the settlements was not money merely, but the means for Indian people to develop their resources and build new lives.

The Department was well aware of these priorities and felt comfortable in its historic role as protector of Indian lands, although public criticism was worrisome. *The Globe and Mail*, for example, reported that of 8,500 employees at its Ottawa headquarters, only twenty were Indian people. The Department responded with a pledge to increase native employment, but by this time, new forces had taken charge. The Trudeau government had brought a new approach to policy making, giving a larger role to the prime minister and his closest advisors and leaving the line departments on the fringes. In the case of the Indian Act, the new group had begun by redefining the purpose of the legislation and, indeed, the whole nature of the Indian problem. In this new view, the basic factors which excluded Indian people from society were racial and cultural discrimination. As to what should be done about it, the new thinking was equally assured in asserting that cultures, like individuals, best make their way in competition with others. From this standpoint, special status, as recommended by Hawthorne, could never be helpful, still less the security embodied in the Indian Act.

Such views, strongly held, were obviously rooted in an individualist philosophy, and they found expression, from time to time, in extravagant terms, such as the "wigwam complex," which spoke volumes. The approach could be seen as a bold, new direction or as a collision course; but the latter seemed more likely when the White Paper went to Parliament in June 1969 with no prior consultations with the people most affected. The essentials were contained in three main provisions:

• the Indian Act, being the basis for legislative and constitutional discrimination, would be repealed within five years (individual bands were to work out new land title arrangements with the provinces and the lands would be protected in the interim); the Department would be dissolved within five years; Indian people would get services through the same channels as other Canadians and additional help, if needed, through ordinary federal departments;

• a new "policy of equality" would be announced, providing measures to effect greater participation in mainstream society;

• the various claims being pressed would not play a major role, being limited to "lawful obligations." In this view, "the importance of the treaties in serving the broad social and economic needs of Indians had steadily diminished over the years to the point where the anomaly of treaties between groups within society and the government of that society will require that these treaties be reviewed to see how they can equitably be ended.[37]

A fourth provision called for "recognition by everyone of the unique contribution of Indian culture to Canadian society," though it failed, as Harold Cardinal remarks, "to point to any way in which such recognition will be accomplished."[38]

Something of the shock which greeted the White Paper may be imagined from its lack of fit with Indian priorities. The tone, as well, seemed to go out of its way to cause offense, as when it curtly dismissed the treaties. "A plain reading," according to the White Paper, "of the words used in the Treaties, reveals the limited and minimal promises which were included in them."[39] Yet the plain reading was precisely what the Indian people were fighting; they wanted the evidence considered from oral histories and other sources which showed how much more was owing. Above all, in failing to make provision for safeguarding the society and the culture, the White Paper ignored the people's most basic wish.

Non-Indians also could see some flaws, such as the belief, for example, that getting rid of special status would end discrimination, or that moving to provincial services would much improve the people's welfare. Indian people could see it still more clearly, for they had firsthand experience with the provincial school systems and were opting out. And they knew their neighbours, the impoverished Métis, better than the men who wrote the White Paper. These authors had also missed or ignored a similar experiment which had taken place south of the border only a decade earlier. Under this experiment, known as "termination," the American equivalent of the Indian Act had been rescinded by Congress, opening the way to termination of the relationship between the federal government and the tribes. The results included new hardships, people cast adrift, and loss of cultural identity, and they were altogether so disruptive that the experiment lasted a mere five years.[40]

The White Paper, however, did not proceed to legislation and was eventually withdrawn in March 1971. By this time, the bands which had reacted with shock and anger were beginning to find a positive side. They had asserted their unique heritage and identity and, with the help of public opinion, had forced the government to back down. Their leaders and organizations had a new prominence and would be given secure funding; Indian priorities got put on the national agenda with the creation of a Land Claims Commission and the bands got funds to research their claims. Additional funds would be forthcoming to promote retention of culture, and a stepped-up timetable for transferring services to the bands was devised.

The legacy of the White Paper in the economic sphere proved less easy to deal with. Hawthorne's recommendation for massive help to get people employed *off* the reserves now seemed politically impossible, so *on*-reserve development would have to be tackled more seriously. But the Department still had no feel for it, while the bands, although continuing to press for development and better training programs, were much occupied with the business of rights and claims – their chief hope for the future. The Canadian public, meanwhile, lost interest. Thus, more years went by, with development hinging on a tiny loans program, while the money went on manpower courses, make-work projects, and welfare.

In 1976, the new Indian policy was at last revealed. The declared purpose – "to promote Indian identity within Canadian society" – could be taken to mean much or little; some scholars have seen it as bringing Indian people within the scope of multiculturalism, thus giving weight to reserve-centred programming and local control.[41] In fact, some promising innovations did follow: encouragement for local government and the gradual transference of program administration to the bands. But the changes were chiefly characterized by their slowness of pace, which reflected the same want of commitment underlying the vagueness of their objectives. The difficulties which the federal government has experienced, both in terms of letting go of control and in facilitating development, is the central topic of the next chapter.

CHAPTER FIVE

The Road Ahead

This chapter surveys the 1980s – a mixture of forward momentum and the continuing frustrations imposed by a century-old system. The first two sections cover these opposing aspects, while a third assesses the outlook, given the new "strategies" now employed. The sticking point remains the people's need to manage their own affairs, and a postscript to the chapter provides a brief glimpse of a group with some of that power: the Crees at James Bay.

TAKING CHARGE

The expanding role of band councils has been a key development of the last two decades, beginning with their authority over schools and gradually spreading to other programs. By the end of the 1980s, some bands were administering the full range of available services; most were administering at least fifty percent; the Department provides program budgets as well as core funding to cover band administration. Working for the band has become a main support of the reserve economy. The larger bands employ several hundred people, including teachers, administrators, accountants, engineers, social workers, office workers, carpenters, maintenance workers, etc., and beyond the employment is a ripple effect, as children see their future in jobs that used to be the exclusive preserve of white people.

Band employment, together with some business development, has been enough to slow the exodus to the cities and, indeed, to launch a movement in the opposite direction. With people moving back as well as out, the net movement has become much smaller. Many of the return migrants are the better educated, who take jobs now available on the reserve, while the stream to the cities continues to include a large component of people ill equipped for city life. Some speak of a renaissance on the reserves and, in a sense, the term is apt; but a true renaissance is hardly possible when the people's affairs are still run by a government department. What is happening now is only a beginning. Fulfilling its potential awaits the time when the people themselves have control of their lives.

Within the present constraints, some innovation is possible, and sometimes the band-run service can be moulded to fit better with the values and the needs of Indian people. The Dakota-Ojibwa, for example, in setting up their own child-welfare agency, developed services based on their own beliefs and culture, including intensive counselling to prevent family breakdown, and serious efforts to contact and reclaim the lost adoptees. The First Nations Confederacy, which represented most Manitoba bands in the early eighties, called for fifty-two new positions in the child- and family-service field; there were only fifteen at the time.[1] The band-run schools have brought in native teachers and added native languages, cultural content, and parental involvement. Opening up a new area of service, the Saddle Lake Band is establishing a tribal court system, using a tribunal of elders and introducing "peacemakers" who will attempt to settle arguments, replacing the police.

The development of larger units which act for groups of bands is another source of strength. The tribal councils, as they are called in Manitoba and Saskatchewan, provide a range of services and usually work on economic development as well. The bands in Alberta tend to form development associations or development corporations. The Native Economic Developers' Association represents four bands in southern Alberta (the Blackfoot, Blood, Piegan, and Sarcee), and has worked out a broad development strategy which includes employment opportunities in the city of Calgary. Indian-owned lending institutions have also made an appearance in Alberta, including a full-scale bank and an investment service which provides loans and advice and operates from five locations, mainly in the small-loans field.

A striking case of innovation is taken from Island Lake, where the tribal council tackled housing, one of the worst aspects of reserve living with seemingly little scope for band action, despite their new powers. For it is the housing budget, set by Ottawa, that determines how much and what quality of housing can be built, together with the ever-present backlog of people in unacceptable housing. Now, the innovators at Island Lake are offering a "rural and remote energy-efficient builders' course" – the first of its kind, and available to northerners and natives across Canada.[2] The four-year course covers new house construction, retrofitting, revision of plans, estimations for materials and labour, tendering, purchasing materials, inventory control, and project management. Between the five-week classroom course in winter and supervised work in house building in the summer, trainees are free to take construction employment, which makes the package quite affordable. Houses built by the first-year graduates were found to be three times better on average than regular reserve housing and comparable to houses built under the federal government's R-2000 program, which promotes the energy-efficient house by providing guidelines and financial support to builders.

It is worth pausing to consider what a similar resolve within the Department could have added to employment on the reserves over the years, besides giving men skills that would have helped them find employment wherever construction skills were needed. Such a program, had it begun when social assistance came in, might have seen the unemployment rate halved by now and the people housed at a standard that has yet to be achieved.

Pursuing the theme of economic growth, two main sources made their appearance in the 1970s, neither of them federal government initiatives. First and most visible were the oil and gas revenues which flowed in vast amounts to some seven bands in Alberta and in a modest way to many more, including a few in Saskatchewan. Some of this wealth went on establishing business enterprises, a full-scale bank being the leading example. The second source might be called private-sector initiatives, although a key role belongs to the provincial governments which pressed the companies to act.

In Alberta, a breakthrough can be traced to the heady days of the Alaska pipeline preparations. Pushed by the Alberta government to hire native people, and perhaps also by conscience and certainly by costly turnover, several of the large resource companies started hiring native people and set up a special corporation, NORTRAN, to provide the training. Although the pipeline was halted, there were still benefits, for many of the trainees got hired by northern employers; at least one of the companies, Nova Corporation, retained its native trainees, adjusting the training programs to match its needs for tradespeople in southern operations. Nova set an objective of having native employment proportionate to the native share of provincial population, and has pretty much met it ever since. It also maintains an outreach program to encourage native high-school students to consider working in the trades.[3] Several Alberta companies, notably in the North, have similarly opened their doors to native people.

Uranium mining in northern Saskatchewan provides a second example of a provincial government insisting on companies employing "northerners," this, too, beginning in the 1970s. The companies, mainly foreign, responded well and, in consultation with band chiefs, worked out solutions to the problems that had defeated Canadian mining companies for so long. At an early stage the uranium companies established special training programs and spent a lot of money on them. They also addressed the problem of bunkhouse life by devising shift systems which allowed the workers to live in their home communities and commute by plane. At one time, fourteen Indian communities had people working in the mines and fifty percent of the workers in one company were native. From this standpoint, uranium mining provides an object lesson in how problems could be solved which once denied employment to native people. From another standpoint, however, the uranium mines are highly controversial, given their contamination of the environment through hazardous wastes and the consequent danger to plants, wildlife, and the people themselves. Northern communities are split on the issue. Some people welcome the high-paid employment; others see it as destroying their land and their own lives.

That something is underway in northern resource industries is further evidenced in a contract signed between Syncrude and the Athabasca Native Development Corporation in the late 1980s. In the section which dealt with measures to maximize native employment in the proposed tar-sands plant, the Development Corporation made clear its primary interest in the trades and management training. Ten years earlier, as their spokesman admitted, their only wish had been to get into the labour force.[4]

Provincial government actions are very much a part of this improving job picture. Human-rights legislation provides a legal framework, while affirmative-action programs require companies to hire native people. Even Manitoba Hydro was pushed to become an equal-opportunity employer, after twenty years of polluting water, destroying habitat, and flooding a few settlements. On its Limestone project, completed in the mid-eighties, twenty-five percent of workers in the construction phase were native and forty percent of these were kept on. The JenPeg program, previously mentioned, provides apprentice training in the trades and jobs for successful completers, not just course certificates.

Increasing opportunities for off-reserve employment have been a boon for some people on the western reserves, but unemployment is still high and the need for jobs is still a major preoccupation with band councils. Thus, among the many things they do, when they can manage it, is to establish and run businesses, one answer to the desperate need for jobs. Six thumbnail sketches will convey something of the range of these businesses – from the first Indian-owned trust company in North America, to two reserves in northern Manitoba where an enterprising spirit combats distinctly unfavourable circumstances.

Peace Hills Trust (Sampson Band, near Edmonton).   Peace Hills is a bank offering the full range of financial services. It opened for business in 1981. An out-of-province branch, in Winnipeg, came later. It was assisted by another trust company in its early stages, but has received no government money.

Redwood Meadows (Sarcee, suburban Calgary).   This is an upscale housing development situated on reserve land, acquired when Calgary Post was a distant speck on the horizon. Urban growth has made the site suburban, and the Sarcee lease the units mainly to non-natives.

Chiniki Restaurant (Stonies, Alberta).   Chiniki is located on the Trans-Canada Highway as it climbs into the Rockies west of Calgary. The restaurant features buffalo steaks from the band's herd, views of stunning beauty, and local handicrafts for sale.

Northern Resource Trucking (Lac La Ronge, Saskatchewan).   The core of this company is long-distance trucking, but it also has interests in wild rice, meat processing, and insurance. At one time Canada's largest Indian development corporation, the company, then known as Sinco, got started during the uranium boom, with most Saskatchewan bands as well as the government putting in money. It experienced some reversals and is now rebuilding.

Crane River (northern end of Lake Manitoba).   This is an isolated location which, nevertheless, has several band enterprises: cattle raising, breeding Simenthal bulls, gravel hauling and road contracts with the province, and a marina and campsite for tourists. With an individually owned store and restaurant as well, the Crane River Band has the winter unemployment rate down to thirty-four percent.

Oxford House (northern Manitoba).   Deep in the north country, beyond the roads, the band is the majority owner of a tourist lodge which is expected to provide fifty jobs in a community of five hundred adults, only eighty of whom have full-time work now. It is hoping for a second joint venture to re-open a wood-products factory which went bankrupt.

These sketches tend to emphasize the upper end of the scale. The three from Alberta involve oil or gas money, which makes them decidedly atypical, but it is important to see what can happen when money is available. The Saskatchewan venture is also atypical, both in size and in its origins. What all six cases have in common is that they are band enterprises, which is not to say that individual enterprise is missing or unimportant, but that it tends to be less visible. Band enterprises take many forms across the West: tourism is a popular choice, along with forestry enterprises and contracting of various kinds; there is also some processing and manufacturing. Individual enterprises are even more widely distributed; most of them are small, many are of the kind encountered in chapter 1 where the owner has to move his supplies across the lake and beats the Bay store by working long hours.

The federal government has played a part in providing seed money for business, but its particular contribution is better suited for discussion under this chapter's second heading. The loans program was revamped, in 1984 and again in 1989, which should make it a more effective instrument. But the real drive comes from the people themselves. The level of activity over the past several years seems to reflect a new confidence that comes from having the management of band affairs, and from a new feeling of responsibility on the part of elected band leaders to get something going. Crane River and Oxford House provide good examples.

From the overall perspective, however, it is still slow going. The outlook is all the more discouraging in that reserves that have experienced significant development still don't have enough. At The Pas, whose highly successful shopping centre has been operating for two decades and employs 250 band members, the unemployment rate is in the same thirty percent range as at Crane River. The rate is still higher on the Blood Reserve, which has several enterprises, among them a factory that has made prefabricated homes for twenty years, and which won the housing contract for the Calgary Olympics.

A few individuals and bands have met the challenge of reserve location by setting up businesses in a neighbouring town. These, typically, are small ventures, but one can be cited that, though still on the drawing board, suggests some distinctly larger possibilities. The plan involves some acreage on the edge of Saskatoon which the Muskeg Lake Band, ninety kilometres to the northwest, acquired as part of a land settlement, and which one of the band members, a business man, proposes to develop for offices, light industry, and retail space. Whether or not this particular venture goes ahead, it suggests that reserve location could become somewhat less restrictive, for off-reserve land could be acquired through purchase as well as settlements, or even through rental agreements.

Taking charge also embraces the effort to get farming onto a sound basis. This too goes back to the 1970s, when reserve farmers managed to attract help from provincial agencies. Now, to take the Saskatchewan program, there are courses and workshops, training programs, credit unions, and assistance towards getting bank credit, all readily available through district offices. In the mid-1980s, Saskatchewan reserves could claim 360 "economic" farms. Though well below potential, since so much of the good land is still leased, this is many times what had been achieved in all the years of dependence on the Department.

Since there are no statistics on employment, it is impossible to say what the overall gains have been, but statistics on unemployment indicate that there is still a long way to go. Clearly, however, there is a new willingness on the part of white society to give Indian people a chance. This is most visible in the activities of large companies, but it can also be seen in the owners of small- and medium-sized businesses who enter into joint-venture agreements to help inexperienced native businessmen.

This new spirit shows itself in some major banks which have programs to help native businessmen. It is even more striking in the Canadian Council for Native Business, established in the early 1980s. The Council signs up member firms and uses their expertise to provide assistance to native businesses. This takes two forms: advice and guidance (never money) at the critical stage of pre-start-up planning, and year-long internship for trainees. The aim is to give business a strong, positive image, to help the people acquire business skills, and to encourage youth to choose a business career. A third project was added recently in the development of a tourist strategy designed to turn a myriad of small lodges into a significant source of jobs. A pilot project in northern Manitoba will determine how to achieve world-class levels in facilities, services, administration, and marketing. With widespread adoption by native lodges, it is estimated that the volume of tourism could increase by a factor of five. It is a notable advance over the consultant studies that have been produced for the Department on just such small, remote lodges and the modest grants which got some of them started or kept them afloat.

The other side of increasing success in the job market has been rising education levels. In the mid-1960s, the highest-scoring band in Hawthorne's Prairie sample had only ten percent still in school at age sixteen. In 1981, statistics for the fifteen- to nineteen-year age group showed forty to forty-seven percent of the registered Indian population attending school; this was roughly twenty percentage points below provincial averages.[5] In the next age group (twenty to twenty-four years), the gap had narrowed: from the twenty-percentage-point range to twelve. This improvement would, in part, reflect Indian students taking longer, but the fact that they are getting through to higher grades would seem more important than the timing. These census data would also miss subsequent improvements, for Indian high-school enrolments moved well up in the 1980s: Canada-wide, grade ten by thirty-nine percent, grade eleven by fifty-six percent, and grade twelve by almost a hundred percent.[6] Similarly, the universities attract increasing numbers, and teachers, lawyers, nurses, and business-school graduates are increasingly available. Some take jobs with the bands and some, like anybody else, with government or the private sector.

In the Saskatchewan case, the relatively greater gains in higher education can be traced back to the 1970s, when the Federation of Saskatchewan Indians made it a major thrust. Their efforts saw Indian colleges established at both provincial universities and given affiliate status and degree-granting powers; later, an Indian Institute of Technology was brought into being and now operates at several locations in the province. The Native Law Centre at the University of Saskatchewan is still the only one of its kind in Canada. Then there is Manitoba, which pioneered a training school for native teachers and saw the graduates employed right across the West – an important contribution to the growth of band schools. The province had more than five hundred native teachers in 1988, and attention had turned to programs for nurses, conservation officers, and engineers. The number of native nurses graduating in Thompson had eliminated the need to recruit offshore, hitherto the mainstay for northern posts.

Improvement in education levels has plainly been assisted by the movement to band schools. When the Alexander Band in Alberta took over the school, the drop-out rate was close to one hundred percent and there had not been a grade twelve graduate for ten years. By 1989, the drop-out rate had fallen to fifteen percent and the school could take the children to the end of grade eleven. People were saying, "We're beginning to believe in ourselves."[7] Band-run schools have brought an enriched curriculum, with room for native languages and culture, as well as native teachers who involve themselves with the children.

Attempting to sum up what has happened in the 1980s, the picture is decidedly mixed. Education levels are rising, a generation of college graduates is taking its place in the work force both on- and off-reserve, yet early drop-out still blights the future for a majority of young people. There is a sense of diminishing isolation and of help being available from new sources, but equally a sense of changes that only go so far. The amount of improvement is encouraging on some reserves, while others, barely touched, continue to battle high unemployment and social problems. Band leadership at Pukatawagen has worked hard to get business started and improve housing and community facilities, but almost seventy percent still have no work.[8]

So it is that "taking charge" includes choices made by band councils faced with high unemployment and deeply troubled individuals and families. Some bet heavily on business ventures, as shown, but others see development as something years away or as unlikely to benefit significant numbers. In many such bands, the choice has fallen on employment associated with works projects or on programs which tackle social problems directly.

The James Smith Band in Saskatchewan has a social-development plan. Once widely known for its level of violence, the band is now described in the press as having turned things around.[9] This plan has been operating on several fronts, but education was given the lead role with the establishment of a new school, a day-care centre, and adult education. Health and alcohol problems came next, with a medical clinic and visiting doctor, and a planned twenty-bed rehabilitation centre. Unemployment, lower on the list, was to be dealt with largely through the Department's "work for welfare" program, which requires community-improvement work from all able-bodied recipients. In the next section, which deals with the constraints facing the reserves, the appeal of this option will become more apparent.

The two sides to the present situation – progress and stagnation – make it difficult to assess the trend. One key question is: to what extent will the development now under way continue? Two answers are possible. The first says that current development is just a beginning, because most of the factors favouring it are recent. These include improved federal programs, provincial and private sector involvement, and growing experience and confidence among the Indian people. The second answer is less optimistic. It emphasizes the reserves' inherent limitations; the extent to which major projects have, in fact, been financed from oil revenues, now diminished; and the government's unwillingness to commit big dollars or to give bands the power to choose programs, much less to run their own affairs.

The point at issue is the strength of the development forces now operating. Are they, for example, strong enough to allow Indian people to achieve something approaching a Canadian standard of living within ten of fifteen years? The answer hinges on the balance between the growth forces just surveyed, and the factors which hold growth back.

OLD CONSTRAINTS

Despite the good things happening on some western reserves, the larger picture could still be described as bleak. This was the verdict of a federal task force as recently as 1985,[10] and only five years earlier, the minister of Indian Affairs had put it in starker terms. Using a Canada-wide perspective, he cited the "appalling reserve conditions" all documented in three reports which he himself had commissioned, all of which concluded that programs had failed to produce significant improvement in the condition of Indian people. He himself declared that "a radically different approach to economic development is necessary because, in plain English, we have failed to help Indian people to help themselves to create and hold jobs."[11] When the Nielsen Task Force subsequently examined the impact of government programs, that impact was deemed "frustratingly marginal."[12] Although $16 billion had been spent on the reserves since 1967, they were still "the worst places to live."

This second section assembles some of the reasons for failure, at long last admitted. It begins with budget and program deficiencies, then moves to the overwhelming government presence and the nature of the relationship between Indian people and the rest of Canadian society, and ends with some questions about stewardship. The list is by no means exhaustive and could be worked in different ways, but the five factors considered here could be said to carry much of the weight.

Low Priority for Economic Development

One factor is the minimal importance assigned to economic development, as indicated by its share in the Department's budget: 4.4 percent, to take the highest level in four recent years.[13] The real money – about eighty percent – goes for schools, housing, various

Table 1
INAC* Expenditure (percentage share)[14]

	Social assistance including services	Economic development
1986–87	21.1	4.0
1987–88	21.6	4.4
1989–90	25.3	3.2
1991–92	26.9	3.9

*Indian and Northern Affairs Canada.

facilities (roads, sewage systems, etc.), and welfare. All of these are needed, but they do nothing to turn the situation around. The schools get too few children educated, while welfare and cheap housing lead nowhere. The Hawthorne Report took the Department to task more than twenty years ago for its neglect of economic development (and for the high cost of accounts and record keeping), but nothing has changed.

Most of the money slated for the reserves goes for services that other Canadians receive through local and provincial governments and pay for with their taxes. Reserve residents can't do this because they have never been connected to an economic base, which is, of course, the essence of their unique situation. The system binds them to places that have not been developed to generate income and, since outside earnings are also small, they are hard pressed to keep food on the table, let alone pay for services. As well, although most reserves could generate more income than they do, the government has not seen this as important. The results are evident in expenditures for recent years, as social assistance commands an ever-increasing share of the Department's budget, while economic development barely maintains its traditional low share (see table 1).

Economic development is somewhat enhanced when other departments are brought into the picture. Particularly encouraging was a new business-loans program – the Native Economic Development Program (NEDP) – under what had become the Department of Regional Industrial Expansion. A year earlier (1983-84), an estimate for "economic development expenditure in the native sector" revealed a grand total of $40 million; the NEDP, averaging $58 million over the next six years, might be seen as a significant addition.[15] Unfortunately, the new commitment may also be seen as grossly inadequate relative to the need. Welfare, as noted, continued to increase its share through the late 1980s; figures released in 1990 suggest that the two departments spending on economic development had got that total up to $145 million, while about five times that went on social assistance. [16] The manpower courses also got more money than economic development.

The question arises: what have manpower courses to do with development of a kind that will truly change the situation? Likewise the various construction and infrastructure projects that have occupied much of the federal programming? This is why stagnation on the reserves has to be seen in terms of ineffective programs, as well as limited budgets.

Ineffective Programs

The Department's loan fund, which goes back to 1970, was for many years the major economic-development initiative. It was also much criticized by Indian organizations, sometimes for its stinginess, more often for neglecting to provide the technical and financial services which could have raised the success rate. The Nielsen Task Force gave the program low marks on this very point. "Too free with the money," said the chairman, who went on to deplore the absence of the counsel and discipline which other businessmen get from their bank managers. [17] This becomes a major point, the contrast between the Spartan services available to fledgling businessmen on the reserves and the wide array of services available to the business community in southern Canada.

Something is very wrong, obviously, for there is little benefit to individuals or community in businesses that fail and much added discouragement, which nobody needs. The situation is inherently difficult, given businessmen with little experience and projects which are hard to assess, and it becomes more so when loan requests originate with band councils which are pulled into the economic-development business by the desperate need for jobs. From their standpoint, too much money has gone into welfare when the need is for jobs, and it would not be surprising if they take too light a view of business risks when they see so much waste in welfare. All of this points to the importance of technical back-up services when assessments are made, and an ongoing commitment to helping businesses through the early years of getting established.

To meet this need, the Department turned to the Canadian Executive Service Overseas (CESO), an organization which provides services of this kind in the Third World, using retired businessmen and executives as volunteers. As it looks to an outside observer, the CESO volunteers have been doing the best they could with their particular expertise, but in an impossible assignment. They confront too many borderline proposals demanding a Solomon's judgment between high risk on the one hand, and the dismaying reserve situation on the other, recognizing the hopes that the proposal has generated. They have been further handicapped by being too few in the field, and by the difficulty of bringing help to distant places as frequently as serious problems arise. One feels that, at some point, a department responsible for seeing money spent to good purpose could have detected the hole which the Nielsen Task Force found readily enough; Nielsen's condemnation led to better back-up services when the new loans program was established in 1984. Meanwhile, fourteen years had gone by, and a great many hopes with them.

A different criticism, made by the bands, provides another dimension. In their view, many good projects have been lost because the Department prefers to pay welfare. As an illustration, the band at Lake Wabasca in northern Alberta has made a loan application for repairs to its aging sawmill, in the hope of preserving an existing business as well as their timber lease. The cost of the repairs ($1.7 million) is only slightly more than the yearly bill for social assistance ($1.5 million) when forty men are working at the mill. Nevertheless, the Department turned the application down, giving as its reason that $2 million have already been spent on the mill over ten years and it has never been economically viable. Said a Department spokesperson to the press, "We try to manage funds in a responsible way."[18]

Without knowing all the facts in the case, it would be rash to say that the decision was wrong; but something does seem wrong when the mill, despite its unprofitability, has been supported for many years, probably for the same reason that could justify further support – namely, the absence of other employment. Perhaps the mill is too old, but there would appear to be little saving for the taxpayer in adding up to forty families to the welfare rolls, while burdening the band with the loss of the timber lease and associated jobs. Arbitrary judgments of this kind have ruled the lives of people on the western reserves since the treaties, and the people cannot be unaffected.

For all its faults, the Indian Affairs loans program is a relatively small item, only one portion of the economic-development expenditures made by the three departments involved. The manpower courses have been much more costly and kept in being over a twenty-five-year period without apparent success. Their low success rate has been established above. The result, as the analysts reported to Erik Nielsen: "training for training's sake, with no expectation to use the skills in a job, appears to have become the norm."[19]

The most disturbing part is the failure to heed the complaints of the Indian organizations, which have stated repeatedly that the courses weren't working for them. The Manpower department has always stood for equal treatment of white or native, grade-eight drop-out or college graduate. All go through the same door and have the same chance. It doesn't even sound sensible. One explanation might be that the Manpower department, like Indian Affairs, expected that only the job-ready could be helped, and that the others didn't matter. Much the same view was expressed by an economic-development officer in one of the tribal councils in the West, as he described the difficulties experienced by young men on welding courses. As he put it, the weakness in trades training for Indian people comes down to the government's overriding interest in the few who are bound for college. Those aspiring to learn a trade are left to get through the courses, whatever their difficulties and irrespective of results.[20] Indeed, so little has come of it over the years that it is possible to believe that, like make-work programs, the manpower courses were used simply to reduce unemployment.

The department responsible for regional development, in its various incarnations, could be said to have a better record in that it includes such successes as Lesser Slave Lake and Special Arda, recorded in chapter 4. But its programs in later years have lacked a clear connection between means and ends. Money has been spent in a sporadic way, although in substantial amounts on some reserves in northern Manitoba and Saskatchewan, mainly on community improvements. These are needed, of course, but the programs have been billed as catalysts for development when, in fact, a few construction projects could hardly generate opportunities and overcome the handicaps that made the reserves what they are. It is hard to imagine the rationale behind this kind of spending, but it may well have been the same as for make-work projects: to put a little money in the community. Or perhaps, more cynically, it has been a show put on for the larger Canadian audience. If so, it has succeeded, for white society tends to see the government as having lots of money for native programs. And how, from the glowing press releases that announce the programs, can their basic inadequacies be perceived?

The low priority given to economic development spills over into education, for if it had been judged important to get young people into jobs, serious efforts would have been made to raise achievement in the schools. A good start had been made in the 1960s with the switch to band-run schools, but it moved all too slowly, with real growth delayed until the 1980s. Even then, at mid-decade, enrolment in band schools had just reached forty percent in Manitoba and Saskatchewan and ten percent in Alberta.[21] The problem may have been weak leadership on the reserves or inertia in some cases, and a genuine preference for integrated schools in others. Nonetheless, making education work better required resources and, as the reserves are not tax-generating communities, the Department was the sole source of the education dollar. One can only conclude, once again, that the Department failed the grasp the importance of education and the overwhelming need to close the gap between Indian and white children.

Even today, the degree of improvement is far from satisfactory and some observers see the situation as essentially unchanged. A 1989 report in Alberta states that seventy-five percent of native students drop out before grade ten.[22] As the education supervisor in Manitoba's frontier region reports, "students know they don't need a high school diploma to collect welfare." In his view, unless teenagers have strong parents, they see themselves in the same position as most adults on the reserve, where no jobs are available, and they have no intention of leaving.[23]

Dependency

The third constraint is simply the overpowering government presence. The people endured the paternalism of the early years; then, in the mid-twentieth century when wage work became hard to find, they were put on social assistance, which raised dependency to a new level. Such a history was bound to mark them and influence the way they saw themselves as individuals and as a society in relation to the dominant whites. Oscar Lathlin, chief of the band at The Pas, put it this way: "Indians have come to accept the negative views that whites have of them. Tell a child all his life and by age 16 he thinks that to be an Indian is to be on welfare, in jail or drunk. That's the programming the Department has done for Indian people."[24] Scholars who study these things agree with Indian leaders that high rates of social pathology are attributable, in large measure, to the status of Indians as people who cannot be trusted to run their own affairs.

The bands began to administer programs more than twenty years ago, but they are still hedged in by restrictions. Endless examples are available, of which one will have to serve. The subject is a band council, again from northern Alberta, with a community-improvement plan whose primary objective is to raise performance in the schools. The plan includes a requirement that social-assistance recipients work on community projects, on the theory that the children would be better motivated by seeing their parents go off to work in the morning. Early results seemed to bear this out; but the Department, citing a rule that welfare eligibility cannot be restricted, put an end to it.

This case is drawn from the *Report of the Special Committee on Indian Self Government*, the outcome of an enquiry established by the House of Commons. The Penner Report, submitted in 1985, provides many illuminating cases and makes a central issue of the limited degree to which Indian people are allowed to run their own affairs. The situation was put succinctly by one of the witnesses at the Committee hearings: "Band councils are just fancy cheque writers for the federal government."[25] Another witness, referring to the monitoring systems insisted upon by the government, said that "easily 75 percent of the time and energy of our band government is spent satisfying the record-keeping, data analysis, reporting, forecasting and evaluating requirements by the many agencies of government which regulate our lives … indeed, we are more truly a branch office of the Indian Affairs Department than we are a tribal government."[26]

At the time of the hearings, program administration had been moving to band governments for more than a decade, and it was widely viewed as a new era in which Indian people would be running their own affairs. In fact, no such thing was happening. It was still the Department that determined what the programs were and what the bands could spend and, even in the narrow area that remained, it still had the power to veto band requests. Each and every band was caught up in negotiations which were time consuming and frustrating, and which often ended in failure. The whole point of devolution had been missed.

These examples are merely one aspect of dependency, limited to the area of administration and government. A high degree of economic dependence – not only on welfare but on all the services which come from the federal government – is also a fact of life. As a *modus vivendi*, it is bound to engender feelings both of incompetence on the one hand, and of being badly treated on the other.

Exclusion

Living separately is itself a constraint because the people on the reserves can see that they count for less than other Canadians. In the West, segregation came into being in a crisis, but it was supported by a plausible plan: after a period of tutelage, the people would be ready for full participation in society. But as time stretched on, the government quietly lowered its sights, and both reserves and wardship took on a permanent character. Nor has white society pressed government to raise either standards or objectives, whether because of indifference, mild prejudice, or a view of Indian people as inferior and even "unworthy."[27] In 1985, the Winnipeg Building Trades Council attacked the government for reverse discrimination, professing itself unable to understand why training programs should be available for natives in categories where skilled workmen were available.[28] In Lethbridge, the Alberta Human Rights Council heard two days of testimony in 1989 concerning discrimination against Indian people in housing, employment, and other areas of daily life.[29]

Canadian society has played a major part in keeping Indian people out, not only through overt discrimination and unsympathetic attitudes but also through a universal willingness to accept that decades of failed programs were the best that could be done. Within the last five years, a radical proposal to change the system – Indian self-government – has barely entered public debate.

Canadians find it easy to ignore appalling conditions on the western reserves. When the big exodus began a quarter-century ago, the cities were flooded with people entirely unprepared for getting jobs and supporting themselves. Any help they got was grudging and inappropriate, centring on welfare when they needed access to the mainstream economy and society. These city problems have been associated with "Indianness," but the real problem is neglect.

A hundred years of exclusion have exacerbated the problems confronting Indian people today, for time has moved at a slower pace on the reserves, while the requirements of the work place have moved upward at a rapid pace. Despite a growing number of young people who have managed to solve the problem for themselves, there remains a large population, for the most part young as well, who cannot do it without help. Few Canadians even see their need for help. The president of a major company in Winnipeg, who has made it his own concern, describes it as "unimaginably difficult for native youth to make it through the present system and emerge with the appropriate skills."[30] The present system cannot change so long as it is based on the principle of exclusion.

Quality of the Stewardship

The weakness in policy has not been the Department's alone. But stewardship, in the narrow sense of safeguarding Indian lands and monies, deserves a word. The Department has been guardian and financial manager for the western bands ever since its relationship with Indian people began. The relationship is similar to that between a trustee and the underage heir whose affairs he manages. A number of departmental actions have cast doubt over the years on the honesty or competence of the trustee, but a single illustration will have to suffice. It concerns the Department's role as manager of the oil and gas revenues in the West.

These revenues were earlier mentioned in the context of Chiniki Restaurant and Peace Hills Trust. The launching of the trust company in itself conveys the enormous dollar flow. Just how much came in is best known to Indian Affairs, which does not publish figures; but it is important from the standpoint of stewardship to derive some rough measure. Consider this: one of the lower ranking of the top seven bands is reported to have gone through $200 million in ten years.[31] If that figure serves as an average for all seven, they took in $1.4 billion over a ten-year period, which would be more than $2 billion in the mid-1980s – say, $200 million a year in current dollars. By comparison, the latest native economic-development program, announced in 1989, covers the entire native population in Canada with an annual budget of $175 million.

With revenues declining through the 1980s, the glory days of the oil boom appear to be past and it is difficult to say what the benefits were. What remains in the oil bands' trust accounts at Indians Affairs ($700 million, according to press reports)[32] suggests that very large amounts have already been spent. But while Peace Hills Trust and other businesses, large and small, are all valuable additions to the reserve economy, they are not nearly enough to account for the revenues which poured in. The reason for this shortfall, if not the amount, is apparent: it lies in the Department's decision to use oil revenues to pay for current services, notably social assistance, and to make per-capita distributions to band members. In later years, when the bands had more control, they also used per-capita distributions, and this too would seem to reflect poorly on the guardian, which could have discussed options with the bands, made contacts with financial analysts and planners, and had the development opportunities assessed. All of this would have been a legitimate charge on the oil revenues, which social assistance was not.

The way the oil revenues were handled is also thought to have contributed to social problems experienced by the oil bands, despite their riches. There was so much money, seemingly no end of it, and the people spending it were often unable to think in terms of assuring their future; nor was there any visible way to do so. Joe Dion, former chief of the Kehewin band, oil-business consultant, and Chairman of the Indian Oil and Gas Task Force, said that oil money "is causing more problems than it is solving on the affluent reserves:

virtually no systematic planning for the future, easy come, easy go, reckless spending of money has in some cases broken families and possibly weakened communities."[33] His report found no evidence that the wealth resulted in improved health on the reserves; on the contrary, suicides, alcoholism, and drug abuse increased.

Finally, there is Indian Minerals West, a branch of the Department which had responsibility for oil and gas production on all the western reserves. This made it one of the larger producers, ranking fourteenth in Canada, yet it was understaffed and underfunded. Another oil-business consultant described it as "incapable of performing some of the most basic management functions."[34] Nor did Indian Minerals West consider that it had a mandate to involve the bands, which resented their passive role and would have welcomed an opportunity to learn about the industry and take part in management – granting leases, approving decisions, etc. Help for Indian people to get training or jobs with the oil industry was similarly absent from the agenda. On all these counts, the federal government was strongly criticized by the 1987 Indian Oil and Gas Task Force.[35]

Indian Minerals West passed into history in the mid-1980s, and its successor, Oil and Gas Canada, has adopted more enlightened policies, including giving band councils the right to participate in the management system, providing employment and training programs, and, as an ultimate goal, transferring full control to the bands. So a new day dawns, but thirty years after the oil and gas flow began, and with the major opportunities perhaps lost forever.

CITY UPDATE

The chapter, thus far, has covered two opposing ways of viewing the present outlook, but omitted an important segment of the population: the one-third to one-half now living in cities and effectively cut off from federal programming. Their prospect matters too, and has to be considered before tackling the question of whether the growth forces now in motion are sufficient to outweigh the formidable constraints.

The account centres on Winnipeg, where the native population is said to exceed 30,000 (the population of Brandon) and registered Indians alone number about 20,000. To a visitor from the East, Portage Avenue conveys a sense that Indian people are "taking charge," for among the crowds of shoppers, office workers, visitors, etc., the number of native people does stand out. Some of them are studying at the university, some work for tribal councils or other native organizations, some for provincial or federal agencies, and others in

the private sector. The visitor is also likely to spot Peace Hills Trust
– as noted earlier, the first out-of-province branch of the first Indian-
owned bank. It is a distinctly favourable first impression; but unfortunately, it must be rounded out with the facts on employment,
housing, schools, dependency, and so on, as documented in surveys
and studies over the past decade.

Unemployment, according to a survey by the Urban Indian Association, stood at seventy percent in 1987, while the number in full-
time jobs was under ten percent.[36] The reference is to the whole
native population, but an Indian Affairs survey limited to status
Indians in Saskatchewan cities, also in 1987, found about eighty-
five percent unemployed and most of the remainder in minimum-
wage jobs.[37] It is not far off the pattern described by Edgar Dosman
a quarter of a century before, just as a majority of the migrants still
lack urban labour-force requirements. To come back to the Winnipeg
survey, the population was predominantly young, the average
education level was grade eight. The same high incidence of single-
parenting found in Regina a decade earlier was also evident: sixty-
five percent of the households surveyed were headed by a single
adult.

Statistics such as these bring a needed perspective to the "good
news" associated with business initiatives on the reserves and jobs
with the band. To see the distance yet to go, one has only to look
at the amount of unemployment which has been transferred from
the reserve to the city, the number of city families on social assistance, and the continuing evidence of family breakdown. Upward
mobility is not much in evidence: Winnipeg's Institute of Urban
Studies reports that the prolonged unemployment associated with
newcomers to the city was experienced in the same degree by native
people who had been in Winnipeg for ten years.[38]

None of this is surprising, given the situation of these migrants
both before and after their move. But it is particularly disheartening
to see that the pain and effort of moving accomplishes so little, even
for the children. Back on the reserve, inadequate education is a prime
cause of joblessness, but the high drop-out rates are often explained
by the poor job prospects. The city, however, does have jobs, yet
the children are dropping out of city schools, which suggests that
the same discouragement applies. Too many city children have
heard the message that they are different, that education won't work
from them.

Early drop-out and marginal literacy are as much in evidence in
the 1980s as are the rising numbers completing high school and
university. This dichotomy fits the pattern Dosman described in the

sixties and stems from the same federal policy which concentrates help on the people who need it the least. Children in families that get established in the city tend to finish school, but far too many families don't get the toe-hold that would permit them to look beyond immediate problems and give their children the encouragement they need.

Failure to get established has been a critical factor, yet government has been blind to the difficulties which the people have been left to handle on their own. Kinew Housing in Winnipeg had a program at one time to help its trainees in such areas as upgrading literacy, dealing with pressures and uncertainties, and the need for punctuality and regular hours on the job. Such simple things, seemingly, but many of the trainees had only worked in casual jobs and were long accustomed to meeting problems with white employers by walking away. The Kinew program worked well, helping many individuals to become truly job-ready, but the money which made this kind of support possible lasted only six years, at which point funds for training were withdrawn altogether. The large majority of Kinew tenants today are on welfare. [39]

For the second generation in the city, the critical factors have been family situation and the schools. The City of Winnipeg has begun to address their problems through Argyle High School, which offers smaller classes, more individual attention, native teachers and cultural content, and courses in native languages and crafts. Native issues have been incorporated into the courses: meetings are held with native youth workers and elders. Not surprisingly, Argyle attracts native students from across the city, many of them adults who will have a second chance to get the education they so plainly need. It is a good start, but no more than that, because Argyle is only one of many Winnipeg schools where native students are well over fifty percent and, in the absence of special help, have had high drop-out rates extending back over years. The Saskatoon system catering to native children operates at the level of grades four to seven, which seems a better time to begin dealing with alienation, absence of motivation, and lack of self-esteem. Still better, of course, would be to begin in grade one, putting such special help into all schools with significant native enrolment; this could be done if Canadian society wished to deal seriously with the problems of Indian people.

Meanwhile, it is important to go after the children and adults who have already dropped out, giving them a second chance with specially designed courses; this is likely to work best when the native community is itself involved. The leading example of this approach is Plains Indian Cultural Survival School in Calgary, which was designed and established by a group of native people who believed

that something could be done about the drop-outs. It has been operating for more than ten years, providing a mixed menu which
blends "algebra and English with lessons in Indian culture and canoe
building," on the theory that troubled children need the cultural
content, since their upbringing has left them feeling that they belong
to neither culture. Clearly, they don't belong with the white people
– the *Calgary Herald* recently reported that two hundred young native
people are living on city streets.[40] But neither were they, growing
up on the reserves, attached firmly to their own. When they come
to have pride in their culture, they feel better about themselves,
begin to take an interest in education, and can get on with their
lives.

Plains has an enrolment of 320 pupils; it spans six grades with
eleven and a half teachers. It has a drop-out rate of about twenty
percent, which compares favourably with the eighty-five to ninety
percent drop-out rate in city schools, and the students do as well
as the provincial average on the departmental exams. These are the
lucky ones, for as Principal Jerry Arshinoff says, "Education, this is
their last stop."[41] Yet Plains operates on a shoestring budget, with
"virtually no funding from the Department."

As noted, Canadian society is more inclined to provide services
than the kind of effort that would be required to make the schools
work for Indian children or get the adults into jobs. Winnipeg has
the Department of Indian Affairs with placement workers, training
courses, and financial assistance for short-term stayers. Employment
and Immigration (the former Manpower department) offers more
training courses; the regional department, now Industry, Science
and Technology Canada, is involved, and the provincial government
claims twenty-five departments which deal, one way or another,
with native people. Yet the objects of all this attention are not rapidly
moving up the ladder towards a Canadian standard of living; they
remain somewhere near the bottom.

Something is clearly wrong with the government services, and
one major error is the continued emphasis on welfare and the various
agencies which are supposed to patch the people up. This kind of
attention, in fact, holds them back and perpetuates their permanent-
client status. Even social workers can't mend a lifetime of frustration
which they can hardly comprehend. Lyle Longclaws, a former grand
chief, describes the cycle which confronts so many young men coming into Winnipeg.[42] They have left the reserves which offer no
work and, once in Winnipeg, are quickly caught up in the core-area
bar scene. They get jobs that don't last and move back and forth
between the city and the reserve, disappointed at first, then becoming angry and resentful. At some point, they become involved with

the police and the various agencies. The next ten or fifteen years, says Longclaws, are spent in and out of various care institutions and prisons. At age thirty, exhausted, they fight to put their lives back together; they take job-training courses, but find them just as frustrating as welfare.

Longclaws hopes to break this cycle with a "child-service centre" which he has established for troubled youth who move to the city. He believes the answer lies in inspiring young people through education and employment opportunities, and his centre offers help in both areas, along with family support and treatment for alcohol and drug abuse.

This is what the centre and similar ventures come down to: Indian people themselves taking action because they know so much better than the government what has to be done. As yet, they can't do much because they don't get the funding; but they are on the right track, giving young people the hope that will get them back into school and the belief that they do have a future.

The situation in Winnipeg is brightening because the province, the city, and the private sector have all shown a new willingness to be part of the solution for native people. The sticking point remains the federal government, still bound by the twelve-month rule, which says, in effect, that however poorly a status Indian has been equipped for life in the 1990s, the act of moving to the city removes any obligation at the senior-government level. Federal foot dragging holds back the other players. Winnipeg, for example, has expressed interest in expanding special school programs, given financial assistance from the federal government. So has the Human Rights Commission in Saskatchewan, but interest at the federal level remains low. It dims hopes for the young people, since the cities are unlikely to take all such responsibilities on themselves. It also defies explanation, given the enormous cost to the federal government of welfare and prisons. Many of the adolescents who don't get the sort of chance offered by Arshinoff or Longclaws will contribute to these costs, and they are formidable. Allowing for lengthy or recurrent incarceration, rehabilitation programs, years on income support, and still another generation being brought up on welfare, the taxpayer is not really getting a bargain. This is brought out dramatically in Arshinoff's estimate, that the reduced tax burden represented by getting just two pupils through Plains pays the cost of education for all the rest.

Limited federal commitment is seen again in the recent "core-area" urban-renewal project, which brought massive federal funding to Winnipeg and included a few programs for native people. The best of these was a skills-training program which, unlike the Manpower courses, guaranteed employment for successful completers. But it was a low-budget affair. The bulk of the core-area money went on restoration of buildings, as the federal member of Parliament himself admitted.[43] It is an old story, and it is easy to see why all three governments would be more interested in eye-catching improvements, when those were what the public preferred as well. Nevertheless, the scarcity of money for Indian needs seems least excusable at the federal level because it is the federal government that is responsible for the ill-prepared state in which Indian people reach the city. And it is also the federal government that could call forth more spending by province and city, simply by sharing in the cost.

NEW STRATEGIES FOR THE NINETIES

Stalemate

The 1980s began with some stock taking and it did look, briefly, as if real changes were imminent. As noted earlier, the minister of Indian Affairs made a public confession of failure and called for a "radically different approach." But when the new policy was announced four years later, it bore a disturbing likeness to the ones which had been condemned. In particular, it ignored the growing feeling that self-government was the essential foundation on which all else depended.

The new policy, grandly called the Native Economic Development Program, was essentially a loans program, but one with more money than its predecessor and better advisory services. Still, it was hardly the radically different approach that the minister seemed to promise. Five years later in 1989, yet another plan had been prepared, this one elevated to a "strategy." But the Canadian Aboriginal Economic Development (CAED) Strategy is, again, much the same thing, centring on loans for business, albeit with a new emphasis on involving the private sector through, for example, joint venturing.[44] It also includes urban Indians for the first time, but they get only manpower courses, adapted in some unspecified way to make them more suitable for native people. There isn't much money – $175 million a year, or one-quarter of the cost of social assistance for registered Indians alone[45] – and CAED covers the entire aboriginal population of roughly 800,000 people.

With a new/old program set to run for another five years, it is time to consider the question posed earlier: whether the future should be seen as rapid progress up the ladder, or bound by historic constraints. The answer is evidently the latter, because so much hinges on a change in the programs, and the CAED strategy contains so little that is new. The most telling failure is the government's continuing refusal to yield on power sharing. In the short term, government will deliver the CAED services, but the real problem runs deeper, namely, that the services were government selected and designed. What is wanted, and what is needed, is the power to say what the programs will be – in other words, self-government.

The CAED strategy does fit the wishes of the people in that it is reserve-oriented, but its narrow focus on business is worrisome. Such a concern was expressed years ago by one of the Indian organizations, which said that the entrepreneur was a rare bird in any society, and Indian society had less business experience than most. The need, it said, was to direct more money towards getting people into wage employment.[46] Many people feel the same way today; many worry about the scarcity of business opportunities and the long wait before business development can improve their lives.

The basic flaw in the CAED strategy is that it is out of touch with the times. A growing body of opinion sees dependency as the real problem, inextricably linked to the problem of economic develop-· ment, so that a shift in power becomes essential if development is to occur. This is quite outside the CAED vision, which still puts the federal government front and centre, assembling a team of players and setting the goals which, as always, are of a general nature: greater participation in the national economy, access to continuing jobs, access to federal development initiatives, etc. The most promising change is the new emphasis on joint venturing and other types of involvement with the private sector, but otherwise, the future is charted in terms of turning over the *delivery* of programs, rather than program choice and design.

As this book is written, the Canadian government is unable either to let go its control or to bring forth new policies that will assist growth in a significant way. Government itself is one of the factors holding back development; it is part of the problem when it should be finding solutions.

Indian people and their leaders have a clearer perception of the problem. They don't see the future narrowly in terms of economic development (although development is wanted, or course), nor do they all want the same thing; but they do know why the programs aren't working. David Courchene caught the essence of it more than twenty years ago: "The real tragedy of the treaties and the practices of public policy by succeeding governments over the past century has been to destroy that element essential to all people for their survival, man's individual initiative and self reliance ... A century of pursuit of [such policies] finds Indian people on the lowest rung of the social ladder, not only suffering deprivation and poverty to a greater extent than any other Canadians but also suffering from psychological intimidation brought about by this almost complete dependence upon the state for the necessities of life."[47]

The qualities which have been eroded under the Department's long reign can only be rebuilt by the people themselves, and then only in a situation which gives them the room to do so. The government can best assist by stepping out of the way and by providing the resources for rebuilding.

Put another way, Indian people need to regain the responsibility they once had for running their own affairs. It is a right claimed by all who see themselves as a distinct society, but the more so in this case, since the dominant society has not found ways to end Indian poverty and alienation. According to the Thalassa Research Group, even the Department recognizes the frustrations in the system and the part it has played in dampening initiative and self-reliance. More than that, it recognizes that "the effect of federal policies has been to foster dependent and alienated societies which demonstrate many of the characteristics of underdeveloped nations in Africa, Asia and Latin America."[48] On the evidence, something is very wrong with the process, not merely the programs, for Indian people would have changed the programs long ago had their views mattered. Thus, it follows that if the process is to change, the Indian people must be part of it – indeed, they should have the lead role.

Indian Self-Government

The Penner Report has shown how little power the bands have to change programs, and their frustration with administering tired old programs that patently don't change the situation. Penner's committee saw this not as peripheral, but as the central problem, requiring a shift from the federal government to the people themselves, giving them the power to run their own affairs. Its major recommendation was "that the federal government establish a new relationship with Indian First Nations and that the essential element be recognition of Indian self government."[49]

The First Nations would have full legislative and policy-making powers on matters that affected them, and full control over territory and resources within their boundaries. They would be free to set their own priorities and be accountable to their own people. And they would be assured of the financial base necessary for independence. Settlement of claims would be a major source of funds, supplemented by initial grants and long-term financial arrangements, the latter embodying the same sharing principle that is the basis for equalization payments to the provinces. The rationale was nicely put: that Canada is obligated to restore a strong economic base to those who shared their land and resources.

Since these recommendations were made, the government has proceeded to define its own version of what self-government should be. Individual bands may now obtain municipal-type powers through a process which involves getting a bill passed in Parliament. While a small number of bands have done this, most find the approach unacceptable. There is no framework which defines who the First Nations are, no recognition of an inherent right to self-government, retained from their long history as a free people. As the Assembly of First Nations explains, their demand is for a "third order" of government, taking its place beside the federal government and the provinces.[50]

The government version also fails to provide for protection of the land – a major concern for most people – and explicitly rules out the possibility that additional money could be associated with self-government. This in itself makes clear the limited nature of the government's objectives. Missing entirely the sense of obligation defined by the Penner Report, the government has also managed to ignore the people's views of what self-government should be. The government is stuck in a time-honoured tradition, pursuing a proposal designed by bureaucrats and lacking in vision or larger objectives, and it is prepared to override any and all objections from the bands and organizations. The Canadian public, not well versed in Byzantine politics, takes at face value the Department's declared support for self-government and willingness to provide assistance. As it happens, the assistance is not financial, but assistance in drafting bills and getting them to Parliament.

Genuine self-government involves vastly more than this and should be seen as central to the process which would see Indian people become full citizens at last. People able to make spending decisions would get money redirected into programs that improve lives. There would be new opportunities for individuals to develop their talents and, as time passes, for band members collectively to experience pride in accomplishment. Services would work better. For example, with respect to the health services delivered by the Department of Health and Welfare, an official recently stated that passing responsibility to Indian people was the only way to deal with the health problems on Saskatchewan reserves.[51] Band managers would have new scope and better feelings about themselves, once they were recognized as serious, competent people and not simply cheque writers. And new ideas would emerge: this happened at James Bay when the Crees got their settlement and were able to solve problems which had long defeated the Department. In brief, transfer of responsibility is the one change that could bring about the redirection of expenditures, the emergence of talents, and the generation of energy from which other changes can flow.

Canadians are unlikely to see these advantages so long as they have faith in the present system, while the problems associated with self-government are all too easily imagined. Such fears are ably dealt with in the Penner Report, which should be required reading in this regard. For example, the bands' managerial abilities got a vote of confidence from the accounting firm which analyzed their performance; indeed, it said that the bands have succeeded "more often because of their own leadership and staff than because of training, advice and monitoring supplied by the Department."[52] The same analysis brought out the high cost of the present system (administrative costs were more than twenty-five percent of the Indian/Inuit Affairs program) and gave equal weight to the mountain of paperwork associated with complex accountability systems. These systems are used for planning, budgeting, and dispersing funds from Treasury Board to the Department's headquarters, then on the regions, districts, bands – and back up the line. Small organizations like Indian bands, said the consultant, do not need these complex and costly procedures, and costs could be significantly reduced.[53]

This does not imply that a switch to self-government would bring an immediate reduction in total costs, for a great many needs cry out for attention. In Penner's recommendations, self-government would be accompanied by new financial resources, to go to First Nations through a combination of claims settlements, transitional grants, and long-term financial arrangements. This aspect is dealt with more fully in the final chapter, where it is shown that under self-government, the costs would, in the longer run, decline.

The remainder of this section will consider some of the daunting problems confronting the First Nations, and some of the solutions that are likely to be tried. It assumes, in other words, that the basic step has been taken to put the bands in charge and that more resources, one way or another, are being made available to them.

Band priorities can be stated in a general way, such as alleviating poverty and dependence, expanding productive activity, and managing economic development in a way that respects the environment. But the bands don't all have the same priorities – nor, indeed, the same situation – so the discussion can only be in general terms. Retaining the term "strategy," I consider two of what are clearly main concerns for most bands – economic development and the need to deal with poverty in other ways as well. The third, help for urban Indians, might be rather lower on the bands' lists, but it is a subject of major importance for many people, whether those in the city now, or those coming later.

Economic Strategies

It is true, as the Canadian Council for Native Business has said, that potential exists on every reserve. That potential will be developed as soon as bands have the power and the funding to do so, but the difficulty comes in saying just how far it will go to strengthen the economy. The answer, obviously, varies greatly from place to place. Recalling Jean Lagassé's despair in the 1950s, there are still places where population is much too large relative to the resources at hand, and places where the band has worked hard to get the unemployment rate down to thirty percent. But the possibilities have opened up since Lagassé wrote – there are band-owned airlines, world-class tourist resorts, and jobs in the private sector, to name a few – and will open more as education levels rise. How far it will carry is impossible to say.

In the United States, an estimate for the reservations put the chances for significant economic development at one in ten.[54] The meaning of "significant," which was not defined, might well exceed the present aspirations of many western bands, and the point is worth stressing for, whatever the long-run prospect, many people on the reserves can be made better off by getting started on development. Indian leaders, rightly, are concentrating on the opportunities they see now which can be translated into immediate employment and income for people, without regard to the reserve's capability in the longer run. This is the present task. And if the amount of development proves insufficient, some of the people will move elsewhere, as they have been doing now for a couple of generations. Those future migrants would also be better off, because the fact that the people have taken charge of their future will have raised both aspirations and education levels.

As well as undeveloped opportunities, there are new approaches to be tried. The Dakota-Ojibwa in southern Manitoba are pursuing the possibility of government contracts that give special preference to business on the reserves. The us Defense department has long had such a policy, to the considerable benefit of the reservations, and the US Small Business Administration has had a minorities-preference policy since the 1950s.[55] Canada may save money in turning down the same tactics, but whether it would amount to more than what gets spent on welfare seems unlikely.

The God's River Band is turning its airstrip into a major airport serving northeastern Manitoba, and an Alberta band is making disposable chopsticks for export to China, which supplied some of the investment. For many bands, control over forestry and mineral resources in the big hope for the future. Another popular strategy is "keeping money in the community," which gives rise to any number of stores and shopping malls. Pukatawagen has recently built a sizeable mall which is expected to bring in $7 to $8 million a year, money that would otherwise have gone to the Bay.

While limits most certainly exist, they cannot be defined until development has been given a chance. The western bands do have potential and they also have ideas. They wait for a kind of self-government which will give them both power and resources.

Poverty Strategies

A second problem area concerns the spread of benefits among band members. There is employment now for people with the right qualifications; but there is also a considerable population which has only worked sporadically or spent ten years on social assistance, to say nothing of unmotivated teenagers. The bands' education officers stress the difficulties that stem from low levels of education and a "give-up" attitude. Whether problems of this kind are seen as factors that limit development or as people who would fail to benefit from development, it comes down to the same thing. Unless special measures are taken, economic development can only go so far.

This is why many Indian leaders want "socio-economic" development to be the first priority. They know that jobs are a distant solution for many people and, in the meantime, they want programs that will help these people pull their lives together and build a fully functioning community. Help of this kind is what the Assembly of First Nations calls a poverty strategy, and it is high on their list of demands. Pointing out that welfare is the fastest growing item in the Department's budget, the Assembly states that, even if business programs generate considerable momentum, the lives and outlook of the very poor will remain unchanged.[56] Nowhere is the gap more serious than in the three Prairie provinces, where the percentage of the population on social assistance is highest, and possibly – in view of the history – the percentage of disaffected people as well.

A poverty strategy would meet these problems head on. It would find ways to show children that they do have a future; it would put more resources into the schools and enlist elders to run cultural programs that instil pride. It would find ways to interest school drop-outs in community endeavours, helping them to find a commitment which may take them back to school or to job training and jobs with a future. There would be clinics where people could become more knowledgeable about nutrition and health and treatment centres for the casualties of a system which has so long ignored human needs; even make-work programs could have a place, providing other things are happening as well. In sum, a poverty strategy is intended to repair the lives of the damaged and disaffected and, at the same time, raise the sights of the several generations involved. It would spend money in ways that could help people combat feelings of inadequacy and hopelessness, and would see welfare costs go down as a result.

Urban Strategies

The problems of urban Indians are not high on band-council agendas. Their mandate is to improve circumstances on the reserves and, from a practical standpoint, there is probably not much they could do for city people. Urban Indian associations are poor and weak, and easily ignored. The CAED strategy, in the spirit of the twelve-month rule, has an urban "component," not a strategy, and this component consists of manpower courses which would be "newly focused" – something which has not been managed in twenty-five years of putting native people on courses.

At issue is up to fifty percent of the registered Indian population in Manitoba and Saskatchewan, twenty-five or thirty percent in Alberta. A disproportionate number are young, undereducated, and underskilled; a high percentage work in casual jobs, spending much time unemployed. The stress, the anger, and the violence they experience have all been touched on. Their problems go unaddressed because, among other reasons, these people fall in a jurisdictional no man's land; the federal government assumes only minor responsibility, while the cities, with provincial help, provide services that are in no way proportionate to the sheer volume of disability and alienation they are dealing with.

The federal government should have an urban strategy. For one thing, it is the federal system for managing the lives of Indian people that has landed so many in the cities without the skills they need. That is obvious enough, but a second reason, no less compelling, is the city's role as an adjunct to the reserve, reducing the Department's welfare costs. Thirdly, the city problems cannot be addressed in a serious way until the resources of the federal government are brought into play.

An urban strategy hinges on federal participation, but it would have to be the Indian people, through the urban Indian associations, that would take the lead role. Otherwise, the result would simply duplicate the experience on the reserves, where people receive services as clients and programs that don't solve the problems. To begin with, then, the problems of the urban Indian associations would have to be addressed. Theirs is a difficult constituency, for Indian people in the city tend to look to the reserve for support, while the contacts they make in the city tend to follow lines of kinship, band, and tribal history. The associations, hard pressed to recruit members, are unable to provide the services that would prove their worth. An urban strategy would put them in a position to give leadership and direction, reflecting the will of their constituency.

An urban strategy would combine elements from both the economic and the poverty strategies. On the economic side, the city has the important advantage of having jobs to offer and this should be capitalized upon. Sensibly designed training programs would play a part, increasing private-sector participation and putting a new emphasis on getting people hired. The Kinew model could be usefully employed. Wage subsidies should be considered, as in Saskatchewan's programs for the long-term unemployed, simply to reduce the stress associated with poverty and give disadvantaged people a better chance to get one foot on the ladder.

Another component is help for Indian business. In Winnipeg, the Urban Indian Association has proposed an economic strategy which incorporates this approach and draws heavily on programs which already exist in Canada or the US.[57] In the latter case, the federal government endorses the principle that a "fair share" of all federal contracts should be "set aside" for minority-owned small business. The Sioux in South Dakota are one of the major beneficiaries, a source of inspiration for the nations to the north. The Winnipeg association also cites the "incubator concept," a device which has been used by Canada's department in charge of regional development (although not for Indian business). The essence is a setting which draws together a number of small businesses and improves their chances by enabling them to share services they might not otherwise be able to afford. Its exponents in Winnipeg see it as the basis for a revived city core, with working families replacing welfare recipients.

Much of the spending required by special training and poverty programs reflects the past and present failure to spend in the ways that would be needed to get the children through the schools. The Prairie cities have made a start, but they would be the first to admit that a great deal more is needed before these children have an equal chance in life. Neighbourhood projects deserve support. The people need to feel that they have a place in the city and, if the urban associations choose to sponsor housing projects, it is to be hoped that the federal government will now recognize their importance.

It may seem more difficult in the city than on the reserves to make room for native people to build initiative and self reliance; but city people need room too. There is an urgent need to reduce the time that people spend as clients in an agency office and to increase the opportunities for becoming independent. With funding, the urban Indian associations could help to meet this need, giving city people the power to say what the programs should be and the opportunity to design and run them. The result would be functions for people, services that work better, and pride in accomplishment. It would be a first step towards building a genuine Indian community in the city and, far from being a ghetto – the government's ostensible fear in the case of the Winnipeg housing project – it would set Indian people on the path to full citizenship in their own society, as well as in the larger Canadian one.

POSTSCRIPT:
SELF-GOVERNMENT AT
JAMES BAY

The Crees at James Bay made headlines in the early 1970s as latter-day Davids battling the Goliath of Hydro Quebec and two governments. But once they had won their settlement, the media lost interest. Their subsequent experience is of interest here because it supplies an actual case of money becoming available to band councils which could spend it as they saw fit. Whether the Crees were fairly treated, whether the gains from the settlement outweigh the losses in terms of land, resources, and way of life, whether the dams should have been built from environmental or other criteria – all such questions are quite outside the narrow scope of this section.

Quebec's decision to harness the rivers flowing into James Bay affected the roughly 5,500 Crees who trapped and hunted along the same rivers, as well as a smaller number of Inuit. These people were not untouched by civilization, for trading posts had been built in the seventeenth and eighteenth centuries and the switch to village life had been made after World War II, much as in northern Saskatchewan. They were, however, untouched by even modest prosperity or the freedom to run their own affairs.

The villages provided some employment; an estimated twenty percent worked in regular jobs, mainly in government agencies. The rest of the adult population either trapped and hunted, or existed through some combination of hunting, short-term jobs and social assistance. Much else besides is reminiscent of Saskatchewan's northern region in the same era: the ubiquitous Bay store; the omnipotent Department; the white people manning the missions, schools, and government offices; the children who quit school early, expecting to follow the same life pattern as their parents. There were the same niceties of racial separation: shortly after he was elected chief of Rupert's House, Billy Diamond was invited to the priest's house for Christmas dinner; he and his wife found themselves seated in a different room, separated from host and other guests alike.[58]

One significant difference between this area and northern Saskatchewan was that the James Bay lands had never been ceded under a treaty. Although the reserves had been declared as such, they were unceded Crown land under Quebec jurisdiction and this was the power base that made it possible for the Crees to oppose the project. Also of advantage to the Crees was the sense they had of belonging to a larger community beyond the home village, the result, in part, of a radio-telephone system that linked the villages and was a part of daily life.[59] The quality of leadership which the threat to their land called into being is another advantage. Chief Billy Diamond at Rupert's House, Chief Robert Kanetewat at Fort George, and Charlie Watt, now a senator and then one of the key spokesmen for the Inuit, were all able men who had come to see the system as the source of their problems. The absurdity of the system was brought home to Billy Diamond, according to his biographer, as he handed out welfare cheques as part of a job he had with the Department after finishing school.[60]

When the struggle began, the Indians of Quebec Association assumed the lead role, but the Crees at James Bay came to see their own objectives as different, and it was with the Grand Council of the Crees of Quebec, along with the Inuit, that the agreement was signed in 1975. The value of what they got has been in dispute ever since, but their achievement deserves recognition, given the forces ranged against them: all the resources of government, including the expertise it could purchase and control of the bureaucratic process.

This the Crees had to master overnight in order to deal with the enormous pressures to act quickly – and the wonder is that they managed as well as they did.

What they got can be summarized as a land settlement (with full rights, including subsurface rights, to some lands and the more limited right to hunt and trap on others) and a financial settlement of $150 million outright (which would be roughly $350 million in 1990 dollars) with a further federal commitment to finance ongoing services (health, education, etc.). Estimates indicate that the value of the services over a ten-year period would be well above the value of the cash settlement.[61]

The Crees moved swiftly to establish their own administrative body, the Cree Regional Authority, along with several boards which would have charge of schools, health services, and housing. These boards were located in the villages, where they provided 1,100 local jobs. This concern for the people's interest had marked Cree leadership throughout. During negotiations, each clause went back to the villages for discussion and approval. A most important innovation – the Crees' answer to welfare – was in place within two years. This was the Income Supplement Plan (ISP) for hunters and trappers.

In chapter 3, the problem with trapping was sketched in a northern Saskatchewan setting, where trapper earnings were so low that most trappers were better off financially staying comfortably at home and drawing welfare through the long, cold winter, much as they hated the life. The ISP did away which such an all-or-nothing choice. Given the supplement, and combined with summer employment, trapping and hunting could once more support a family. The old pursuits became viable. Elsewhere in the reserve economy, it has long been argued that given a real choice, people would choose the traditional life over welfare, and so it proved at James Bay. By the early 1980s, the social-assistance caseload had been reduced by two-thirds; welfare ruled no longer.

Here is tangible evidence of the good results that can flow from self-government: the Department has resolutely stuck with social assistance as the only answer for people unable to support themselves, although it has received proposals for income supplementation (such as ISP) which, not surprisingly, the people prefer. Nor did the energy released by self-government stop there. Subcontracting was launched in the forest industries. A Cree construction company was established which, besides building houses, trained construction workers and provided unskilled jobs for hunters in the summer. Funds for the crash housing program were borrowed, in the belief that people shouldn't have to spend another fifteen years in bad housing. Richard Salisbury of McGill University, writing in the 1980s, spoke of a contemporary way of life with a stove, refrigerator, and TV in every household, along with piped-in water and indoor plumbing.[62] In 1982, the Crees acquired an airline by buying fifty-one percent of Austin Airways, the only regional airline which had hired the Crees as groundworkers in the days before the settlement. The business went well; much of its original traffic consisted of workers who needed to be ferried to and from northern work camps and, by 1988, the Crees were able to buy Austin out.

The Crees did not get enough money to break the bonds of dependence on the larger society. Much of the employment is with the various Cree agencies, hunting is subsidized, and government funding is still the basic source of support. They have new powers to decide how funds will be spent, but are still constrained in the matter of planning and budgeting. At the same time, their achievements are considerable. Salisbury highlights the Cree Regional Authority, which they see as their own, and the building of a larger community through linkages between the villages. The reduction in welfare must surely be added, and the revival of a traditional way of life which so many people prefer. It all leads to the point which is relevant to other Indian nations: that real changes become possible once decision making passes to the band.

The housing program alone gives pause for thought. The many millions spent on housing on the western reserves could have seen thousands trained in the building trades, ready to take employment when they went to the cities. Reducing welfare has also been a primary objective in the West, but western nations have not had the power to try something new. Their band councils are caught up in an entirely different process: administering programs which the Department has selected; attending meetings; seeking approval for projects which, as likely as not, will be turned down. It is a process which frustrates and exhausts, with little to show for itself, whereas the Crees at James Bay must have been inspired and invigorated by the challenges they took on. Stripped to its essentials, the James Bay process differs fundamentally from the way things are managed on the western reserves, and it can only be seen as a significant advance.

CHAPTER SIX

Changing Course

The hundred-year history since the treaties were signed is one that reflects badly on Canadian society. Even today, any gains are made slowly and the reserves still shock foreign visitors. The government has its own agenda, barely hearing what the bands have to say, and the public, not much interested, leaves it to the government. In this last chapter, the focus switches to public opinion and how it might help to turn the situation around.

PERSPECTIVES OF WHITE SOCIETY

Public opinion has always been a factor in Indian policy, usually by providing passive support; but in the West, at least initially, it shaped the basic direction. It seems to have become strongly influential again in the mid-twentieth century, when the reserve economy collapsed and the government held to the original white understanding that Indian people would not spill over to compete with them in the labour market. And while white people did manage to accept integrated schools, they made it hard on children.

Majority opinion has continued to support the government on Indian policy, although, thanks to the media, Canadians are not unaware of the high unemployment on the reserves, deep poverty, and eight-year-old children sniffing glue. Indian leaders have commanded little attention and some columnists have come to call them "complainers." It all contrasts oddly with the kind of public pressure that pushed the government to play a prominent role on the international stage in the matter of apartheid in far-away South Africa, for while apartheid may be worse, the misery on the reserves is bad enough and fully our own responsibility.

Sympathy and support for Indian people are also present, as opinion polls taken over more than a decade show; indeed, they were much in evidence during the summer crisis at Oka in 1990. But this kind of support never takes the next step of challenging government policy, which presumably reflects a widespread feeling that government is doing the best it can. This is a feeling based on trust, for few Canadians actually know anything about the programs for Indian people, other than welfare. If they had greater knowledge, this trust would surely be shaken. Indian leaders have made this point, that the public never hears about the tiny budget for economic development or the piecemeal projects, and because the program shortcomings are never revealed, the public goes on blaming the Indian people for failing to rise up the ladder.[1] L.I. Barber, the first Indian claims commissioner, put it this way: "Indian people don't get public sympathy because they have never been able to present their side effectively."[2]

GOVERNMENT AS THE PROBLEM

Although the modern age has eliminated the worst mistakes of the colonial era, it tolerates welfare as the chief answer to joblessness and has wasted twenty-five years on programs that are patently not working. The reluctance to deal in a straightforward way on the matter of self-government shows the basic inertia in the system. Either the government fails to grasp the nature of the problem, or it is hanging on to power for reasons that have little to do with the welfare of Indian people. Probably both factors apply, and it can be difficult for those administering the programs to be entirely clear on the rationale. One official, speaking to his colleagues, said: "We must be careful not to increase dependency and subsequent erosion of the sense of responsibility and motivation to ensure self-accomplishment, respect and a reasonable livelihood. The financial assistance and services provided to Indian individuals and families are to enable them and their dependents to maintain health, safety, dignity and family unity."[3]

In the West, government has been the central feature in people's lives for more than a hundred years, and the shortcomings of the early administrators may be the easiest to excuse because they were rooted in a worldwide belief system that saw civilization as a gift. "We will lift you up," said Governor Morris in all sincerity, believing it to be a simple matter.[4] But no such belief survives today, nor is there a new ideology which could give credence to the modern-day management of the reserve system. The government hangs on to its powers, lacking a rationale or a sense of direction, and by its very presence blocks the key change that is needed if solutions are to emerge.

This key change, it has already been said, is simply for the government to step back, allowing Indian people the room to build initiative and self-reliance. The government, on the other hand, sees self-government as one of many demands; blind to the larger purpose, it has no sense of the urgency that goes with it, or of the need for funds. It also continues to see itself as the lead player, which is the heart of the difficulty.

Government as lead player comes through very clearly in the CAED strategy, which overflows with the good things that government has devised for the benefit of aboriginal people. In the recently produced CAED handbook,[5] the central theme is partnership, which could mean either a larger role for aboriginal people, or a device for preserving government control. There are to be many partnerships – between government and aboriginal people, and among several federal departments, provincial and territorial governments, and the private sector – while the programs cover community development, resource development, business development, and job training. Looking at the area of job training, there is the obligatory statement of good intentions: "to invest in and develop, in partnership with the aboriginal people, a trained aboriginal labour force for participation in unique aboriginal labour markets and the broader Canadian labour market."[6] But much hinges on the "how" of doing it. The CAED strategy offers "delivery mechanisms" which will be "managed and arranged through aboriginal infrastructures," while the actual training package is none other than the Canadian Jobs Strategy, the most recent name for the cluster of manpower courses available from CEIC, which have never yet been adapted to the particular needs and wants of aboriginal people.

The handbook begins by saying that the CAED strategy "incorporates the recommendations of aboriginal peoples on how federal economic development programs can best support their needs. These recommendations came out of a two-year consultation with aboriginal peoples and their organizations throughout Canada."[7] Doubtless they did, but given the overwhelming power on the government's side, this is hardly proof that the programs reflect native wishes, while the meagre results attaching to the same programs in the past argue otherwise. Summing up, while the CAED strategy may seem to be a step forward, the heavy emphasis on delivery, the small budget, and the government's insistence on the manpower programs do not augur well for the future.

This unwillingness to let go is not a rare characteristic among governments and should be recognized for what it is. The Canadian government has not much to show for all its years of running Indian programs, yet it has never lost faith in the programs or the bureaucrats who design them. The bureaucracy is itself a considerable force sustaining the *status quo*; this was explored by Penner's Committee on Indian Self-Government. At the time of the hearings, roughly twenty years had passed since the bands were admitted to program administration and the Committee sought answers as to why the process had got stuck, never going on to transfer decision-making power. The accounting firm that analysed the administration and budgets pointed to the bureaucracy, describing its vested interest as follows: "Just as control of the purse is fundamental to the evolution of our own parliamentary system, it is fundamental to the survival and growth of government bureaucracies. Thus Indian self-government comes into conflict with bureaucratic process and it is not surprising that real decision-making power, which depends on having unrestricted funding, has not been transferred to Indian bands and councils."[8]

Recent years have seen a government which missed the whole point of self-government as recommended by the House Committee, imposing an inappropriate substitute; they have also seen the government make savings through problematic measures such as cutting funds for Indian organizations and ending funds for Indian newspapers. In summary, neither the record nor present actions support the view that the Canadian government can be counted on to see what would work best for the Indian people. We come back, therefore, to the importance of public opinion: if Canadians could come to see that, far from being incurable, the problems are simply not being addressed. The toll in human lives is ongoing and it does not seem right in a country that prides itself on caring.

THE CONSTITUTIONAL ROUTE

Beginning in the 1970s, some Canadians began to see a solution in the movement, initiated by aboriginal organizations, for constitutional protection of their rights, including the right to self-government, which eventually became a central focus. Through several conferences and the repatriation of the Canadian Constitution, proposals for recognition of rights received good coverage in the newspapers.

One approach, called "top-down", favours constitutional recognition first, followed by negotiations with provinces and municipalities on form and substance; the other ("bottom-up") would begin with the local agreements and later see them entrenched in the Constitution. The 1983 First Ministers Conference saw an accord signed on some of the processes involved, but did not advance the cause very far. Subsequent conferences in 1984, 1985, and 1987 have been characterized as failures.[9]

Meanwhile, a more direct route had been opened up by Keith Penner's report in its recommendation for recognizing Indian First Nation governments through an act of Parliament. This should not be seen as a substitute, for the highest importance attaches to constitutional recognition of rights, but as something which should be easier to achieve quickly – an important consideration under the circumstances. Unfortunately, the more direct approach has not seen much progress either. The government's bill, which "did not capture the spirit of the Committee's recommendations," died on the order paper and was not reintroduced.[10] Subsequently, the government switched to negotiating self-government on an individual-band basis, as described in chapter 5.

So compressed an account of the constitutional proceedings may be taken to reflect my view that constitutional entrenchment, essential as it is, should not occupy centre stage to the exclusion of all else. It seems likely that much of the Canadian public now sees the solutions, including self-government, as waiting on constitutional agreement, and hence sees the future in terms of continuing negotiations over years, if not decades. So long a view is bound to reinforce the tolerance with which the present circumstances are viewed. "What can't be changed must be endured" – easy enough to contemplate when the enduring is confined to the Indian peoples.

The path to self-government through act of Parliament should be quicker, and would be, if the government did not insist on imposing its own version. One wonders: Why this insistence? According to Keith Penner, aboriginal leaders see it as the government's preference for a municipal model, whose powers are delegated. He himself has added another factor in the Department's instinct for self-preservation: "after wandering about in a public policy desert for decades, [the Department] has now embraced Indian self-government and given itself a new lease on life ... Their conception of self-government would have them playing a major role for years to come."[11] Consulting the time schedule under present policy, he estimated that the achievement of self-government would take a hundred years, and said it was exactly what his Committee had anticipated when it argued for a new, small federal agency, as evidence of the government's desire to begin a new era of cooperative coexistence.[12]

It is now more than fifteen years since the James Bay Agreement introduced the unconditional grant, a considerable advance at the time, which gave the Cree governments a firmer base. But as Billy Diamond explained recently, the new system still maintained the "old client relationship whereby bands have no control, no certainty, no opportunity to plan or budget in accordance with the bands' priorities and needs."[13] The Department, Diamond argued, sees itself continuing to determine the nature and type of financing that will be available. More than that, the process whereby self-government is addressed – the First Ministers Conferences that argued the thing back and forth through the 1980s – "fails to recognize as the primary condition the requirement for adequate and guaranteed financial resources to make sure that aboriginal self-government works."[14]

CONSIDERATIONS OF COST

In the course of the stand-off with the Mohawks in the summer of 1990, the minister of Indian Affairs made a statement on the cost of federal programs for aboriginal people, which came to just over $4 billion in 1990–91, most of it earmarked for registered Indians.[15] This was surely intended to show that the government was committed, digging deep into its pockets to improve Indian lives; that would be what most Canadians took from it. It may even be what the government believes. Nothing, of course, could be further from the truth. What wasn't said in the minister's statement is that the $4 billion is mainly a holding action: it pays the grocery bills for people who can't get jobs, hires social workers for their problems, and covers schooling for children who will drop out early and repeat the cycle of their parents. When the minister's figures are broken down, economic development comes in at less than four percent.[16]

These figures provide a good perspective for the discussion of self-government, revealing a high-cost enterprise which keeps much of the Indian population in a state of dependency and offers neither a better life nor a reduced need to spend. Self-government is the change that would break the pattern. With this change, programs that don't work would be curtailed or abandoned. Band and tribal councils would be free to pursue development opportunities, make training arrangements with employers, enrich programs to keep children in school and go after the drop-outs; they could find ways to heal people who have spent too many years on welfare, too many years fighting the system.

The cost of the new programs could be met in part through the cost savings associated with self-government; the main ones are cutting out ineffective programs and ending duplication in administrative services. Such savings may be relatively small in the short run because many programs – welfare, for example – can't be much reduced until full-time employment is more generally available, and that will take time. Also, there will be strong pressures to improve living circumstances, such as housing, to raise the spirits as well as health and give the children a better chance at school. A century of neglect cannot be overcome quickly or without spending money. This is why the House Committee recommended transitional grants, to be managed unconditionally by the bands and modelled on the equalization payments which go to the poorer provinces.

Later, as the new programs take hold, more people will be working; aspirations and self-confidence will rise; the costs of welfare, social services, and the rest will go down. This is the magic of self-government. It really can bring the change that is most needed: the redirection of spending into useful channels, which also marks the beginning of a reduced need to spend. A dramatic illustration of cost effectiveness is the cost of training a tradesman at the Thompson Centre in northern Manitoba – $10,000 in the mid-1980s.[17] This was close to the annual cost of maintaining a northern family on welfare at that time, yet training is a one-time outlay that sees a man employed, presumably for most of his working life, while welfare tends to be a continuing cost, extending, in some problem families, on to the next generation. Thus, the shift to self-government becomes highly cost effective in the longer run.

To speed this day would make more sense that clinging to the present cluster of costly programs, and a faster pace is possible if Canada will commit more funds along with self-government. The House Committee recommended a combination of short- and long-term funding in addition to settlement of outstanding land claims: this seems to get it right.

Settlement of claims stands in a special category because the lands and monies involved are substantial, and because the government has been stalling for far too long. The land that is owing would add significantly to the resources under aboriginal control, increase the security of their position as nations, and enhance the development prospect. The Assembly of First Nations rightly calls it "the key to the future." However, while the importance of claims is impossible to exaggerate, from the standpoint of financing self-government, the claims suffer from two limitations. One is that not all bands have claims to make; the other is that the success rate in the settlement process and the timing of the verdicts are unknowns. For these reasons, the settlements are only part of the solution and self-government in the early years would require the unconditional grants, as recommended by Penner's committee.

The question of adequate funding for Indian self-government is the real test of Canada's willingness to end the blight on the reserves, for if the will is there, the government has the ability to come up with very large sums of money. For example, in two consecutive years, offers went out to the Dene/Métis and the Inuit under the comprehensive-claims process, each of them in excess of $500 million, which suggests that $1 billion is not an impossible sum. Applied to the much larger population in the three western provinces, it would, of course, seem less; on the other hand, claims settlement is a one-time payment, whereas grants for self-governing bands would be spread around in smaller amounts and continue over a period of years. To take a figure, why not $1 billion a year for five years?

The suggestion is not outrageous – it amounts to the equivalent of two comprehensive-claims settlements, or one-third of the foreign-aid budget, which was $2.9 billion in 1990. Nor should it shock when Canadians accept the annual $4 billion package which consists largely of welfare and services. That acceptance, of course, is based on false premises, a belief that present programs represent the best that can be done. Once the package can be recognized for what it is, money to launch self-governing nations should come more readily.

If Canadians were to insist on real commitment to improving Indian lives, it could be done and the cost would not be unbearable. Spending one-third of the foreign-aid budget to end Canada's own Third World in three provinces seems modest enough, all the more so because it would be advantageous to Canada, ending the hemorrhage through welfare and programs that help no one. In a call for Indian self-government with strong financial support, John Beaver, vice-president of Atomic Energy of Canada Ltd, claimed that without economic development, the future will see Canada "wasting four or five times what we are wasting now."[18]

SOMETHING OWING

Cost saving is one argument for changing the policies, but since it would only be realized in the longer run, it is probably not enough to effect a major shift in public opinion. A Canadian businessman, who showed his own deep commitment by launching the Canadian Council for Native Business, expressed his view in the foreword to *Canada's Native People*, volume 2: "The aboriginal people of Canada have long suffered indignities, both from a lack of recognition of their contributions to our heritage, culture and social structure, and from limitations imposed on them that have inhibited their development."[19] Something is owing, Murray Koffler is saying, and the Council is one way that like-minded Canadians can begin to make amends. Others can join the movement in various ways, first and foremost by sending a clear signal to the government that present policies are seen as bankrupt.

Opinion polls suggest there is a "deep well of goodwill" as well as a willingness to recognize and deal with native rights. From a poll in October 1989 comes the word that more than fifty percent of Canadians are becoming "more sympathetic to the native plight, [and] believe their right to self-government should be entrenched in the Constitution."[20] This goodwill is as yet unfocused, but it is there to be drawn upon if Indian people can get their message across.

It may be useful to recall a native cause that did catch public attention not so long ago, in the mid-1970s. The Dene in the Mackenzie Valley, who were still living in something approaching their traditional way, found themselves threatened by the massive intrusion of an oil pipeline and its destruction of their way of life. Their good fortune was to have a spokesperson, Chief Justice Thomas Berger, who understood their fears and saw the importance of giving them time, so that adjustments could be made at a slower pace. Berger was also in a position to give them the time, and his decision drew little criticism; indeed, it may even have had widespread support, reflecting the goodwill that pollsters find now.

The case is relevant to the present because it reveals a willingness to help native people that might not otherwise have come to light. In the profound questions that were raised at the time, Thomas Berger saw the justice of the Dene cause, their concern for the future, and the relationship of that future to our own:

They are challenging the economic religion of our time, the belief in an ever-expanding cycle of growth and consumption ... They argue that their own culture should not be discarded, that it has served them well for many years and that the industrial system of the white man may not, here in the North, serve them as well for anything like so long a time ... With the guarantees that can be provided only by a settlement of their claims and with the strengthening of their own economy, they wish to ensure that their cultures can continue to grow and change – in directions that they choose for themselves.[21]

Precisely the same wish infused the people of the Plains in the 1880s; they saw themselves as a distinct society, with values and a culture they would continue to uphold and pass on to their children. But they had no sympathetic spokesperson, no public understanding of their position, and the Canadian government set about extinguishing everything they wished to preserve. The unfortunate people were expected to shed their identity and, with the white man's clothes, put on his beliefs and values. Insofar as they could, they resisted: "Indian people who once dwelt proud and sovereign in all of Canada have resisted with stubborn tenacity all efforts to make them like everybody else ... Indians have constantly insisted and will continue to insist that they are a special people who have an inherent right to a special status as a nation within a nation."[22]

Again, something is owing here, for however well it can be explained by colonial administrators and outdated beliefs, the people have been put through a terrible history. Their resistance has never been understood and Canadians, as a nation, have no collective memory of the harshness of the western experience.

In one last comparison with the Dene, it may be recalled that the decision to halt the pipeline was taken – despite the thousands of jobs at stake and the powerful interests involved – because the Chief Justice saw disaster for a small group of native people. Compensation for a disaster that happened long ago ought to seem less threatening to interest groups; if the Dene could be given time, it should not be impossible to give western bands the compensation they deserve for past injury. The problem is in seeing that we have an obligation to do so. Something is owing, and not merely for the policies of the distant past, for the damage done in early years has been compounded in our own times: we have put two generations on welfare and ignored such universal human needs as opportunity, pride, and independence. Even today, there is no sense that it is an urgent matter to slash the welfare rolls, raise retention in the schools, or move swiftly to settle claims.

Settlement of claims can hardly count as compensation, since the money is owed, where validated, for specific reasons. Most of the land claims in the Prairie provinces revolve around treaty acreage that was never allocated and to the extensive sell-offs that came later. In effect, the government is withholding what was promised or taken away. In Saskatchewan, the settlement process has validated claims to one million acres, and claims for an almost equal amount (933,000 acres) are still outstanding.[23] A full settlement would more than double the present reserve acreage. The Manitoba nations have an additional source of grievance in that the formula used in their treaties yielded only one-quarter of the land that was granted from Treaty Six on. Their reserve acreage today is only one-third that in the other two provinces, although population is much the same. Manitoba leaders want this ancient inequity corrected and, in all three provinces, leaders want the calculations adjusted for the (larger) modern populations.

A 1985 "Status Report" on treaty land-entitlement claims shows seventy-seven bands in Manitoba and Saskatchewan with outstanding claims, of which fifty-three have been accepted for negotiation.[24] Eleven bands are recorded for Alberta, with another five making claims for expropriation and illegal surrender (the number in Saskatchewan is not specified). Alberta also has the Lubicon, who never signed a treaty; they filed a claim under aboriginal rights in 1980 and have been negotiating ever since.

The sell-offs are a particularly unsavoury piece of the history, involving the loss of good farm land as white speculators made fortunes and Department officials facilitated the sales. In one outrageous case in Saskatchewan, an entire reserve was sold off and the band dispatched to a reserve already occupied by people of a different nation who had very little land worth farming.[25]

A process was established roughly twenty years ago to settle land and other claims, but it moves much too slowly, and the time that people have waited must be counted as something else that is owing. Not only do most claims involve the land, which is uniquely important to the people, but the whole settlement process, so long drawn out, has greatly raised the level of suspicion and mistrust among Indian people, extending it beyond government to the whole Canadian society. Claims Commissioner Lloyd Barber spoke to this point more than a dozen years ago (1978):

Until very recently, their grievances have not been fully brought to light because of serious weaknesses in communication and the very one-sided nature of the relationship between Indians and others in this country. Indian grievances are not new to Indians nor are they new to the Department of Indian Affairs. The rest of us, however, have not known much about them, and the Indians have never been in a position to put their claims forward in a clear and forceful way which would make them fully understandable to us. For this reason alone, it is valid that these very old grievances be dealt with now ...

There is an additional and overriding reason why the grievances must be dealt with in a just and equitable manner. Over the years, the relationships between Indians and the Government have been such that strong feelings of distrust have developed. This distrust goes far beyond distrust of government to the entire society which has tried, since day one, to assimilate Indian people.[26]

Ironically, much or perhaps most of the money saved by foot dragging on claims still has to be paid out in the form of welfare and other services which only maintain the *status quo*. Settlement of claims, on the other hand, would see real money invested in the people and in the resources they possess.

BENEFITS TO CANADIAN SOCIETY

Making room for an independent and prosperous Indian society offers benefits beyond large savings in cost. One of the more important would be in the area of resource use, for our new partners would bring to it a feeling for nature and a concern for future generations that does not mark our own approach to resources. The world at the end of the twentieth century faces problems that did not plague our forefathers and what to them seemed a civilization that could solve all problems has now revealed itself as poorly equipped. Nowhere is this more evident than in the matter of reconciling our endless appetite for goods with a seriously deteriorating environment.

Indian civilization offers a value system in which the land and all nature are supreme; the goods of modern civilization, while desirable, are ranked lower down. The responsibility to future generations is also central to Indian culture, so that land and resources must be used in a way that ensures their preservation. It is a view of life that could vastly improve the prospects of our own children's children. In the forest regions which cover much of Canada, a fledgling environment movement struggles to protect a diminishing resource, confronting powerful forest companies and a public which counts jobs and income above all else. The Barrière Lake Band, which lives in LaVérendrye Park, supplies a different perspective. Much as Chief Mis-Ta-Wa-Sis declared at Treaty Six that his people were looking ahead to their children's children, so Chief Jean Maurice Matchewan at Barrière Lake is attempting to negotiate a conservation plan which will ensure the survival of the forests and wildlife. As he says: "If Canadians can support saving the rain forest in Brazil, they should be able to support a forest which is in their own backyard."[27]

Millions of people the world over worry about unstoppable development and depletion of resources. John McMurtry of Guelph University linked world interest in the Oka dispute with a longing for a truce: "for a stop to the endless devastation of the world's remaining forests, free places and natural habitats."[28] Canada's Indian problems and environment problems are intimately linked, he writes, and must be solved together.

The effects of unstoppable development are all too keenly felt in distant northlands where few whites but many native people live. At Fort Chipewyan on Lake Athabaska, some of the most toxic chemicals known to man can be found in the fish, borne there by the Athabaska River from the pulp mills and other industries to the south. Fish is a staple for the native people. Far to the east, at the other end of Lake Athabaska, other Chipewyan live where uranium was mined for thirty years and the wastes from the mines – millions of tons of them – dumped without treatment onto the land and into the lakes. This mine is now closed, but the uranium industry still runs at full tilt in northern Saskatchewan. One of the mines is at Wollaston Lake, the pride of Saskatchewan's northern fishery a generation ago, and the mill uses two hundred tons of concentrated sulphuric acid per day, discharging seven million litres of wastewater which makes its way to the lake.[29] Radioisotopes, including radium, are released into the environment, with effects on the fish, the moose that graze on contaminated plants, and the people who eat the moose and the fish. A petition from the local council reads in part: "The land is still very much a part of us and we would like to see it protected for us and our children and their children."[30]

At Cigar Lake, also in northern Saskatchewan and reportedly the world's largest high-grade uranium deposit, the radioactivity is so high that its development may hinge on the use of robots. A spokesperson for the mining industry, quoted in *Saskatchewan Business*, notes the importance of a compliant population, stating that he preferred to face the technical problems of mining Cigar Lake than "the political hassle of developing a uranium mine in Australia."[31] The compliant population in Canada lives well outside the danger zone, for the most part, although some resident native people accept the industry for the sake of jobs. But given local control over resources, the balance of power would likely shift. Band and village councils would have at least some power to protect the environment and, incidentally, themselves, and we would all be better off for their actions.

Reverence for the land, which is the driving force that the Indian nations would bring to environmental issues, is just one part of a belief system that offers help on other daunting problems of modern society. Living in harmony with other members of society as well as with nature is another prime value that has been practised for thousands of years. Architect Douglas Cardinal describes Indian culture as "a different way of being human."[32] Colonel Butler sensed this in the 1870s, when he camped with the bands still living the free life, admiring their contentment with what they had, which included spiritual as well as material possessions, and the importance they placed on seeing to it that the needs of all were met.

The other way of being human, as put by Cardinal, is the way of the "society of the ego man … in conflict with the environment, with himself and with the spirit."[33] The natural man can help bring balance to this ego society because, "as human beings linked with the life cycle, we feel the effects that all nature is feeling in this highly industrialized and technologized society."[34] In the development of Indian culture, Cardinal sees harmony reintroduced to the land.

It is worth thinking about. Our Euro-Canadian ancestors handed down a view of life well suited to spanning the Prairies with steel rails, harvesting boundless resources, and building industries that made this country one of the world's richest. Today's world is very different. Our resources are limited and, in most cases, deteriorating. We live with salinization of soils, pollution in lakes and rivers, and smaller trees growing in our forests. New perils such as global warming have arisen and can only be dealt with in cooperation with other nations. And the problem of poverty, never solved by our forefathers, becomes the more unconscionable, given the wealth of the nation as a whole. Highly sophisticated technology in industry and the marketplace contrasts with numbing poverty in city cores, a drug culture, and alienated people. The Indians' sharing principle could help us here, just as it ensured their survival through all the millenia before the white man came.

Notes

CHAPTER ONE

1 Statistics Canada, "The Socio-Demographic Condition of Registered Indians," *Canadian Social Trends* (Winter 1986), 3. The estimate for immigration was based on data in Foot, *Canada's Population Outlook*, 4.
2 *Calgary Herald*, 12 December 1989.
3 *Winnipeg Free Press*, 14 October 1988.
4 The terms "registered" and "status" are interchangeable. They refer to persons whose names are recorded on the register maintained by Indian and Northern Affairs Canada (INAC) and its predecessors, stretching back to colonial times. The new Dominion passed the Indian Act in 1876 and, with many revisions, this is still the basis for maintaining a special category of people.

The definition is a legal one, never strictly racial, as it is in the United States. It rests on the right to live on Indian lands, which was decided – at least, in the three Prairie provinces – on an individual-band basis at the time when the bands first took up residence on the reserves. The entitlement extends to wives and widows, and descends to children through the male line. Until the 1950s, status women who married non-Indians automatically ceased to be "Indian."

Entitlements include such things has housing, health services, education, social assistance for non-earners, and exemption from income tax. By and large, these apply only to people living on the reserve, with a twelve-month grace period on moving to the city. The education entitlement is not so restricted.

There are also a number of restrictions associated with status, notably in the case of land. The title to all reserve land is vested in the Crown (intended to prevent loss of land through individual sales to

speculators) and this has posed a major problem for business and farming, since land cannot be used as security for loans.
See also Frideres, *Native Peoples in Canada*, 6–10.

5 The statistics are from Stephen Sharzer, "Native People: Some Issues", 550.

6 Some urban groups suspect bias stemming from the link between government grants and on-reserve population.

7 Statistics Canada, *Social Security, National Programs, Other Programs*, 74.

8 *Ottawa Citizen*, 21 January 1989.

9 Items one and two: Canada, Indian and Northern Affairs, Corporate Policy, Research Branch, *An Overview of Registered Indian Conditions in Manitoba*, 67, 143; and *An Overview of Registered Indian Conditions in Saskatchewan*, 70, 134. Item three: *Calgary Herald*, 7 October 1986.

10 Canada, Energy, Mines & Resources, *Energy Performance of On-Reserve Housing*, Appendix A. Subsequent reference to the Piapot Reserve is from Appendix B. Reference to "positive attitudes to housing" in the next paragraph is from the Main Report, 10.

11 *Calgary Herald*, 6 October 1989.

12 Thalassa Research Associates, *The Economic Foundations of Indian Self-Government*, 119–20. The second item was taken from an INAC discussion paper which is identified in the Thalassa Report.

13 McCourt, *Saskatchewan*, 4.

14 Canada, Indian and Northern Affairs, *A Survey of the Contemporary Indians of Canada* (the Hawthorne Report), vol. 1, Table I, 49.

15 *Winnipeg Free Press*, 10 February 1987.

16 Thompson, *Chief Peguis and His Descendants*.

17 Personal communication to the author, October 1989.

18 Paulette Bear, "A History of Band No. 99," 11.

19 Brant and Brant Native Development Consultants, *Indian Band Economic Development Potential*, 92.

20 *Winnipeg Free Press*, 10 February 1987.

21 Robertson, *Reservations are for Indians*, 34–7.

22 Island Lake Tribal Council, *Island Lake*.

23 Ibid. 17.

24 Manitoba, Department of Agriculture and Immigration, *The People of Indian Ancestry in Manitoba*, Main Report, 142.

25 Brant and Brant, *Indian Band Economic Development Potential*, 47.

26 Manuel, *The Fourth World, An Indian Reality*, 101.

27 Personal communication to the author, October 1989.

28 Courchene, in Annette Rosensteil, ed., *Red and White*, 173.

29 Canada, House of Commons, *Indian Self-Government in Canada – Report*.

30 Don Logan (Native Economic Developers' Association), quoted in *Alberta Native Business News*, Summer 1989.

CHAPTER TWO

1 Kennedy, *Recollections of an Assiniboine Chief*, 10.
2 Milloy, *The Plains Cree*, chapter 2.
3 Ibid., 28.
4 Ibid., 106.
5 Sealey, "Indians of Canada: A Historical Sketch," 21.
6 Kennedy, *Recollections of an Assiniboine Chief*, 72.
7 Carter, *Lost Harvests*, 43.
8 Cardinal, *The Unjust Society*, 28.
9 Quoted in Taylor, "Two Views on the Meaning of Treaties Six and Seven," 16.
10 Quoted in Saskatchewan Indian Cultural College, *Treaty Six*. N.P.
11 Quoted in Taylor, "Two Views," 20.
12 Ibid., 23.
13 Morris, *The Treaties*.
14 Quoted in Saskatchewan Indian Cultural College, *Treaty Six*.
15 Ibid.
16 Ibid.
17 Manitoba, Culture, Heritage and Recreation, Historic Resources Branch, *Chief Peguis*, 7.
18 Carter, *Lost Harvests*, 40.
19 Meyer, *The Red Earth Crees*, ch. 4.
20 Miller, *These Too Were Pioneers*, 43.
21 Chance, "Strategies of Developmental Change Among the Cree," 23.
22 McCourt, *Remember Butler*, 68.
23 Manitoba Indian Brotherhood, *Treaty Days*, Preface.
24 Surtees, *The Original People*, 55.
25 Danziger, Jr, *The Chippewas of Lake Superior*, 214.
26 Dempsey, "One Hundred Years of Treaty Seven," 27.
27 Cuthand, "The Native People of the Prairie Provinces," 39.
28 Grant, *Moon of Wintertime*.
29 Ibid., 118.
30 Dr. Laurie Barron, quoted in *Saskatoon Star Phoenix*, 30 January 1988. Dr. Barron is head of the Department of Native Studies at the University of Saskatchewan.
31 Grant, *Moon of Wintertime*, 166.
32 Stocken, *Among the Blackfoot and Sarcee*, 46.
33 Stanley, "Displaced Red Men: The Sioux in Canada," 70.

34 Barman, Hêbert, and McCaskill, "The Legacy of the Past, An Overview," 74.
35 Manitoba, Department of Agriculture and Immigration, *The People of Indian Ancestry in Manitoba*, Main Report, 115.
36 Sindell, "Some Discontinuities in the Enculturation of Mistassini Cree Children," 84–92.
37 Cardinal, *Canadian Confrontations*, 20.
38 Manitoba Indian Brotherhood, *Treaty Days*, 49.
39 Ibid., 51.
40 CBC *Ideas* series, "Literacy: The Medium and the Message," Winter 1988–89.
41 Barman, Hêbert, and McCaskill, *The Legacy of the Past*, 8.
42 Ibid., 9.
43 Cuthand, "The Native People," 36.
44 Hanks and Hanks, *Tribe under Trust*, 8.
45 Carter, *Lost Harvests*, 76.
46 Ibid., 101. The examples which follow from the Cowessess and Day Star's Bands are also from this source.
47 Elias, *The Dakota of the Canadian Northwest*, 73.
48 Carter, *Lost Harvests*, 175.
49 Elias, *The Dakota of the Canadian Northwest*, 80.
50 Carter, *Lost Harvests*, 210.
51 Ibid., 211.
52 Titley, *A Narrow Vision*, 34.
53 Carter, *Lost Harvests*, 216.
54 Goodwill and Sluman, *John Tootoosis*, 125.
55 Cuthand, "The Native People," 35.
56 Elias, *The Dakota of the Canadian Northwest*, 88.
57 Ibid., 90.
58 Carter, *Lost Harvests*, 231.
59 Dosman, *Indians: The Urban Dilemma*, 60.
60 Carter, *Lost Harvests*, 256.
61 Ibid., 246.
62 Hurt, *Indian Agriculture in America*, 234.
63 Goodwill and Sluman, *John Tootoosis*, 85.
64 Ibid., 121.
65 Ibid., 125. Ahenakew graduated from the University of Saskatchewan, was active in the League of Indians of Western Canada in the 1930s, and pushed hard for local schools and better qualified teachers.
66 Humber, ed., *Canada's Native Peoples*, vol. 2, 19.
67 Rosensteil, ed., *Red and White*, 101.
68 Blanchard, *Kahnewake, A Historical Sketch*, 16–22.
69 Cuthand, "The Native People," 71.

70 Hanks and Hanks, *Tribe under Trust*, 8. See also Samek, *The Blackfoot Confederacy*, Goldfrank, *Changing Configurations*.
71 Dempsey, *Crowfoot, Chief of the Blackfeet*, 135.
72 Stocken, *Among the Blackfoot and Sarcee*, 81.
73 Dempsey, *Crowfoot, Chief of the Blackfeet*, 81.
74 Hanks and Hanks, *Tribe under Trust*, xiv.
75 Ibid., 170.
76 Ibid., 149.

CHAPTER THREE

1 Buckley and Campbell, *Farming at Mistawasis*.
2 Edgar Dosman, *Indians: The Urban Dilemma*, 6.
3 Kehoe, "The Dakotas in Saskatchewan," 153, 160.
4 Deprez and Sigurdson, *The Economic Status of the Canadian Indian*, 51–2.
5 Bone, Shannon, and Raby, *The Chipewyan of the Stony Rapids Region*, 63.
6 Deprez and Sigurdson, *The Economic Status of the Canadian Indian*, 10.
7 Freyman and Armstrong, *The Role of the Indian*, 644.
8 Stan Fulham (Manager of Kinew Housing, Winnipeg) personal communication to the author, October 1989.
9 Manitoba, Committee on Manitoba's Economic Future, *Manitoba, 1962–1975, A Report to the Government of Manitoba*, xi–3–10.
10 Canada, Indian and Northern Affairs, *A Survey of the Contemporary Indians of Canada*, vol. 1, Table XII, 95.
11 Robertson, *Reservations are for Indians*, 192–6.
12 *Indian News*, July 1981.
13 Manitoba, Department of Agriculture and Immigration, *The People of Indian Ancestry in Manitoba*. The quotes in the text are from the Main Report.
14 Ibid., 167.
15 Ibid., 141.
16 Statistics Canada, *Social Security, National Programs*, 74.
17 In a 1981 study, for example, mother-led single-parent families comprised fifty-three percent of all native family households in Winnipeg. See Canada Employment and Immigration Commission, *Issues Concerning the Role of Native Women in the Winnipeg Labour Market*, 69.
18 Johnson, *Native Children and the Child Welfare System*, 33.
19 Canada, Indian and Northern Affairs, *A Survey of the Contemporary Indians of Canada*, vol. 1, 327.
20 Canada, Indian and Northern Affairs, *Indian Conditions, A Survey*, 3.
21 Bird, *Problems of Economic Development*, 73.
22 Daikey, *Alcohol and Indians of Ontario*, 115.

23 Johnson, *Native Children and the Child Welfare System*, 77.
24 Stymiest, *Ethnics and Indians*, 70.
25 Canada, Indian and Northern Affairs, Manitoba Region, *A Presentation to the Deputy Minister and the Assistant Deputy Minister*, 19, 20.
26 Dosman, *Indians, The Urban Dilemma*, chapter 3.
27 R.W. Dunning, "Some Problems of Reserve Indian Communities: A Case Study," 3–38.
28 Dunning, "Ethnic Relations," 117–22.
29 Lithman, *The Community Apart*.
30 Ibid., 82.
31 Ibid., 83.
32 Ibid., 85.
33 Ibid., 62.
34 Ibid., 63.
35 Stymeist, *Ethnics and Indians*.
36 Ibid., 71.
37 Ibid., 70.
38 Ibid., 79.
39 Ibid., 78.
40 Ibid., 78.
41 Ibid., 76.
42 Ibid., 75.
43 Shimpo and Williamson, *Socio-Cultural Disintegration Among the Fringe Saulteaux*.
44 Ibid., 7.
45 Ibid., 121.
46 Ibid., 254.
47 Dosman, *Indians, The Urban Dilemma*.
48 Krotz, *Urban Indians*, 101.
49 Clatworthy and Hull, *Native Economic Conditions in Regina and Saskatoon*, 52.
50 Ibid., 97, 56.
51 Krotz, *Urban Indians*, 93.

CHAPTER FOUR

1 Stevens, *A Review of Changes on the Manitoba Indian Reserves*, 23–34. Figures are for 1968 and the measure is retention – i.e., the percentage of pupils entering grade 1 retained at grade 8.
2 Canada, Indian and Northern Affairs, *Survey of Contemporary Indians*, vol. 2, 131.
3 Cardinal, *The Unjust Society*, 59.

4 Canada, Indian and Northern Affairs, Education and Social Development Branch, *Indian Education Paper (Phase I)*, Appendix C, 7.

5 National Indian Brotherhood, *Indian Control of Indian Education*, 1–3.

6 McEwen, *Community Development Services for Canadian Indian and Métis Communities*.

7 Canada, Indian and Northern Affairs, *Survey of Contemporary Indians*, vols. 1 and 2.

8 Federation of Saskatchewan Indians, "A Strategy to Increase Employment of Indian People," 8.

9 The figures for numbers on courses are from Canada Employment and Immigration Commission, *Report of the Task Force on Manpower Services to Native People*, while those on course costs (1973/74) were produced for the Nielsen Task Force and are available in Canada, Task Force on Program Review, "Improved Program Delivery," *A Study Team Report*, vol. entitled *Indians and Natives*.

10 The statistics are derived from the CEIC's "follow-up" survey, which provides estimates of the percentage of course completers employed three months after the course and again after twelve months. Employment and Immigration Canada, *Estimates, Part III – Expenditures Plan 1989–90*, 2–30.

We consider the so-called "skill-utilization rate," which is the percentage both employed and using the skill acquired. The basic data from which these rates are calculated are obtained from a mail survey – worth noting because mail surveys tend to have low response rates and a problem with "bias" (i.e., respondents' situations fail to represent those of non-respondents). In this particular case, the person who got a job could be seen as more likely to fill in government surveys and mail them back.

In the statistics cited, the skill-utilization rate for aboriginal people (in the higher-skill category) is 80 percent, very close to the 83 percent for all course takers. The lower rate of 62 percent for entry-level skills is also close to the general population. A skeptic will note that the statistics do not reveal the *number* of trainees represented. Thus, the 80 percent (higher skills) might represent 1,600 course completers, or only 16 – the percentage in itself is meaningless. Difficulties that aboriginal people have with the courses and the amount of higher-skill training done by employers suggest that the numbers are, in fact, rather low.

This same follow-up survey has been used for many years and seems an unsuitable vehicle for measuring what training courses are doing for aboriginal people.

11 Stan Fulham, personal communication to the author, October 1989.

12 Federation of Saskatchewan Indians, "A Strategy to Increase Employment of Indian People," 10.

13 Canada, Task Force on Program Review, *Report*, 113.

14 Alberta, Northern Alberta Development Council, *Socio-Economic Review of Northern Alberta*.

15 Canada Employment and Immigration Commission, *Report of the Task Force on Indian and Native Employment*.

16 Alberta, Northern Alberta Development Council, *Socio-Economic Review*, 213. *Inter alia*, the phrase is encountered in many sources.

17 Expenditure on make-work programs in 1977–78 is given in Canada, Indian and Northern Affairs, *Indian Conditions, A Survey*, 74, 75. The author was unable to get economic-development expenditures for the same year, but a rough measure can be had, using a straight-line interpolation between the two estimates from the Nielsen Task Force ($22 million in 1973–74 and $40 million in 1983–84), yielding $31 million; see Canada, Task Force on Program Review, "Improved Program Delivery," *A Study Team Report*, 52. Allowing for manpower courses – then, as now, part of the economic-development budget – would reduce the development element.

Expenditures from the Indian Economic Development Fund in 1977–78 were $3.1 million (Stevens, *A Review of Changes on the Manitoba Indian Reserves*, 64).

18 Canada, Task Force on Program Review, *Report*.

19 Canada, Task Force on Program Review, "Improved Program Delivery," *A Study Team Report*, 113.

20 Driben and Trudeau, *When Freedom is Lost*.

21 Canada, Indian and Northern Affairs, Program Evaluation, Alberta Region, *Developmental Application of Social Assistance Funds*.

22 Now Industry, Science and Technology Canada (ISTC).

23 Federation of Saskatchewan Indians, *A Plan for Economic Development*, 10.

24 Buckley, Kew, and Hawley, *The Indian and Métis in Northern Saskatchewan*.

25 Krotz, *Urban Indians*, 58.

26 Ibid., 62.

27 Bill Hanson, personal communication to the author.

28 Dosman, *Indians, The Urban Dilemma*, 126.

29 Krotz, *Urban Indians*, 147.

30 Based on the account by Waldram, *Modernization or Underdevelopment?*

31 Canada, Mackenzie Valley Pipeline Inquiry, *Northern Frontier, Northern Homeland*. The Berger Report.

32 Canada, Indian and Northern Affairs, Manitoba Region, "Backgrounder," *The Northern Flood Agreement*.

33 *Globe and Mail*, 12 March 1989.
34 *Globe and Mail*, 29 February 1990.
35 This section relies heavily on Weaver, *Making Canadian Indian Policy, The Hidden Agenda, 1968–70*. The reference to public criticism includes the Law Reform Commission, R.W. Dunning, some members of Parliament, the Indian-Eskimo Association, and the *Globe and Mail*.
36 Cardinal, in Rosensteil, ed., *Red and White*, 172.
37 Weaver, *Making Canadian Indian Policy*, 167.
38 Cardinal, *The Unjust Society*, 143.
39 Ibid., 153.
40 Fixico, *Termination and Relocation*.
41 Frideres, *Native Peoples in Canada*, 251.

CHAPTER FIVE

1 Johnson, *Native Children*, 110.
2 Island Lake Tribal Council, *Rural and Remote Energy Efficient Builders' Course*.
3 Author's interview with officers of Nova Corporation, October 1989.
4 *Alberta Native Business News*, Winter 1988–89, 4.
5 Census data in Canada, Indian Affairs and Northern Development, Corporate Policy, Research Branch, *An Overview of Registered Indian Conditions in Manitoba*, 75. Similarly, see *An Overview of Registered Indian Conditions in Saskatchewan*, and *An Overview of Registered Indian Conditions in Alberta*.
6 Canada, Indian and Northern Affairs, Education and Social Development Branch, "Student Enrolment in Federal (Provincial, Band-operated) High Schools, by Year, 1959–60 – 1987–88".
7 *Red Deer Advocate*, 4 January 1989.
8 *Winnipeg Free Press*, 7 February 1987.
9 *Saskatoon Star Phoenix*, 29 April 1987.
10 Canada, Task Force on Program Review, *Report*.
11 *Indian News*, January 1980. The three reports were: Canada, Indian and Northern Affairs, *Indian Conditions, A Survey*; National Indian Brotherhood, *Strategy for the Economic Development of Indian People*; and National Indian Brotherhood, *A Strategy for the Socio-Economic Development of Indian People: National Report*.
12 Canada, Task Force on Program Review, *Report*, 21.
13 Canada, Indian and Northern Affairs, *Estimates, Part III, 1986–87, 1989–90, 1991–92*. The estimates cover both current and capital accounts, the latter including loans and guarantees through the Indian Economic Development Account (Canada, Indian and Northern Affairs, *Estimates, 1987–88*, 2–12).

Only twenty-four percent of the economic-development dollar goes into the business program (figures for 1989–90) and the largest component consists of the Department's manpower courses.

14 Ibid.

15 The 1983–84 figure is from Canada, Task Force on Program Review, "Improved Program Delivery," *A Study Team Report*, 52, while the expenditure under the NEDP is taken from Canada, *Canadian Aboriginal Economic Development Strategy*, 20.

16 An expenditure breakdown covering "all federal programs directed to aboriginals" was published by the *Globe and Mail*, 13 November 1990:

	($ millions)
INAC – economic development	93
INAC – other programs	2,875
National Health and Welfare	550
Employment and Immigration	138
Industry, Science and Technology	79
All other departments	277
TOTAL:	4,012

The figures permit only a rough estimate for economic development. The INAC contribution is $66 million when its manpower courses are excluded; ISTC, the other department involved in the NEDP and its successor, is likely to have made non-development expenditures as well, but they cannot be measured. Taking the whole of the ISTC entry the two departments would have spent $145 million on economic development. This is less than the manpower courses ($165 million counting CEIC and INAC) and well below the $700 million that INAC spent on social assistance.

The Canadian Aboriginal Economic Development Strategy (see page 149) does increase the allocation for economic development, but apparently had not done so in time for these 1990 figures.

17 Canada, Task Force on Program Review, *Report*.

18 *Edmonton Journal*, 3 February 1984.

19 Canada, Task Force on Program Review, "Improved Program Delivery," *A Study Team Report*, 113.

20 Personal communication to the author, October 1989.

21 Figures supplied by Canada, Indian and Northern Affairs, Education and Social Development Branch, Indian and Inuit Affairs, January 1989.

22 "Urban Native Education Project," *Calgary Herald*, 27 March 1989.

23 *Winnipeg Free Press*, 14 October 1988.

24 Ibid.

25 Canada, House of Commons, *Indian Self-Government in Canada – Report*, 86.
26 Ibid., 87.
27 Braroe, *Indian and White*.
28 *Winnipeg Free Press*, September 1985.
29 *Calgary Herald*, 6 October 1989.
30 Kerry Hawkins (president and chief executive officer of Cargill), *Winnipeg Free Press*, 10 February 1987.
31 *Calgary Herald*, 6 December 1988.
32 *Ottawa Citizen*, 28 September 1988.
33 *Calgary Herald*, 4 February 1986.
34 Consultant Russel Banta, quoted in the *Calgary Herald*, 27 May 1986.
35 Canada, Indian and Northern Affairs, *Report of the Indian Oil and Gas Task Force*.
36 Figures from Urban Indian Association survey, Winnipeg, 1987, supplied by Stan Fulham.
37 *Saskatoon Star Phoenix*, 24 June 1987.
38 Clatworthy, *The Effect of Length of Urban Residence*, 41–2.
39 Stan Fulham, personal communication to the author.
40 *Calgary Herald*, 3 June 1988.
41 Jerry Arshinoff (principal of Plains Indian Cultural Survival School), personal communication to the author, winter 1991.
42 *Winnipeg Free Press*, 14 October 1988.
43 *Winnipeg Free Press*, 17 October 1988. Lloyd Axworthy states that the core-area initiative, designed as job training, became focused on capital improvements.
44 Canada, Indian Affairs and Northern Development, *Canadian Aboriginal Economic Development Strategy*.
45 Canada, Indian and Northern Affairs, *Estimates, Part III, 1991–92*. This source lists "Social Assistance," including associated services and management, at $710 million.
46 Federation of Saskatchewan Indians, *Plan for Economic Development*.
47 Courchene, "Problems and Possible Solutions," 179.
48 Thalassa Research Group, *The Economic Foundations of Indian Self-Government*, 46.
49 Canada, House of Commons, *Indian Self-Government in Canada – Report*, 41.
50 Assembly of First Nations staff officer, personal communication to the author, August 1989.
51 *Saskatoon Star Phoenix*, 22 April 1988.
52 Canada, House of Commons, *Indian Self-Government in Canada – Report*, 88.
53 Ibid., 90.

54 Cohen, "Business: Tribal Enterprise," *Atlantic Monthly*, October 1989.
55 Richard Scott Fulham, *Economic Strategy for Urban Indians*, chapter 2. Also, author's interview with the economic-development officer of the Dakota-Ojibwa Tribal Council, Winnipeg, October 1989.
56 Assembly of First Nations staff officer, personal communication to author.
57 Fulham, *Economic Strategy*, chapter 3.
58 McGregor, *Chief, The Fearless Vision of Billy Diamond*, 47.
59 Salisbury, *A Homeland for the Cree*, 47 ff.
60 McGregor, *Chief*, 41.
61 Ibid., 141.
62 Salisbury, *A Homeland for the Cree*, 98.

CHAPTER SIX

1 National Indian Brotherhood, "What's Wrong with the Economic Development Program?" 1.
2 Barber, "Indian Land Claims and Rights," a speech delivered at a 1978 symposium on Amerindians, sponsored by the Royal Society of Canada, 13.
3 Canada, Indian and Northern Affairs, Manitoba Region, *Presentation to the Deputy Minister and the Assistant Deputy Minister*, 16.
4 Quoted in Saskatchewan Indian Cultural College, *Treaty Six*.
5 Canada, Indian and Northern Affairs, *Canadian Aboriginal Economic Development Strategy Handbook*.
6 Ibid., I-17.
7 Ibid., I-1.
8 Canada, House of Commons, *Indian Self-Government in Canada – Report*, 82.
9 This brief section relies largely on two sources: Hawkes, *Negotiating Aboriginal Self-Government*, Background Paper No. 7; and Hawkes and Peters, *Issues in Entrenching Aboriginal Self-Government*.
10 Hawkes, *Negotiating Aboriginal Self-Government*, 10.
11 Hawkes and Peters, *Issues in Entrenching Aboriginal Self-Government*, 22.
12 Canada, House of Commons, *Indian Self-Government in Canada – Report*, 60.
13 Hawkes and Peters, *Issues*, 95.
14 Ibid., 96.
15 *Ottawa Citizen*, July 1990.
16 See note 16, chapter 5. The source did not provide full information and probably did not include the CAED funds which will strengthen the economic-development budget but within narrow limits.
17 *Winnipeg Free Press*, 18 December 1985.

18 John Beaver, *Indian News*, January 1981.
19 Murray Koffler, "Forward," in Humber, ed., *Canada's Native People*, vol. 2.
20 The Angus-Reid poll (October 1989), *Ottawa Citizen*, 3 January 1990.
21 Canada, Mackenzie Valley Pipeline Inquiry, *Northern Frontier, Northern Homeland*, vol. 1, 199.
22 Barber, "Indian Land Claims and Rights," 13.
23 Thalassa Research Associates, *The Economic Foundations of Indian Self-Government*, 55.
24 Canada, Indian and Northern Affairs, "Land Claims: Status Report."
25 Saskatchewan, Education, Community Education Branch, "The Pheasant's Rump and Ocean Man Scam," in *Native Studies – Student Resource Guide*, 361.
26 Barber, "Indian Land Claims and Rights," 13.
27 *Ottawa Citizen*, 17 September 1990.
28 John McMurtry, letter to the editor, *Ottawa Citizen*, September 1990.
29 Goldstick, *Wollaston, People Resisting Genocide*, 105, 106.
30 Ibid., 141.
31 Ibid., 77.
32 Douglas Cardinal, "How Indian Culture Can Heal White Society," *Ottawa Citizen*, 20 January 1990.
33 Ibid.
34 Ibid.

Bibliography

GOVERNMENT SOURCES

CANADA

Canada Employment and Immigration Commission. *Community-Based Development*. Technical Study no. 3 prepared for the Task Force on Labour Market Development by P.D. Brodhead, M. Decter, and K. Svenson. Ottawa: Canada Employment and Immigration Commission, 1981.

– *Estimates, Part III – Expenditure Plan*. Ottawa: Supply and Services Canada, 1989/90.

– *Issues Concerning the Role of Native Women in the Winnipeg Labour Market*. Technical study prepared for the Task Force on Labour Market Development by S.J. Clatworthy. Ottawa: Canada Employment and Immigration Commission, 1981.

– *Report of the Task Force on Indian and Native Employment*. Ottawa: Canada Employment and Immigration Commission, 1981.

– *Report of the Task Force on Manpower Services to Native People*. Ottawa: Manpower and Immigration, 1977.

Canadian Aboriginal Economic Development Strategy. Cat. no. C2 118/1989. Ottawa: Supply and Services Canada, 1989.

Department of Energy, Mines and Resources. *Energy Performance of On-Reserve Housing*. Ottawa: Supply and Services Canada, 1987.

Department of Indian and Northern Affairs. *The Canadian Aboriginal Economic Development Strategy Handbook for On-Reserve Services*. Ottawa: Indian and Northern Affairs Canada, 1990.

– Agriculture. *Interim Policy and Guidelines for Agriculture*. Ottawa: Indian and Northern Affairs Canada, 1974.

– Alberta Region. *Alberta Indian Agricultural Development Corporation Evaluation, Final Report*. Ottawa: Indian and Northern Affairs Canada, 1986.

– Alberta Region. Program Evaluation. *Developmental Application of Social Assistance Funds*. Edmonton: Indian and Northern Affairs Canada, 1979.

- Corporate Policy. Research Branch. *An Overview of the Educational Characteristics of Registered Indians in Canada*. Prepared by Jeremy Hull and the Working Margins Consulting Group. Winnipeg: Indian and Northern Affairs Canada, 1987.
- Corporate Policy. Research Branch. *An Overview of Registered Indian Conditions in Alberta*. Prepared by George K. Jarvis and Lithwick Rothman Schiff Associates. Winnipeg: Indian and Northern Affairs Canada, 1987.
- Corporate Policy. Research Branch. *An Overview of Registered Indian Conditions in Manitoba*. Prepared by Jeremy Hull and Lithwick Rothman Schiff Associates. Winnipeg: Indian and Northern Affairs Canada, 1987.
- Corporate Policy. Research Branch. *An Overview of Registered Indian Conditions in Saskatchewan*. Prepared by George K. Jarvis and Lithwick Rothman Schiff Associates. Winnipeg: Indian and Northern Affairs Canada, 1987.
- Education and Social Development Branch. *Indian Education Paper, Phase I*. Ottawa: Indian and Northern Affairs Canada, 1982.
- Education and Social Development Branch. "Student Enrolment in Federal (Provincial, Band-operated) High Schools, by Year, 1959–60, 1987–88." Ottawa: Indian and Northern Affairs Canada, 1989.
- *Estimates, Part III – Expenditure Plan, Indian and Inuit Affairs Program*. Ottawa: Supply and Services Canada, 1986–87, 1987–88, 1989–90, 1991–92.
- *Indian Conditions – A Survey*. Ottawa: Indian and Northern Affairs Canada, 1980.
- Indian Economic Development. *Report of the Task Force to the Deputy Minister*. Ottawa: Indian and Northern Affairs Canada, 1985.
- *Report of the Indian Oil and Gas Task Force*. Edmonton: Indian and Northern Affairs Canada, 1987.
- *Land Claims: Status Report*. Ottawa: Supply and Services Canada, 1985.
- Manitoba Region. *Manitoba Indian Agricultural Program, 1975–80*. Winnipeg: Indian and Northern Affairs Canada, 1982.
- Manitoba Region. *Indian Reserves, Community Profiles*. Winnipeg: Indian and Northern Affairs Canada, 1983. Rev. ed. 1990.
- Manitoba Region. "Backgrounder." *The Northern Flood Agreement*. Winnipeg: Indian and Northern Affairs Canada, 1984.
- Manitoba Region. *A Presentation to the Deputy Minister and the Assistant Deputy Minister*. Winnipeg: Indian and Northern Affairs Canada, 1980.
- Research Branch. *Indian Coverage in Canadian Daily Newspapers 1977: A Content Analisys*. Prepared by Heather Sim for the Policy Research Group, Indian and Northern Affairs Canada, Ottawa, 1978.
- Saskatchewan Region. *Saskatchewan Indian Agricultural Program, 1975–80*. Regina: Indian and Northern Affairs Canada, 1982.

- *Schedule of Indian Bands, Reserves and Settlements, Including Membership and Population, Location and Area.* Ottawa: Indian and Northern Affairs Canada, 1990.
- Statistics Branch. *Overview of Demographic/Social and Economic Conditions among Canada's Registered Indian Population.* Prepared by Andrew J. Siggner. Ottawa: Indian and Northern Affairs Canada, 1979.
- Statistics Branch. *Overview of Demographic/Social and Economic Conditions among Canada's Registered Indian Population, Canada and Saskatchewan.* Prepared by Andrew J. Siggner. Ottawa: Indian and Northern Affairs Canada, 1980.
- Statistics Branch. *Overview of Demographic/Social and Economic Conditions among Canada's Registered Indian Population, Manitoba.* Prepared by Andrew J. Siggner. Ottawa: Indian and Northern Affairs Canada, 1983.
- Statistics Branch. *Regional Comparison of Data on Canada's Registered Indian Population.* Prepared by Andrew J. Siggner. Ottawa: Indian and Northern Affairs Canada, 1982.
- *A Survey of the Contemporary Indians of Canada – A Report on the Economic, Political and Education Needs and Policies.* 2 vols. The Hawthorne Report. Ottawa: Queen's Printer, 1967.
Department of Industry, Science and Technology. *Consultation Paper on DRIE Native Economic Programs.* Ottawa: Industry, Science and Technology Canada, July 1987.
House of Commons. Special Committee on Indian Self-Government. *Indian Self-Government in Canada – Report of the Special Committee on Indian Self-Government* (the Penner Report). Ottawa: Supply and Services Canada, 1983.
Mackenzie Valley Pipeline Inquiry. *Northern Frontier, Northern Homeland – The Report of the Mackenzie Valley Pipeline Inquiry.* Vol. 1. The Berger Report. Ottawa: Supply and Services Canada, 1977.
Royal Commission on Equality in Employment. *Equality in Employment – A Royal Commission Report, Research Studies.* Ottawa: Supply and Services Canada, 1985.
Statistics Canada. *Social Security, National Programs, Other Programs.* Ottawa: Statistics Canada, 1983.
- "The Socio-Demographic Conditions of Registered Indians." Paper by Andrew J. Siggner in *Canadian Social Trends* (Winter 1989).
Task Force on Program Review. "Improved Program Delivery." In *A Study Team Report to the Task Force on Program Review.* Vol. entitled *Indians and Natives.* Ottawa: Supply and Services Canada, 1985.
- *Report of the Task Force on Program Review.* The Nielsen Report. Ottawa: Supply and Services Canada, 1985.

ALBERTA
Department of Agriculture. *Alberta Indian Agricultural Development Corpo-*

ration Evaluation – Final Report. Edmonton: Government of Alberta, 1986.

Northern Alberta Development Council. *Profiles of Regions and Small Communities in Northern Alberta*. Edmonton: Northern Alberta Development Council, 1983.

– *Socio-Economic Overview of Northern Alberta*. Prepared by Co-West Associates. Edmonton: Northern Alberta Development Council, 1981.

MANITOBA

Department of Agriculture and Immigration. *The People of Indian Ancestry in Manitoba*. Main Report and two Appendices, *The People of Indian Ancestry in Greater Winnipeg* and *The People of Indian Ancestry in Rural Manitoba*. Prepared by Jean Lagassé. Winnipeg: Agriculture and Immigration, 1959.

Committee on Manitoba's Economic Future. *Manitoba, 1962–1975 – A Report to the Government of Manitoba*. Winnipeg: Committee on Manitoba's Economic Future, 1963.

Department of Culture, Heritage and Recreation. Historic Resources Branch. *Chief Pequis*. Winnipeg: Culture, Heritage and Recreation, 1984.

SASKATCHEWAN

Saskatchewan Report. Natives in Business. Regina: October 1989.

Education. Community Education Branch. *Native Studies – Student Resource Guide*. Regina: Education, 1990.

Human Resources, Labour and Employment. *The Native Career Development Program*. Regina: Human Resources, Labour and Employment, n.d.

– *New Careers*. Regina: Human Resources, Labour and Employment, n.d.

BOOKS AND ARTICLES

Ahenakew, Edward. *Voices of the Plains Cree*. Toronto: McClelland and Stewart Ltd, 1973.

Andrist, Ralph K. *The Long Death, the Last Days of the Plains Indians*. New York: Collier Books, 1969.

Armstrong, Robin. "Factors of Indian Economic Development on-Reserve: An Initial Analysis." *Native Issues*. Vol. 1, *Native Socio-Economic Development in Canada: Adaptation, Accessibility and Opportunity*. Winnipeg: University of Winnipeg, Institute of Urban Studies, 1989.

Barbeau, Marius. *Indian Days on the Western Prairies*. Ottawa: National Museum of Canada, 1960.

Barber, L.I. "Indian Land Claims and Rights." Speech delivered at a symposium on Amerindians, sponsored by the Royal Society of Canada, 1978.

Barman, Jean, Yvonne Hébert, and Don McCaskill. "The Legacy of the Past – An Overview." *Indian Education in Canada*. Vol. 1, *The Legacy*. Nakoda

Institute Occasional Paper no. 2. Vancouver: University of British Columbia Press, 1986.

Bear, Paulette. "A History of Band No. 99." Paper produced for the University of Saskatchewan, College of Education, Department of Indian and Northern Education, 1974.

Berger, Thomas R. *Village Journey – The Report of the Alaska Native Review Commission*. New York: Hill and Wang, 1985.

Bird, Bradley. *Problems of Economic Development on Manitoba's Indian Reserves*. Winnipeg: Social Planning Council of Winnipeg, 1983.

Blanchard, David S. *Kahnewake, A Historical Sketch*. Kanawake, Québec: Kanien'kehaka Raotitiohkwa Press, 1980.

Bone, Robert. "Economic Development and Country Food." *Native Issues*. Vol. 1, *Native Socio-Economic Development in Canada: Adaptation, Accessibility and Opportunity*. Winnipeg: University of Winnipeg, Institute of Urban Studies, 1989.

Bone, Robert M., and Milford B. Green. "Accessibility and Development of Métis Communities in Northern Saskatchewan." *Canadian Geographer* 30, no. 1 (1986): 66–71.

Bone, Robert, Earl Shannon, and Stewart Raby. *The Chipewyan of the Stony Rapids Region*. Saskatoon: University of Saskatchewan, Institute for Northern Studies, 1973.

Brant and Brant Native Development Consultants. *Indian Band Economic Development Potential and Its Implications for Indian Self-Government*. A report to Indian and Northern Affairs Canada. Deseronto, Ontario: Brant and Brant Native Development Consultants, April 1985.

Braroe, Nils. *Indian and White, Self-Image and Interaction in a Canadian Plains Community*. California: Stanford University Press, 1975.

Breton, Raymond, and Gail Grant, eds. *The Dynamics of Government Programs for Urban Indians in the Prairie Provinces*. Montreal: Institute for Research on Public Policy, 1984.

Buckley, Helen, and Sheriden Campbell. *Farming at Mistawasis*. Saskatoon: University of Saskatchewan, Centre for Community Studies, 1963.

Buckley, Helen, M. Kew, and J. Hawley. *The Indian and Métis in Northern Saskatchewan*. Saskatoon: Centre for Community Studies, University of Saskatchewan, 1963.

Canadian Council for Native Business. *Annual Report*. Toronto: Canadian Council for Native Business, 1988.

Canadian Welfare Council. *Indian Residential Schools – A Report for DIAND* Ottawa: Canadian Welfare Council, 1967.

Cardinal, Harold. *The Unjust Society: The Tragedy of Canada's Indians*. Edmonton: M.G. Hurtig, 1967.

Carter, Sarah. *Lost Harvests, Prairie Indian Reserve Farmers and Government Policy*. Montreal-Kingston: McGill-Queen's University Press, 1990.

Chance, Norman A. "Strategies of Developmental Change Among the Cree." In *Conflict in Culture: Problems of Developmental Change Among the Cree*, edited by Norman A. Chance. Ottawa: Université Saint Paul, Centre canadien de recherches en anthropologie, 1969.

Clatworthy, S.J. *The Effect of Length of Urban Residence on Native Labour Market Behaviour*. Winnipeg: University of Winnipeg, Institute of Urban Studies, 1982.

Clatworthy, S.J., and J.P. Gunn. *Economic Circumstances of Native People in Selected Metropolitan Centres in Western Canada*. Winnipeg: University of Winnipeg, Institute of Urban Studies, 1981.

Clatworthy, S.J., and J. Hull. *Native Economic Conditions in Regina and Saskatoon*. Winnipeg: University of Winnipeg, Institute of Urban Studies, 1983.

Cohen, David. "Business: Tribal Enterprise." *Atlantic Monthly*, October 1989.

Courchene, David. "Problems and Possible Solutions." In *Indians without Tipis: A Resource Book by Indians and Métis*, edited by D. Bruce Sealey and Verna J. Kirkness. Winnipeg: William Clare, 1973.

Cuthand, Stan. "The Native People of the Prairie Provinces in the 1920s and '30s." In *One Century Later*, edited by Ian Getty and Donald B. Smith. Vancouver: University of British Columbia Press, 1978.

Daikey, R. *Alcohol and Indians of Ontario*. Toronto: Alcohol and Drug Addiction Foundation, 1962.

Danziger, Edmund J., Jr. *The Chippewas of Lake Superior*. Norman, Oklahoma: University of Oklahoma Press, 1978.

Dempsey, Hugh. *Crowfoot, Chief of the Blackfeet*. Edmonton: Hurtig Publishers, 1972.

– "One Hundred Years of Treaty Seven." In *One Century Later*, edited by Ian Getty and Donald B. Smith. Vancouver: University of British Columbia Press, 1978.

Deprez, Paul. *Education and Economic Development: The Case of Indian Reserves in Canada*. Winnipeg: University of Manitoba, Centre for Settlement Studies, 1973.

Deprez, Paul, and Glen Sigurdson. *The Economic Status of the Canadian Indian: A Re-Examination*. Winnipeg: University of Manitoba, Centre for Settlement Studies, 1969.

Dosman, Edgar J. *Indians: The Urban Dilemma*. Toronto: McClelland and Stewart Ltd, 1972.

Driben, Paul, and Robert Trudeau. *When Freedom is Lost: The Dark Side of the Relationship between the Government and the Fort Hope Band*. Toronto: University of Toronto Press, 1983.

Dunning, R.W. "Ethnic Relations and the Marginal Man in Canada." *Human Organization* 18, no. 3 (1959): 117–22.

- *Social and Economic Change among the Northern Ojibwa*. Toronto: University of Toronto Press, 1959.
- "Some Aspects of Governmental Indian Policy and Administration." *Anthropologica* 4 (1962).
- "Some Problems of Reserve Indian Communities: A Case Study." *Anthropologica* N.S. 6, no. 1 (1964): 3–38.

Elias, Peter Douglas. *The Dakota of the Canadian Northwest: Lessons for Survival*. Winnipeg: University of Manitoba Press, 1988.

Federation of Saskatchewan Indians. *A Plan for Economic Development*. Regina: Federation of Saskatchewan Indians, 1970.

- *A Strategy to Increase Employment of Indian People*. Regina: Federation of Saskatchewan Indians, 1972.

Fixico, Donald Lee. *Termination and Relocation – Federal Indian Policy, 1945–1960*. Albuquerque, New Mexico: University of New Mexico Press, 1986.

Foot, David K. *Canada's Population Outlook*. Toronto: James Lorimer and Co. Publishers, in association with the Canadian Institute for Economic Policy, 1982.

Freyman, Andrew J., and Graham T. Armstrong. *The Role of the Indian and Eskimo in the Canadian Mining Industry*. Toronto: Canadian Institute of Mining and Metallurgy Bulletin, June 1969.

Frideres, James S. *Native Peoples in Canada: Contemporary Conflicts*. Scarborough: Prentice-Hall Canada, 1988.

Friesen, John. "Expansion of Settlement in Manitoba, 1870–1900." In *Historical Essays on the Prairie Provinces*, edited by Donald Swainson. Toronto: McClelland and Stewart Ltd, 1970.

Fulham, Richard Scott. *Economic Strategy for Urban Indians*. Winnipeg: Urban Indian Association, 1987.

Fulham, Stanley A. *In Search of a Future, A Submission on the Migration of Native People*. Winnipeg: Manitoba Métis Federation Press, 1971. Rev. ed. 1981.

Getty, Ian, and Donald B. Smith, eds. *One Century Later*. Vancouver: University of British Columbia Press, 1978.

Goldfrank, Ester S. *Changing Configurations in the Organization of a Blackfoot Tribe During the Reserve Period (The Blood of Alberta*, Canada). Seattle, Washington: University of Washington Press, 1945.

Goldstick, Miles. *Wollaston – People Resisting Genocide*. Montreal–New York: Black Rose Books, 1987.

Goodwill, Jean, and Norma Sluman. *John Tootoosis*. Winnipeg: Pemmican Publishers, 1984.

Grant, Gail. *The Concrete Reserve: Corporate Programs for Indians in the Urban Work Place*. Montreal: Institute for Research on Public Policy, 1983.

Grant, John Webster. *Moon of Wintertime*. Toronto: University of Toronto Press, 1984.

Hanks, Lucien M., Jr, and Jane Richardson Hanks. *Tribe under Trust, A Study of the Blackfoot Reserve in Alberta*. Toronto: University of Toronto Press, 1950.

Hanson, Bill. *Dual Strategies, Dual Realities: The Future Paths of the Aboriginal People's Development, A Programmer's Handbook*. Saskatoon: Bill Hanson, Consultant, 1985.

Hawkes, David C. *Negotiating Aboriginal Self-Government – Developments Surrounding the 1985 First Ministers Conference*. Background Paper No. 7. Kingston: Queen's University, Institute of Intergovernmental Relations, 1985.

Hawkes, David, and Evelyn Peters. *Issues in Entrenching Aboriginal Self-Government*. Kingston: Queen's University, Institute for Intergovernmental Relations, 1987.

Hlady, W.M. *A Community Development Project Amongst the Churchill Band at Churchill, Manitoba, September 1959–March 1960*. Saskatoon: N.p., December 1960.

Humber, Charles J., ed. *Canada's Native Peoples*. Canada Heirloom Series, vol. 2. Mississauga: Heirloom Publishing Company, 1988.

Hurt, R. Douglas. *Indian Agriculture in America – Prehistory to the Present*. Laurence, Kansas: University Press of Kansas, 1987.

Indian-Corporate-Government Conference. *Indian Development for the 80s: A New Partnership*. Proceedings of the Indian-Corporate-Government Conference held in Banff, Alberta, 25–27 September 1979.

Island Lake Tribal Council. *Island Lake*. Winnipeg: Mikisiw Asiniy Printers, 1989.

– *Rural and Remote Energy Efficient Builders' Course*. Winnipeg: N.p., n.d.

Jackson, James A. *The Centennial History of Manitoba*. Toronto: McClelland and Stewart Ltd, 1970.

Johnson, Patrick. *Native Children and the Child Welfare System*. Toronto: James Lorimer and Co., in association with the Canadian Council on Social Development, 1983.

Kehoe, Alice B. "The Dakotas in Saskatchewan." In *The Modern Sioux*, edited by Ethel Nurge. Lincoln, Nebraska: University of Nebraska Press, 1970.

Kennedy, Dan (Ochankugahe). *Recollections of an Assiniboine Chief*. Toronto: McClelland and Stewart Ltd, 1972.

Krotz, Larry. *Urban Indians: The Strangers in Canada's Cities*. Edmonton: Hurtig Publishers, 1980.

Lithman, Yngve Georg. *The Community Apart*. Winnipeg: University of Manitoba Press, 1984.

– *The Practice of Underdevelopment and the Theory of Development: The Canadian*

Indian Case. Stockholm Studies in Social Anthropology. Stockholm: University of Stockholm, 1982.

McArthur, Douglas. "The New Economic Development Institutions." Native Issues. Vol. 2, *Native Socio-Economic Development in Canada: Adaptation, Accessibility and Opportunity*. Winnipeg: University of Winnipeg, Institute of Urban Studies, 1989.

McCourt, Edward. *Remember Butler*. London: Routledge and Kegan Paul, 1967.

– *Saskatchewan*. Toronto: MacMillan, 1968.

McEwen, E.R. *Community Development Services for Canadian Indian and Métis Communities*. Toronto: Indian-Eskimo Association of Canada, 1968.

MacEwan, J.W. Grant. *Portraits from the Plains*. Toronto: McGraw-Hill Co. of Canada, 1971.

McGregor, Roy. *Chief – The Fearless Vision of Billy Diamond*. Markham, Ontario: Viking Press, 1989.

Malone, Marc. *Financing Aboriginal Self-Government in Canada*. Kingston, Ontario: Queen's University, Institute of Intergovernmental Relations, 1986.

Manitoba Indian Brotherhood. *Treaty Days (Centennial Commemorations Historical Pageant)*. Winnipeg: Manitoba Indian Brotherhood 1971.

Manuel, George. *The Fourth World, An Indian Reality*. New York: The Free Press and MacMillan, 1974.

Meyer, David. *The Red Earth Crees, 1860–1960*. Mercury Series. Ottawa: National Museum of Man, 1985.

Miller, Harry B. *These Too Were Pioneers – The Story of the Key Indian Reserve and the Centennial of the Church, 1884–1984*. Melville, Saskatchewan: Seniors Consultant Service, 1984.

Milloy, John S. *The Plains Cree: Diplomacy and War, 1790 to 1870*. Winnipeg: University of Manitoba Press, 1988.

Morris, The Honourable Alexander, P.C. *The Treaties with the Indians of Manitoba, the Northwest Territories and Keewatin in the Dominion of Canada*. 1880. Reprint. Toronto: Belfords Clarke and Co., Publishers, 1971.

National Indian Brotherhood. *Indian Control of Indian Education*. Ottawa: National Indian Brotherhood, 1972.

– *Strategy for the Economic Development of Indian People*. Ottawa: National Indian Brotherhood, 1977.

– *A Strategy for the Socio-Economic Development of Indian People. National Report*. Ottawa: National Indian Brotherhood, 1977.

Nurge, Ethel, ed. *The Modern Sioux*. Lincoln, Nebraska: University of Nebraska Press, 1970.

Peters, Evelyn. *Native Households in Winnipeg: Strategies of Co-Residence and Financial Support*. Winnipeg: University of Winnipeg, Institute of Urban Studies, 1971.

Ponting, J. Rick, and Rodger Gibbons. *Out of Irrelevance – A Socio-Political Introduction to Indian Affairs in Canada*. Toronto: Butterworth's, 1980.

Price, John A. *Indians of Canada – Cultural Dynamics*. Scarborough: Prentice-Hall of Canada, 1979.

Price, Richard, ed. *The Spirit of the Alberta Treaties*. Toronto: Institute for Research on Public Policy, 1979.

Robertson, Heather. *Reservations are for Indians*. Toronto: James Lewis and Samuel, 1970.

Rosensteil, Annette, ed. *Red and White, Indian Views of the White Man, 1492–1982*. New York: Universe Books, 1983.

Salisbury, Richard. *A Homeland for the Cree: Regional Development in James Bay, 1971–81*. Montreal: McGill-Queen's University Press, 1986.

Samek, Hana. *The Blackfoot Confederacy, 1880–1920: A Comparative Study of Canadian and US Indian Policy*. Albuquerque, New Mexico: University of New Mexico Press, 1987.

Saskatchewan Indian Cultural College. *Treaty Six*. Saskatoon: Saskatchewan Indian Cultural College, n.d.

Sealey, D. Bruce. "Indians of Canada: A Historical Sketch." In *Indians without Tipis: A Resource Book by Indians and Métis*, edited by D. Bruce Sealey and Verna J. Kirkness. Winnipeg: William Clare, 1973.

Sealey, D. Bruce, and Verna J. Kirkness, eds. *Indians without Tipis: A Resource Book by Indians and Métis*. Winnipeg: William Clare, 1973.

Sharzer, Stephen. "Native People: Some Issues." In *Equality in Employment – A Royal Commission Report, Research Studies*. The Royal Commission on Equality in Employment (Judge Rosalie Abella, Commissioner). Ottawa: Supply and Services Canada, 1985.

Shimpo, Mitsuru, and Robert Williamson. *Socio-Cultural Disintegration among the Fringe Saulteaux*. Saskatoon, Saskatchewan: University of Saskatchewan, Centre for Community Studies, 1965.

Sindell, Peter S. "Some Discontinuities in the Enculturation of Mistassini Cree Children." In *Conflict in Culture*, edited by Norman A. Chance. Ottawa: Université Saint Paul, Centre Canadien de Recherches en Anthropologie, 1969.

Spearman, L.B. *Comparison of Social Welfare Needs with Service Network in Northern Manitoba Communities*. Winnipeg: University of Manitoba, Centre for Settlement Studies, 1975.

Stanley, George F.G. "Displaced Red Men: The Sioux in Canada." In *One Century Later*, edited by Ian Getty and Donald B. Smith. Vancouver: University of British Columbia Press, 1978.

Stevens, Harvey. *A Review of Changes on the Manitoba Indian Reserves*. Winnipeg: Social Planning Council, 1982.

Stevens, William C. *Factors Determining Success and/or Failure for Economic Development Projects on Indian Reservations in Canada*. Cambridge, Massachusetts: Harvard University, John F. Kennedy School of Government, Harvard Project on American Indian Economic Development, 1988.

Stocken, H.W.G. *Among the Blackfoot and Sarcee*. Calgary, Alberta: Glenbow Institute, 1976.

Stymiest, David. *Ethnics and Indians, Social Relations in a Northwestern Ontario Town*. Toronto: Peter Martin and Associates, 1975.

Surtees, Robert. *The Original People*, Toronto: Holt, Rinehard and Winston of Canada, 1972.

Swainson, Donald, ed. *Historical Essays on the Prairie Provinces*. Toronto: McClelland and Stewart Ltd, 1970.

Tanner, Adrian, ed. *The Politics of Indianness – Case Studies of Native Ethnopolitics in Canada*. St. John's, Newfoundland: Memorial University of Newfoundland, Institute of Social and Economic Research, 1983.

Taylor, John Leonard. "Two Views on the Meaning of Treaties Six and Seven." In *The Spirit of the Alberta Treaties*, edited by Richard Price. Toronto: Institute for Research on Public Policy, 1979.

Thalassa Research Associates. *The Economic Foundations of Indian Self-Government – A Report Prepared for the House of Commons Special Committee on Indian Self-Government*. Victoria: Thalassa Research Associates: 1983.

Thompson, Chief Albert Edward. *Chief Pequis and his Descendents*. Winnipeg: Pequis Publishers, 1973.

Titley, E. Brian. *A Narrow Vision – Duncan Campbell Scott and the Administration of Indian Affairs in Canada*. Vancouver: University of British Columbia Press, 1986.

Waldram, James B. *Modernization or Underdevelopment? The Grand Rapids Hydro Project and the People of Easterville, Manitoba*. Paper prepared for the Kanata Institute's Economic Development Conference, Winnipeg, 25–29 May 1981.

Walsh, Gerald. *Indians in Transition*. Toronto: McClelland and Stewart Ltd, 1971.

Weaver, Sally M. *Making Canadian Indian Policy – The Hidden Agenda, 1968–70*. Toronto: University of Toronto Press, 1981.

Western Association of Sociology and Anthropology. *Canadian Confrontations*. Banff: Western Association of Sociology and Anthropology, 1969.

Index

agents, 38, 40, 43, 53, 55, 57, 63, 71; phased out (1960s), 101
Ahenakew, Rev. Edward, 58
Alaska pipeline, 117, 128
Alberta, 3–27 *passim*; nineteenth century, 37–8, 41–2, 47; 1960s, 1970s, 69, 77, 79, 100, 108–9; 1980s, 127ff, 138–40, 155–6, 172. *See also* oil and gas revenues
Alberta Human Rights Council, 142
Alexander. *See* bands/reserves
Algonkian nations, 59
apartheid, 233. *See also* South Africa
Archibald, Lieutenant Governor, 32
Argyle High School (Winnipeg), 146
Arshinoff, Jerry, 146–8
Assembly of First Nations (AFN), 152, 153–4, 155, 168
assimilation, 6, 43, 60, 121
Assiniboine. *See* First Nations
Athabasca Native Development Corporation, 129

Athabaska River, 174

Badger, Chief, 36
bands/reserves (unless specified otherwise, the names are the same):
– Alberta: Alexander, 133; Bigstone Cree (Wabasca) 138; Blackfoot, 28–30, 34, 37–8, 45, 47, 50, 61ff, 127; Blood, 12, 28, 61, 63, 127, 131; Fort Chipewyan, 174; Kehewin, 143; Lubicon, 172; Piegan, 17–18, 28, 62–3, 127; Saddle Lake, 38, 127; Sampson, 130; Sarcee, 127, 130; Sawridge, 12; Stoney, 30, 99, 130
– Manitoba: Buffalo Point, 12; Chemawawin, 117–18, 121; Crane River, 130–1; Cross Lake, 118ff; Fairford, 37, 70, 72; Fort Alexander, 37; God's Lake, 14; God's River, 14, 155; Island Lake (three reserves: Garden Hill, St Theresa Point, Wasagamack), 14, 20–1, 127; Mathias Columb (Pukatawagen Reserve), 4, 134, 155; Nelson House (South Indian Lake Reserve), 118ff; Norway House, 18–19, 20, 21, 45, 49, 118ff; Oak River (Lake), 54; Oxford House, 130–1; Peguis, 15–16, 37; Red Sucker Lake, 14; Roseau River, 37; Shamattawa, 14; Split Lake, 118ff; The Pas, 70, 73, 131, 140; York Factory (York Landing) 118ff
– Saskatchewan: Coté, 56, 90–3; Cowessess, 52; Day Star, 52; James Smith, 134; John Smith (Muskoday Reserve), 16–17, 22, 51; Key, 38; Lac La Ronge, 130; Mistawasis, 57, 67ff; Muskeg Lake, 131; Pasqua, 51; Piapot, 9; Poundmaker, 53, 57; Red Earth, 38
– Eastern Canada: Barrière Lake, 173; Kahnewake, 60, 83–7, 98; White Dog and Grassy Narrows, 108. *See also* Reserves.
bands/tribal councils, development corporations: general reference, 10, 19–20, 22, 154; band-administered programs, 25,

101, 126–8, 129, 131, 133–4, 139, 140–1, 152–3, 155, 160–1; bands in business, 16, 20, 70, 130–1, 155
Barber, Lloyd I., 163, 171, 172
Barrière Lake. *See* bands/ reserves
Bear, Paulette, 17
Beaver, John, 169
Berger, Thomas, 117, 170ff
Big Bear, Chief, 67
Big Child, Chief, 34
Bird, Bradley, 80
Blackfoot (and Blackfoot Confederacy). *See* bands/reserves, First Nations
Blood. *See* bands/reserves, First Nations
Blue Quills Native Education Centre, 100; residential school, 47
Bow River, 31, 37
Brandon, 144
Brant, Joseph, 59
Brass brothers, 38
Brochet, 21
Brocket, 17
Buffalo Point. *See* bands/ reserves
Butler, Colonel R.A., 41–2, 60, 174–5

Calgary, 127, 130, 146
Canada Employment and Immigration Commission (CEIC) 104, 139, 147, 164. *See also* Manpower courses, Manpower offices, Manpower policy
Canadian Aboriginal Economic Development (CAED) Strategy, 149, 150, 156, 164, 167; *CAED Handbook*, 164
Canadian Council for Native Business, 132, 154, 169–70

Canadian Executive Service Overseas (CESO), 137ff
Canadian Jobs Strategy, 164
Canadian National (CN), 89
Canadian Pacific Railway (CPR), 38–9, 42
Cardinal, Douglas (architect), 174, 175
Cardinal, Harold, 32, 99, 123. *See also* Indian Association of Alberta
Carter, Sarah, 53, 54
Central Mortgage and Housing Corporation (CMHC), 9
Chemawawin. *See* bands/ reserves
child-care services, 79–80, 127
Chiniki restaurant, 130, 143
Chipewyan. *See* First Nations
Chippewa, 33
Churchill, 4, 70
Church Missionary Society, 45
Cigar Lake, 174
cities, the Indian experience, 93–6, 113–16, 144–9, 156–8. *See also* Indian and Northern Affairs Canada, Neeginan, New directions (urban strategies), Regina, Saskatoon, Winnipeg
"civilizing," 25, 43–4, 53
claims. *See* land and other claims, settlement of claims
Columbus, Christopher, 5
Committee on Manitoba's Economic Future (COMEF), 74
community development (CD), 102–3
Confederation, 3, 34, 47, 59

conflict of interest: examples, 116–20; analysis, 120–1, 163, 165
constitutional negotiations, 165–6, 170
cooperatives, 102, 111
cost: estimate for mid–1980s, 135; for 1990, 189n.16; Indian and Northern Affairs only, 135–7, 153
Coté. *See* bands/reserves
Courchene, David, 24, 150
Cowessess. *See* bands/reserves
Crane River. *See* bands/ reserves
Cree Regional Authority, 160ff
Crees. *See* bands/reserves, First Nations
Cross Lake. *See* bands/reserves
Crowfoot, Chief, 34–6, 38, 46, 61

Dakota (Sioux). *See* First Nations
Day Star. *See* bands/reserves
Dempsey, Hugh, 62, 63
Dene. *See* First Nations
Department of Indian Affairs. *See* Indian and Northern Affairs Canada (INAC)
dependency, 8, 10, 23–4, 25, 27, 43–4, 55, 57, 63, 77–8, 82, 116, 135, 138, 140–1, 161, 163, 167
Diamond, Chief Billy, 159, 167
Dion, Chief Joe, 143–4
Dosman, Edgar, 93, 95, 115, 145
Dunning, R.W., 82, 185n.35

Easterville, 118
economic development. *See* government policy, reserves (economy)

education: Indian philosophy of, 100–1; performance measures, 133, 182n.1; relationship to economic policy, 112–13, 139–40; results of low education, 24; in settlement days, 43–4, 47–51, 56; tax burden associated with dropout, 148; in twentieth century, 8–10, 18–19, 61, 69, 71, 83, 85–6, 89, 96, 97–101, 133, 140, 145–7. *See also* Plains Indian Cultural Survival School, residential schools

Emanuel College, 46

employment, 7, 19, 23, 72–4, 76, 84–5, 88, 97, 103, 126, 128–9, 131–2

Evans, James, 45, 49

exclusion, 3, 6, 10–12, 22–3, 26, 42, 72, 81, 83, 86–7; analysis, 89–90, 92–3, 98, 112–13, 142

Fairford. *See* bands/reserves

Family Allowance, 71, 72, 77, 98

farming, 16–17, 22, 26; 1870s to World War II, 39, 45, 51–8, 61–6; 1950s and subsequently, 67–9, 71, 101; Indian organizations/ provincial help, 101–2, 132; US farm policy, 57. *See also* land leasing

Federation of Saskatchewan Indians (FSI), 104, 106, 110, 133, 150

First Ministers Conference, 166ff

First Nations, 4, 151ff, 166
– Assiniboine (Nakota), 4, 28–30
– Blackfoot (Siksaka), 4, 28–30, 34, 37–8, 45, 47, 61ff, 127; Blackfoot Confederacy (Blackfoot, Blood, Piegan), 17, 28–30, 61
– Blood (Kainai), 4, 28, 61, 63, 127
– Chipewyan, 4, 28, 71, 72, 174
– Crees, 4, 14, 17, 19, 21; early history through nineteenth century, 28–31, 33–4, 38–9, 45–6, 49, 62; 1950s to 1970s, 67, 71, 117; James Bay, 38, 48, 126, 158–61
– Dakota (Sioux), 4; nineteenth century 28, 31, 52–5, 63; 1950s, 70; 1980s, 127, 154, 157
– Dene, 169ff
– Inuit, 102, 159, 169
– Mohawk, 59, 167
– Ojibwa, 4, 14; in Ontario, 30, 33, 36, 43
– Piegan, 4, 17–18, 28, 62–3, 127
– Sarcee, 4, 127, 130
– Saulteaux, 4, nineteenth century, 30, 37, 63; since 1960, 83ff, 90ff, 127, 154

First Nations Confederacy, 127

fishing. *See* trapping/fishing

Fort Alexander. *See* bands/reserves

Fort Carleton, 55, 67

Fort Chipewyan. *See* bands/reserves

Fort Edmonton, 33

Fort Garry, 16

Fort George, 159

Fort Pitt, 55

Fort Qu'Appelle, 38, 52

Frideres, James S., 125, 177n.4

Fulham, Stan, 73, 105, 146

fur trade, 28–9, 59, 71–2, 112–13

God's Lake. *See* bands/reserves

God's River. *See* bands/reserves

Goodwill, Jean, and Norma Sluman, 57

government/bureaucracy: seen as the problem, 121, 153, 163–5, 166–7

government economic programs, 101, 103–10, 121–2, 131, 163; percent of budget, 135–6; some reasons for failure, 136–40. *See also* Canadian Aboriginal Economic Development Strategy, Indian Economic Development Fund, Native Economic Development Program

government policy, 6, 39, 42–5, 50, 61, 96–7, 103–4, 113, 121–2; economic, 101–10, 135–7, 167; education, 97–101; policy statement, 125; self-government, 152; urban, 114–16, 121–2. *See also* Indian and Northern Affairs Canada

Grand Council of the Crees of Quebec, 159

Grant, John, 45, 46

Grassy Narrows. *See* bands/reserves

Hanks, Lucien and Jane, 64, 65, 66

Hanson, Bill, 115

Harper, Elijah, 14

Hawthorne, H.B., 78

Hawthorne Report, 15, 74, 78ff, 103ff, 111, 122ff, 133, 136

Head-Smashed-In Buffalo Jump and Interpretive Centre, 18

Health and Welfare Canada, 152

health services, 6, 8–9, 75–6, 110–11, 152

housing, 8–10, 13, 19–20, 74–5, 77–8, 101, 114, 127–8, 161, 168. *See also* Neeginan
Hudson Bay, 28, 59, 83
Hudson's Bay Company, 28–9, 33, 38, 52, 59
Hurt, Douglas, 57
hydro projects, northern Manitoba, 70, 73–4, 97, 116–21
Hydro Quebec, 158

Ile à la Crosse, 45, 111
immigrant experience, comparisons with Indian, 3, 113
Income Supplement Plan (ISP) at James Bay, 160
Indian Act, 56, 122ff, 177n.4
Indian agents. *See* agents
Indian and Northern Affairs Canada (INAC): nineteenth century, 12, 43–5, 51–7, 61–5; consequences of these policies, 23–5; in the 1920s, 57–8; 1950s to 1970s, 67–70, 74, 77–8, 97ff, 101–4, 113, 116ff, 121–3, 125; in the 1980s, 126, 128, 132, 135–8, 140–4, 147, 152–3, 166–7; mandate and responsibilities, 177n.4; and other aspects of urban policy, 95, 113–14, 115–16, 147–8, 156; present role, 8–10, 19; twelve-month rule, 115, 148. *See also* cost
Indian Association of Alberta, 8, 32, 123
Indian associations. *See* native associations
Indian bands. *See* bands/reserves
Indian culture/values, 12, 39–42, 45, 48, 65, 66, 80, 100–1, 114, 124,

125, 127, 146–7, 156, 170–1, 173–5
Indian Economic Development Fund, 104, 137–8
Indian Minerals West, 144
Indian Oil and Gas Task Force, 143–4
Indian, origin of name, 5. *See also* "Status" Indian
Indian priorities: at time of Indian Act Review, 122–5; *circa* 1990, 153ff, 170ff. *See also* Indian self-government, settlement of claims
Indian reserves. *See* bands/reserves
Indian self-government: benefits to white society, 173–5; an inherent right, 170–1; government resistance, 142, 152, 165–7; at James Bay, 158–61; need for, 120–1, 150–3, 163–5, 167–9.
Indian views: of government programs, 78, 98, 104–6, 107–8, 110, 138–9, 143–4, 150–1; of white society, 11, 29, 56, 64, 78, 84–6, 90, 93, 107
Indian women and children, 6, 8, 24, 72, 75–6, 78–9, 80, 85–6, 89, 92, 94–5, 96, 114–16, 145–6, 177n.4. *See also* childcare services
Indians of Quebec Association, 159
Industry, Science and Technology Canada, 147, 186n.16. *See also* "regional" department
Institute of Urban Studies (Winnipeg), 145
Interlake Region, 15, 70
Inuit. *See* First Nations
Iroquois Confederacy, 59

Island Lake. *See* bands/reserves
Island Lake Tribal Council, 20, 127

James Bay, 28, 39, 48, 49, 158ff
James Bay Agreement, 167
James Bay Crees. *See* First Nations
JenPeg Program: cost effectiveness compared with welfare, 168; training in northern Manitoba, 119, 129
John Smith. *See* bands/reserves
Johnson, Patrick, 79

Kahnewake. *See* bands/reserves
Kamsack, 90ff
Kanetewat, Chief Robert, 159
Kehewin. *See* bands/reserves
Kehoe, Alice, 70, 71
Key. *See* bands/reserves
Kinew Housing, 105, 116, 146, 157. *See also* Stan Fulham
Koffler, Murray, 170
Krotz, Larry, 95, 96

Lac La Ronge. *See* bands/reserves
Lacombe, Father, 38, 45, 46
Lac Ste Anne, 37–8, 45
Lagassé, Jean, 21–2, 76, 102, 154
Lake Athabaska, 72, 174
Lake Wabasca, 139
Lake Winnipeg, 37, 38
land and other claims, 18, 93, 123, 125, 152, 168–9, 171–3. *See also* settlement of claims
Land Claims Commission, 125. *See also* land

and other claims, settlement of claims
land leasing, 16, 22, 67–8, 101. *See also* farming
land surrenders (selloffs), 13, 16, 22, 56–7, 63, 123, 172
Lathlin, Chief Oscar, 141
Leaf Rapids, 73
Lebrett residential school, 47
Lesser Slave Lake, 109, 139
Lethbridge, 11, 17, 142
Lewis, Stephen, 4
Lithman, Yngve, 83–4, 87
Longclaws, Grand Chief Lyle, 147–8
Lubicon. *See* bands/reserves

Mackenzie Valley Pipeline Inquiry, 117, 170
McMurtry, John, 173
make-work program, 104, 108, 139, 156; cost of, compared to economic development, 184n.17
Mandans, 29–30
Manitoba, 3–27 *passim*; nineteenth century, 37, 45, 52, 54; 1960s, 1970s, 70–1, 74, 98, 117–19; 1980s, 120, 127ff, 154–6, 171–2. *See also* Winnipeg
Manitoba Aboriginal Justice Inquiry, 7, 119
Manitoba Hydro, 73, 117–20, 129
Manitoba Indian Brotherhood, 24, 41–2, 49
Manpower courses, 104–8, 109, 115, 137–9, 147–9, 164; Indian views of, 104, 106–7, 139, 149
Manpower offices, 74, 95, 107, 114–15
Manpower policy, 104ff, 139
Manuel, George, 23
Markle, W.A., 54, 57, 63–4

Matchewan, Chief Jean Maurice, 173
Meech Lake Accord, 14
Métis, 5, 6, 47–8, 94, 112, 124; nineteenth century: 30–2, 37–8, 42, 45; Dene-Métis claims, 169; northern Manitoba communities, 21–2, 73, 76, 117
migration to cities, 3, 6–7, 14, 87, 93, 101. *See also* cities, the Indian experience
Migratory Birds Act, 123
Milloy, James, 29
mining industry, 72–4, 97. *See also* uranium mining
Mis-Ta-Wa-Sis, Chief, 34, 36, 67, 173
Mistawasis. *See* bands/reserves
Morris, Governor, 33, 35, 163
mortality rates: current, 9; in 1960s, 76, 111; settlement era, 50, 61
multiculturalism, 125
Muskeg Lake. *See* bands/reserves

National Indian Brotherhood, 100, 135, 163
National Transcontinental Railway, 87
native associations. *See* Assembly of First Nations (AFN), bands/tribal councils, development corporations Federation of Saskatchewan Indians (FSI), First Nations Confederacy, Grand Council of the Crees of Quebec, Indian Association of Alberta, Indians of Quebec Association, Manitoba Indian Brotherhood, National Indian Brotherhood,

dian Brotherhood, Urban Indian Association
Native Economic Developers' Association, 127
Native Economic Development Program (NEDP), 136, 149
Native Law Centre (University of Saskatchewan), 133
Native Metals, 107
Neeginan, 114, 158
Nelson House. *See* bands/reserves
New directions: economic strategies, 154–5; poverty strategies, 155–6; urban strategies, 157–8
Nielsen, Erik, 108, 138
Nielsen Report, 104, 106, 107, 135ff, 184n.17
Northern Alberta Development Council, 106, 108
Northern Flood Agreement (1977), 119ff
Northern Resource Trucking, 130
North Saskatchewan River, 34, 38, 62
North West Mounted Police, 33, 38, 41
Nortran Corporation, 128
Norway House. *See* bands/reserves
Nova Corporation, 128

Oak River (Lake). *See* bands/reserves
Oblate Fathers, 45
Oil and Gas Canada (INAC), 144. *See also* Indian Minerals West
oil and gas industry, employment in, 128, 129
oil and gas revenues, 13, 128; estimates of, 143; financing Indian business, 128, 130–1, 135; government mismanagement, 143–4

Ojibwa. *See* First Nations
Oka, 163, 173
Oldman River, 18
O'Soup, Louis, 52, 54, 56
Oxford House. *See* bands/
reserves

Palliser, Captain John, 31,
37
Pasqua, Chief, 51
Pasqua. *See* bands/re-
serves
Peace Hills Trust, 130,
143
Peguis, Chief, 16, 37
Peguis. *See* bands/re-
serves
Penner, Keith, 153, 165,
166
Penner Report, 25, 82,
141, 151ff, 165–6, 169
permit system, 53–4, 58
Piapot. *See* bands/re-
serves
Piegan. *See* bands/re-
serves, First Nations
Plains Indian Cultural
Survival School, 146–8.
See also Jerry Arshinoff
Poundmaker, Chief, 34,
38, 67
Poundmaker. *See* bands/
reserves
Precambrian Shield, 13,
37
private-sector involve-
ment, 25, 128–9, 132
Provencher, Bishop
Joseph, 45
Provencher, Lieutenant
Colonel, 35
provincial government in-
volvement, 25, 101–2,
128–9, 132, 146. *See also*
private-sector involve-
ment
public opinion: impor-
tance of, 121, 142, 162,
165; lack of knowledge,
163; view of Indian sit-
uation today, 4–5, 26–
7, 141–2, 170; views

from 1950s and 1960s,
69, 73–4, 76, 80, 83, 85–
6, 88–90, 92–3, 103,
112; views from settle-
ment days, 40–2, 49,
53, 61
Pukatawagen. *See* bands/
reserves

Red Earth. *See* bands/re-
serves
Red Fife wheat, 52
Red River, 16ff, 30–2, 34–
5, 37–8, 42, 45, 55
Red Sucker Lake. *See*
bands/reserves
Redwood Meadows, 130
Reed, Hayter, 52–3, 57
Regina, 8, 57, 95–6, 107,
145
"regional" department:
Regional Economic Ex-
pansion (DREE), 104,
109, 139; Regional In-
dustrial Expansion
(DRIE), 136–7, 139. *See*
also Industry, Science
and Technology Can-
ada (ISTC)
Registered Indian. *See*
"Status" Indian
Reserves, 6–26 *passim*
– economy (1950s to
1970s), 69–74, 77, 83–5,
92, 97, 101; (1980s),
128–9, 132, 134–7, 139,
150–1, 154–5
– land and resources, 12–
13, 21–2, 55, 123, 151–
2, 168; legal status of
land, 33, 55. *See also*
bands/reserves, land
surrenders
residential schools, 47–9
Riel Rebellion, 32, 34, 46,
62
Robertson, Heather, 19,
74
Robinson Treaties, 34, 36,
42
Roseau River. *See* bands/
reserves

Royal Proclamation
(1763), 33

Saddle Lake. *See* bands/
reserves
Salisbury, Richard, 159,
161
Sampson. *See* bands/re-
serves
Sarcee. *See* bands/re-
serves, First Nations
Saskatchewan, 3–27 *pas-*
sim; nineteenth cen-
tury, 34, 38, 46–7, 51ff,
56; 1950s to 1970s, 70,
72, 77, 79, 90ff, 102,
110–13; 1980s, 127ff,
133–4, 139, 152, 156,
171–2. *See also* Regina,
Saskatchewan Govern-
ment Plan (1950s), Sas-
katoon
Saskatchewan Govern-
ment Fish Marketing
Service, 112
Saskatchewan Govern-
ment Plan (1950s),
110–13
Saskatchewan Human
Rights Commission,
148
Saskatchewan Indian In-
stitute of Technology,
133
Saskatoon, 93ff, 131, 146
Saulteaux. *See* First Nations
Sawridge. *See* bands/re-
serves
Scott, Duncan Campbell,
44, 53
self-government. *See* Indian self-government
Selkirk settlers, 37, 45
settlement of claims, 123–
5, 152, 168–9, 171–3.
See also land and other
claims
Settlement Plan (1870s to
1890s), 39–40, 42–58,
60; contrast with east-
ern Canada, 42–3, 58–

60. *See also* "civilizing," farming, residential schools

Shamattawa. *See* bands/reserves

Shimpo, Mitsuru and Robert Williamson, 90

Sioux. *See* First Nations: Dakota-Sioux

smallpox epidemics, 30

Smith, Adam, 55

social assistance ("welfare"), 7–8, 10, 13–14, 16–17, 19, 22, 27, 58; percentage of population, 1972, 77, 78–9; 92, 97, 128; 136, 145, 155, 161, 163

social problems, 7–8, 11, 24–5, 78–82, 90, 97, 116, 118, 143–4, 147–8, 162, 181n.17

something owing, 169–73

South Africa, 15, 162

"Special Arda," 109, 139

Split Lake. *See* bands/reserves

Squaw Rapids Dam (Manitoba Hydro), 117

Starblanket (Ahtukakoop), Chief, 34

"Status" Indian (also known as Registered Indian): defined, 177n.4 as percentage of provincial population, 1; relinquishing status, 6. *See also* bands/reserves, First Nations

Steinhauer, Henry, 37

Stevenson, Chief Louis, 15

stewardship, 52–8, 77, 116–21, 142–4, 152, 166, 171–3. *See also* conflict of interest, land surrenders

Stocken, Henry, 47, 63

Stoney (Stonies). *See* bands/reserves

Stymiest, David, 81, 87–90

sugar-beet pickers, 69, 74, 83, 97

Sunderland, Victor, 54–5, 67

surrenders (sell-offs). *See* land surrenders

Sweetgrass, Chief, 33, 34

Syncrude, 129

termination (us experiment in 1950s), 124

The Pas. *See* bands/reserves

Third World, 3, 15, 77, 102–3, 111, 137, 169

Thompson, David, 16, 30

Thompson Centre, 168

Tootoosis, John, 57–8

Touchwood Hills, 52

"traditionalists," 80, 82, 91, 94, 115, 117, 130–2, 135, 164

trapping/fishing, 71–2, 74, 104, 110–12

Treaties. *See* Robinson Treaties, Western Treaties

Upper Canada, 59

uranium mining, 112, 129, 174

Urban Indian Association, 145, 157

wage work, 22, 54, 58, 63, 65, 69, 70, 71, 73–4, 83–4, 94–5, 128–9, 157

Watt, Senator Charlie, 159

welfare. *See* Social assistance

West, John, 45. *See also* Church Missionary Society

Western Treaties, 3, 5, 6, 28, 31–6, 46, 123–4, 162; oral tradition, 36; Treaty One, 32, 83; Treaty Three, 34; Treaty Four, 52; Treaty Six, 22, 33, 34, 46, 51, 55, 67, 171ff; Treaty Seven, 34, 37, 62

White Dog. *See* bands/reserves

White Owl, Chief, 55

"White Paper", 107, 122–5

white settlement, 39–40, 42. *See also* immigrant experience, land surrenders

Winnipeg, 8, 70, 95, 96, 105, 114, 116, 130, 142, 144–9, 157–8, 181n.17

Winnipeg Building Trades Council, 142

Winnipeg River, 28, 37

Wollaston Lake, 174

York Landing. *See* bands/reserves